Breonna Taylor and Me

OMPLICATED

A Book Series of Curriculam studies

William F. Pinar.
Series Editor

Volume 61

Breonna Taylor and Me

Black Women, Racial Justice and Reclaiming Hope

Edited by
Angela Y. Douglas and Emmanuel Harris II

PETER LANG

New York · Berlin · Bruxelles · Chennai · Lausanne · Oxford

Library of Congress Cataloging-in-Publication Data

Names: Douglas, Angela Y., editor. | Harris, Emmanuel, editor.
Title: Breonna Taylor and me : Black women, racial justice, and reclaiming
   hope / edited by Angela Y. Douglas, Emmanuel Harris II.
Description: New York : Peter Lang, [2024] | Series: Complicated
   conversation, 1534-2816 ; vol. 61 | Includes bibliographical references.
Identifiers: LCCN 2024006066 (print) | LCCN 2024006067 (ebook) |
   ISBN 9781636675428 (paperback) | ISBN 9781636679211 (hardback) |
   ISBN 9781636675435 (pdf) | ISBN 9781636675442 (epub)
Subjects: LCSH: Taylor, Breonna, 1993-2020. | African American
   women—Social conditions—21st century. | Women, Black—Social
   conditions—21st century. | Racism—United States. | Racism.
Classification: LCC E185.86 .B6948 2024 (print) | LCC E185.86 (ebook) |
   DDC 305.48/896073—dc23/eng/20240220
LC record available at https://lccn.loc.gov/2024006066
LC ebook record available at https://lccn.loc.gov/2024006067
DOI 10.3726/b21764

Bibliographic information published by the Deutsche Nationalbibliothek.
The German National Library lists this publication in the German
National Bibliography; detailed bibliographic data is available
on the Internet at http://dnb.d-nb.de.

Cover design by Peter Lang Group AG

ISSN 1534-2816 (print)
ISBN 9781636679211 (hardback)
ISBN 9781636675428 (paperback)
ISBN 9781636675435 (ebook)
ISBN 9781636675442 (epub)
DOI 10.3726/b21764

© 2024 Peter Lang Group AG, Lausanne
Published by Peter Lang Publishing Inc., New York, USA
info@peterlang.com - www.peterlang.com

Table of Contents

Acknowledgements

The pandemic and the summer of 2020 brought forth a profound impact on the Black community, underscoring the many struggles faced by Black women in the fight for justice. Black women bore the brunt of both the health crisis and the enduring weight of systemic oppression. In this pivotal moment, it became essential to recognize the experiences of Black women who have long been overlooked and sidelined in their unwavering pursuit of equality and justice. To these resilient and courageous champions, I offer my deepest gratitude. Your contributions and sacrifices inspire hope and drive progress in shaping a more inclusive and equitable future. Breonna, your life and legacy will endure forever.

I also extend my sincere thanks to the contributors of this volume. Your invaluable insights and diverse perspectives elevate this conversation far beyond the confines of these pages. A very special thanks to my colleague and brother in "scholactivist" education, Emmanuel Harris II, for his unwavering support. Together, we amplify voices, empower communities, and drive positive change.

Within my own life, I am blessed by the presence of remarkable Black women. Unfortunately, I cannot name everyone but know I love and thank you all! My beloved mother, Rosa M. Douglas, your love and guidance transcends death. My sisters, Kim Anderson and Clarissa Douglas, you both exemplify true sisterhood. Together, we have faced challenges and celebrated triumphs. Our bond is unbreakable.

This volume envisions a brighter future, where my nieces and grandnieces thrive and become agents of change. You all are cherished, and I pray the stories of courageous Black women before you will inspire your own journeys. Auntie A. loves you much and for always.

-Angela Y. Douglas

Coming out of the pandemic, the Black community was struck dispro-portionately when measured by the number of us that we lost, were seriously ill or afflicted. It seems like before, during, and even now we are still dealing with more than light afflictions, setbacks, loss, health, and mental struggles. The editors and contributors of this volume are no exception. Thus, I appre-ciate beyond measure the work of all the contributors and my colleague and sistah (who'll always be Senator to me) Angela Douglas. Simply put, without each of you, this endeavor would never have happened. Your patience, per-sistence, dedication, and invaluable hard work have given life to this edited volume. ¡Mil gracias! A thousand thanks.

Sincere and heartfelt gratitude is also extended to Alison Jefferson and Joshua Charles at Peter Lang. We appreciate you and your support in realiz-ing this vision.

And to my family, I thank you too. There's not enough time or space to name everyone, but I give special thanks to the women in my family, my mother, Jeri Harris, and the ancestors, Mama Queen Bogues, Mama Margaret Wilks, Mama Nancy Harris, and Mama Shirley Harris. To my children Kalani Harris, Kalomé Harris, my daughter by marriage Gabi Greenberg, and my father Mann Harris, I also extend love and heartfelt gratitude. And finally, to my wife, Donna Payne Harris, thank you for saying yes. This is for Breonna Taylor so that she may soar and that the children will know her name.

-Emmanuel Harris II

List of Illustrations

Introduction: Breonna Taylor and Me: Black Women, Racial Justice, and Reclaiming Hope

The pivotal role of Black women in American history is unequivocal though severely underappreciated and underrecognized. Indeed, Black women's contributions, sacrifices, and influences permeate nearly every aspect of our society and most of the world, as evidenced in and around 2020. Among many others making noteworthy contributions during this time frame, women of African descent would come to the forefront, such as Dr. Kizzmekia Corbett in COVID-19 vaccine research, Uganda climate activist Vanessa Nakate, Vice President Kamala Harris, LaTosha Brown of "Black Voters Matter" or the tireless elections work of Stacey Abrams in Georgia. The year 2020 characterized an era when these Black women truly shined in what may be considered a Summer of Reckoning, all while in the grip of a pandemical lockdown. Throughout the nation and, in fact, the globe, reactions to George Floyd's death were characterized by demonstrations, affirmations, and calls for social justice. The video of his tragic murder became the primary catalyst, as it showed a corrupt police officer defiantly staring at a camera while kneeling for over nine minutes on the handcuffed, Black man's neck. Many do not realize that a young, Black woman, then 17-year-old Darnella Frazier, filmed Floyd's murder, forever scarring her and the millions of people who viewed the footage. Without that film, most argue, there would have been no conviction, much less the international movements that followed.

Whereas Floyd came to symbolize systematic racism and institutionalized violence, especially against people of color, the absence of coverage of another Black person's death, Breonna Taylor – which occurred months earlier also in 2020 and similarly at the hands of the police – further illuminates the marginalization, erasure, or omission of Black women in racial, social, and political contexts. It was not until months after George Floyd's assassination that an international uproar encompassed Breonna's plight, even prompting billboards and advertisements from prominent figures such as Oprah Winfrey and numerous other dignitaries. Eventually, Breonna Taylor's image graced the cover of *O The Oprah Magazine* and *Vanity Fair*, as well as murals in parks and public places. Initially, however, the officers involved were not charged.

When African American lives are lost at the hands of the police or implicitly endorsed by authorities, too often, the names that are remembered are only those of the men. *Invisible No More* by Andrea Ritchie is described by Angela Davis as a book that "challenges us to acknowledge the human dimension of this violence, which should not be effaced in abstract statistical accounts." (x) Ritchie, the author and principal investigator in the work, provides the following observations in her text's Introduction:

> Pulled over in a traffic stop and beaten by the side of the road. Placed in a banned choke hold by a New York City police officer. Violently taken into police custody, never to come out alive. Shot first, questions asked later.
>   The stories and images that immediately leap to mind in connection with these scenes are those of Black men – Rodney King, Eric Garner, Freddie Gray, and Philando Castile.
>   But these are also the stories of Black women. (1)[1]

In many ways, *Breonna Taylor and Me: Black Women, Racial Justice, and Reclaiming Hope* builds on the work of Ritchie, as well as Audre Lourde's *Sister Outsider*, a compilation of essays and speeches initially published in 1984 though still extremely relevant today. Lourde argues, "Each one of us here is a link in the connection between antipoor legislation, gay shootings, the burning of synagogues, street harassment, attacks against women, and resurgent violence against Black people." (139) The tragedy that marks Breonna Taylor's killing and other Black women like her deserves to be recognized, humanized, and memorialized.

The following collection centers on the experiences of Black women, celebrates the efforts and accomplishments of Black female leaders in the movements for positive social change, critiques established norms regarding the treatment of women of African descent around the globe, and encourages hope in a world of systemic racial oppression. Nikole Hannah-Jones' profoundly informative work in *The 1619 Project*, which also gives voice to Breonna Taylor's plight, underscores the importance of Black social justice in general. She states, "Black rights struggles paved the way for every other rights struggle, including women's and gay rights, immigrant and disability rights." (11) Later, Jones adds the following: "The truth is that as much democracy as this nation has today, it has been borne on the backs of Black resistance and visions for equality." (33) Likewise, writer and CNN White House correspondent April Ryan had the audacity to title her book, *Black*

Women Will Save the World and then had the perspicacity to support her argument with facts.[2]

The title *Breonna Taylor and Me* additionally pays homage to the progress achieved thanks to the #MeToo movement, popularized by another African American woman, Tarana Burke. Though the events surrounding Breonna Taylor may not constitute sexual violence, they do pertain to violence, nevertheless. Furthermore, in terms of the treatment of Black women, *The 1619 Project* highlights a 2001 review of prosecutorial decisions in sexual-assault cases in Kansas City and Philadelphia, finding that prosecutors were 4.5 times more likely to file if the victim is white as opposed to if the victim is Black; if the plaintiff is Black there is a better chance of acquittal for the accused, and if convicted, receiving a lighter sentence. In that region, only 1 in 15 Black women report being assaulted. The writers conclude, "Many Black women and girls see the criminal legal system as offering little recourse for the sexual violence they experience." (Roberts 58) Violence is violence, and the pain can transcend generations. However, as Audre Lourde states, "Pain is an event, an experience that must be recognized, named, and then used in some way in order for the experience to change, to be transformed into something else, strength or knowledge or action." (171)

The scholars in *Breonna Taylor and Me* come from a variety of disciplines to create transformative research, knowledge, and action. In the first part, political scientist Athena M. King argues that Breonna Taylor's murder at the hands of law enforcement indicates the political system's general ignorance toward African American women's needs, concerns, and voices. Historian Aaron Treadwell and educator Bisola A. Wald articulate many foundational underpinnings surrounding violence against African American women. Africana Studies scholar Emmanuel Harris II reaffirms that Breonna Taylor's life matters as he outlines relevant aspects of her upbringing, character, and untimely death.

While centering on the 2020 Summer of Reckoning, the second part expands on the effects of Breonna Taylor's tragedy. It contains two educators: Julia Lynch, who depicts a poetic narrative qualitative study that explores the lived experiences of Black women teachers in rural northern United States during a national (re) awakening, and Keryn Vickers, who explains the groundwater or systemic issues that give rise to events like the one in Louisville as he also humanizes those who were involved, including individuals in law enforcement. Meanwhile, social work scholar Tiffany Lane advocates for her co-disciplinarians to remain present to have critical conversations related to the intersection of race and gender. Additionally, anthropologist and African American Studies specialist Kimberly Eison Simmons presents a reflective chapter that explores coursework assignments and discussions with students about "Black Lives Matter" while contemplating the historical and contemporary racialized experiences of Black people in the United States, particularly Black women. In another chapter by Harris, he highlights the 2020 publication of Puerto Rican writer and activist Yolanda Arroyo Pizarro as an exemplary, feminist literary creation that celebrates *afroamor* or Black love.

The third and final part builds from the previous two and presents some of the legacies of Black women while emphasizing respect, empowerment, and hope. The political scientist pracademic (practitioner and academician) Angela Y. Douglas uses Breonna Taylor's death and a few notable cases and settlements to highlight ideological connections in devaluing Black women – visibility, activism, and accountability. That same visibility and awareness may be applied to Afro-Uruguayan writer and linguist Cristina Cabral as she internationalizes the importance of Black sisterhood in the African diaspora. The historian Louis L. Woods complements Cabral's essay by making the international quite personal, allowing us to be privy to an open letter to his daughters. Part III also contains two chapters that reaffirm hope. In their chapter, the educator team of Sheka Houston and Tammy Taylor propose to interrupt the narrative around the adultification of Black girls and focus on how embracing our deep Africana heritage can change the trajectory of these young ladies on their journey to becoming productive and successful women. Public health specialist Sabrina T. Cherry emphasizes the importance of intentionally seeking opportunities to foster hope, joy, and community amid the dual pandemics of COVID-19 and persistent racial and gender injustice.

This collection of scholarly writings, in many ways, builds on the words, wisdom, and works of the ancestors and the elders as it centers the life of Breonna Taylor. We let the words of sister Maya Angelou in *Letters to My Daughter* bring us home:

> When I find myself filling with rage of the loss of a beloved, I try as soon as possible to remember that my concerns and questions should be focused on what I have learned or what I have yet to learn from my departed love. What legacy was left which can help me in the art of living a good life?
> *Did I learn to be kinder*
> *To be more patient,*
> *And more generous,*
> *More loving,*
> *More ready to laugh,*
> *And more easy to accept honest tears?*
> *If I can accept those legacies of my departed beloveds, I am able to say, Thank You to them for their love and Thank You to God for their lives.* (65–66)

Together our narratives form a part of the continuum of works that celebrate, illuminate, and educate about the lives of Black and African American women. Rest in peace and power Breonna Taylor.

Notes

1 The women Andrea Ritchie names as victims of these injustices were Sandra Anton in 1996, Rosann Miller in 2014, Alesia Thomas in 2012, and Mya Hall in 2015 (1). Like Ritchie in *Invisible No More*, throughout this anthology, the terms "woman" and "women" emphatically include transgender women.
2 As part of her compelling argument, Ryan states, "The culture is starting to recognize and acknowledge our power. 'Black women saved the Democrats. Don't make us do it again,' declared the Washington Post in the run-up to the 2020 general election. 'Last night in Georgia, Black women saved democracy,' exclaimed the Brookings Institution after President Donald Trump's defeat in November 2020. 'Black women prove to be the backbone of American democracy,' the Houston Chronicle underscored after the January 6 insurrection." (6)

Bibliography

Angelou, Maya. *Letters to My Daughter.* New York: Random House, 2009.

Davis, Angela Y. Foreword. *Invisible No More: Police Violence against Black Women and Women of Color.* Andrea Ritchie. Boston: Beacon Press, 2017.

Hannah-Jones, Nikole et al Editors. *The 1619 Project: A New Origin Story.* New York: One World, 2021.

Lourde, Audre. *Sister Outsider: Essays and Speeches.* 1984. New York: Crossing Press, 2021.

Ritchie, Andrea. *Invisible No More: Police Violence against Black Women and Women of Color.* Boston: Beacon Press, 2017.

Roberts, Dorothy. "Race" *The 1619 Project: A New Origin Story.* Nikole Hannah-Jones et al Editors. New York: One World, 2021.

Ryan, April. *Black Women Will Save the World: An Anthem.* New York: Amistad, 2022.

Part I Breonna Taylor and Me: Historical Contexts and Black Women

1 Breonna Taylor Matters: We Remember Her Name

EMMANUEL HARRIS II

To Know Her Is to Love Her

Tamika Palmer, Breonna Taylor's mother, sits in her living room and reads from her daughter's high school scrapbook, "I'm a strong, intelligent, beautiful Black woman, who has grown so much."[1] The story of Breonna's life, her humanity, and her complexity, despite the now international recognition, often understates or completely omits the person she was. Her mother describes her daughter, "To know her is to love her. She's so much like me, but she's so much better than me."[2] We remember her name, celebrate her, and continue to feel her presence and influence today. The facts surrounding her life and her untimely death have become clouded by false narratives, lies, and hearsay. This chapter emphatically and enthusiastically proclaims that Breonna Taylor matters, and it encourages us all to not forget her and the enduring effects of her murder, especially in the continuum of Black folks – Black women in particular – dying at the hands of police officers.

Breonna[3] was born in Grand Rapids, Michigan, on June 5, 1993, where her mother and Trory Herrod raised her. Her mother recalls in an interview with the *New York Times* the way that her daughter always sought to help people. "I can remember her being seven years-old saying to my mother 'Let me check your blood sugar' … my mother would let her stick her finger and check her blood sugar and [Breonna] was so pumped up to do it and help her do her insulin"[4]. Her family moved to Louisville near the beginning of her high school years.[5] Regarded by the parents of her peers as the more responsible one in her friend group, "[s]he woke them up to get to school on time after sleepovers, practiced mock interviews for an after-school job in ninth grade in Louisville, where her family had moved."[6] That young person would continue to aspire to help others throughout her brief life and inspire and uplift well beyond her time on Earth. In an interview, Ju'niyah Palmer, Breonna's sister, explains, "Just being around family gave her a lot of joy. She loved to be around family."[7] Kenneth Walker, Breonna's longtime boyfriend, affirms, "She was the star of the show for the family, basically. And she kept everybody going,"[8] She liked having fun and wanted those around her to be lifted. "When you're around her, you're going to enjoy it. You're going to have the time of your life, even if it's just riding to the Chick-fil-A and getting macaroni and cheese. You're really going to have a good time,"[9] says Katrina Curry, Breonna's cousin. Another cousin who grew up more like a sister to her, Preonia Flakes, chimes in, "Literally. She's going to turn her music up. She's going put the pedal to the medal and we're going to ride to Chick-fil-A and get some macaroni and cheese. And that's just what it's going to be."[10] Her personality undoubtedly left an indelible mark on those that knew her.

"She was just goofy. She was always posting funny stuff,"[11] Kenneth Walker explains. Kenneth was with Breonna the night of the tragedy. They met via Twitter while the two were in college – she was a nursing student at the University of Kentucky, and he was a student at Western Kentucky. Their relationship was off and on for several years before eventually becoming firmly established. He explains, "I'm a Gemini, and she was also a Gemini. So, you know, some days it was, 'Yeah let's, let's get married and have a kid,' and another day it's like, 'No, let's be single and live carefree lives.'"[12] There are videos of the two of them discussing their plans of eventually raising a family together. They even bought baby sneakers for the child they hoped to have one day. "We definitely talked about babies, and she wanted a girl." He adds, "These are the [Air Jordans] shoes for whenever we finally got to have a baby. So, these are kind of special" says Kenneth, as he holds the tiny shoes. He continues, "For the future, we had a lot planned. Actually, we planned on buying a house and she already had got a new car that she wanted."[13] His love for Breonna is undeniable as he discusses her. He adds, "She did like to sing all the time." Her aunt, Bianca Austin, would agree, "Even though she couldn't sing. She could 'sang', if you know what I mean," she says with a laugh.[14]

In high school, Breonna's teachers remember her vividly. Nureka Dixon taught her math at Western High School, says both Breonna's personality and intellect stood out to her:

> She had a math mind. She had a beautiful mind. And she was very helpful to others. A lot of times we would start a lesson and kids would be confused or they wouldn't understand. I'd be like, "Oh, what am I going to do?". Bre would be like "I got it Ms. Dix. I'll work with them. I'll help them." She was always willing to help others. She was a leader.[15]

Dixon continues:

> This is my nineteenth year in education, and we've taught lots of students. I've taught lots of students, but I remember brilliant minds. She was brilliant and fast! And efficient and she just had my back, you know. In the classroom, with kids, if anyone was disrespectful to me, she would shut that down.[16]

After awareness of the tragedy spread nationally, the news media's characterization of Breonna motivated several of her former instructors, including Leah White, to hold a press conference. Stephanie Holton, whose job as youth service center coordinator at Western includes assisting emotionally distressed students with a myriad of issues, states the following: "Breonna would many times find someone crying in the bathroom and bring them to me and assure them that I was going to help them and take care of them or come in and grab something for a student that needed it."[17] White's words concur:

> I remember in class, I would always get her to help upperclassmen. And that's kind of hard, because she was younger, but she would help seniors and help them with their math. I think that was such a sign of maturity and resolve to be able to help upperclassmen, being new to this school and this environment and jumping right in. She just had that confidence.[18]

Breonna's high school scrapbook shows a young person with a vision and goals for her life. "Graduating this year on time is so important to me because I will be the first in my family to accomplish this,"[19] she wrote in her scrapbook during her senior year, next to a photo of herself in a cap and gown. "I want to be the one who finally breaks the cycle of my family's educational history. I want to be the one to finally make a difference."[20] She would also write about how she envisioned that her diploma would only be the beginning of her journey toward adulthood and greater responsibilities in life.[21] Part of that journey entailed pursuing a nursing degree at the university before becoming a certified emergency medical technician in Louisville and later a patient care assistant. She tended to people recovering from trauma at Frazier Rehabilitation Institute, under the University of Louisville Health Hospital.

The media's narrative about Breonna's life after the tragedy often conflicted with the reality of who she really was. Her former teacher Leah White expresses the reality clearly:

> For me, I feel like the world needs to know what a wonderful person she was. Not just saying it. We have these experiences with her as her teacher, mentor and the world needs to know that she was a beautiful person and just a light, a delightful, pleasant person. She loved helping people. And that's not always what you're hearing. And that's where the frustration, anger and emotion come in because you're like, "I knew her." … She was just a wonderful person.[22]

Friends and family recall how her smile could light up a room, and she was quick to laugh. White recalls, "What I remember most is that she loved to laugh. And she had this beautiful smile. She would just crack up – we would crack up in class and just giggle and giggle and giggle. She was just a pleasure to be around. Everyone loved her. She was just an angel." Nureka Dixon, the former assistant principal at Western points out, "Just to hear her name, I can't help but literally hear her laughter." She adds "That is something that was just synonymous with her, that huge smile and that laughter."[23]

2020 Deff Gonna Be My Year WATCH!

At the time of her murder, Breonna Taylor was 26 years old and with no criminal record. A *New York Times* article, "Breonna Taylor's Life Was Changing. Then the Police Came to Her Door" chronicles many of the events that transpired on March 12 and the early morning of March 13, 2020. Earlier that year, Breonna had tweeted, "2020 deff gonna by my year WATCH" and indeed, many of the plans she had put into place were starting to come to fruition. She had her own apartment and purchased a new car, a black Dodge Charger. The strength in her relationship with Kenneth Walker provided them the security and freedom to begin to discuss marriage and children seriously. She seemed to put her ex-boyfriend, Jamarcus Glover, behind her finally. He was under police surveillance, had been convicted for drug dealing, and at one point had received packages addressed to him at Breonna's apartment.[24] The Louisville Metro Police Department (LMPD) watched her home at apartment number four, 3003 Springfield Drive, purportedly to track Glover, though he had not been seen there for weeks prior to her murder.[25]

The LMPD established a strike force to target supposed drug trafficking in which Breonna's ex-boyfriend was believed to be involved. After months of surveillance of him and his associates, five locations were targeted. Three centered around and included an abandoned house on 2424 Elliot Ave, where Glover was thought to reside, and a house which was a two-minute drive from it on 2605 W. Muhammad Ali Blvd. Breonna's home, also targeted, was in an established residential apartment area at 3003 Springfield Drive #4.[26] On the night of March 12, 2020, over sixty officers executed raids on the five properties, and Glover was arrested prior to the raid on Breonna's apartment.[27] Former Louisville Metro Police Detective Kelly Hanna Goodlett, involved in the raid on Breonna's apartment, came forward and later pleaded guilty that the details for the search warrant for her house were indeed falsified.[28] The original warrant called for plain-clothes officers to conduct a no-knock, no announce entry. In an interview, David James of the Louisville Metro Council President and a former 14-year narcotics officer states that such a warrant would usually be reserved for entering a reinforced dwelling of a high-flight risk, violence-prone suspect.[29] The *New York Times* confirms there had never been any observance of drug trafficking or distribution at Breonna's apartment, nor had she received any packages with drugs, or had any packages addressed to Glover been received within thirty days before the raid on her home.[30]

On the evening of the raid on Breonna's home, the no-knock warrant was changed to a knock-and-announce warrant. However, whether this information was communicated to the eight officers executing the entry remains unclear or unclarified. Around 12:40 am on the morning of March 13, four officers banged, openhanded, on the door of apartment number four on Springfield Drive, where Breonna and Kenneth were sleeping. The couple had just enjoyed a dinner date at Texas Roadhouse, Uno card games, and a movie. There is confirmation that the plain-clothes officers banged on the door. However, there are discrepancies as to whether or not they announced themselves as being the police. According to several neighbors who heard the banging on the door, including Kenneth, only one neighbor heard the officers say they were police.[31] Kenneth described his reaction to hearing the loud bang at the door at nearly one o'clock in the morning: "It's too late for anybody to be knocking at the door, so I grab my gun and we proceed to go answer the door. . . and then when we get right in the doorway of the bedroom, the door flies open."[32] Upon seeing the intruders, Kenneth, a licensed gun owner, fires one shot which strikes Sargent Johnathan Mattingly in the leg. The officers would return over 30 rounds of fire.[33] Kenneth states, "Breonna, she couldn't say anything. She was scared to death, as was I. But she did scream at some point in time when she got hit. That's the last sounds that she made."[34]

In an interview, the district attorney Thomas Wine would later state, "There's now no question that they knocked. But the question is, did they announce themselves as police before they came in and even after they came in, before the shooting started."[35] Former officer James explained, "As you listen to the 911 call, it's silence in the background. There's no such a thing as a knock and not announce search warrant. That is the most dangerous thing you could ever do, especially in a state like Kentucky where we have stand your ground laws"[36] and an individual has a right to defend him or herself, thus creating a predicament in which the policy regarding self-defense contrasts the policy of no-knock search warrants.[37] In the officers' hail of bullets, five struck and killed Breonna, the fatal shot striking her in the chest, causing her to bleed to death.[38] There were bullet holes everywhere, including in the clock, the bathroom soap dish, and several neighboring apartments. Kenneth called his mother, then 911, and afterwards Breonna's mother. He said, "While I was talking with Breonna's mother, I told her on the phone, 'Well, I think it's the police outside.' But I was really thinking that the police came to help."[39] In his truly unsettling emergency call, one hears the fear and utter misery in his voice as he cries out for help and prays aloud for Breonna's well-being.[40]

Kenneth was immediately arrested and held in jail for over two weeks. The ambulance that eventually arrived on the scene never attended to Breonna but instead, the officer who was struck in the leg. Breonna was left to bleed to death in the hallway of her apartment. Her mother, Tameka Parker, was never informed of her daughter's demise that night. After receiving Kenneth's call, she went to the apartment, where over twenty police cars had arrived, including a SWAT unit. After being informed by one of the officers that she may have been transported to the hospital, she went there and waited, inquiring for hours without receiving any information about Breonna, until finally, she returned to Springfield Drive. In an interview, she states, "It was about eleven o'clock in the morning when [an officer] comes back over and says they were almost done. And I said, 'Okay, that's fine, but where's Breonna?' That's when he says, 'Well ma'am, she's still in the apartment.' So, I knew then what that meant."[41] For over ten hours, Breonna's body remained on site exactly as she was when murdered. Her mother adds, "No one ever really told me what happen there though. I didn't find out that she was shot by a police officer until I saw it on the news."[42] Drugs or drug money were never found in the apartment. After the shooting started, the officers never searched for either. The inflated letters of the word "HOME" were still on the front door, and the many motivational messages and stickers could still be seen posted throughout the house, as well as the bloodstained carpet where Breonna Taylor breathed her last breath.

I Was God's Blessing to My Mother

After days of calling LMPD for answers, Tameka Parker contacted a lawyer to assist her. The initial notification about the murder of Breonna Taylor was one where, in the public briefing the evening of March 13, the Louisville Police Department celebrated the bravery of the officers involved and gave thanks that no other officers were harmed.[43] In the news, Kenneth was treated as someone who attempted to kill a police officer and Breonna, an accessory to the crime. The official police incident report stated there was no forced entry, and Breonna was not wounded. Tameka Parker and family hired legal counsel and fought relentlessly to seek answers and justice to the events surrounding March 13.[44] It was not until the country, entrenched in a pandemical lockdown, saw 18-year-old Darnella Frazier's video recording of George Floyd's murder that unheeded cries of #JusticeForBreonna began to be heard nationally and internationally.

With the calls for justice, state and federal investigations took place. Officer Hutchinson was later indicted, not for the murder of Breonna Taylor but for wanton endangerment for blindly firing shots that entered the neighbor's apartment where a family of three lived. Several jurors have come forward publicly stating that Attorney General of Kentucky, Daniel Cameron, did not provide them the opportunity to deliberate homicide charges for the officers for the death of Breonna Taylor.[45] Additionally, Hutchinson, according to numerous sources, had a history of misconduct.[46] After three hours of deliberations, the jury acquitted Hutchison, the only officer indicted at the state level.[47] It would be years before the Federal Justice Department would bring four of the LMPD to trial.[48] In June 2020, Kentucky would prohibit no-knock police entries, a policy commonly known as Breonna's Law. In October 2020, Grand Rapids, Michigan, approved naming Breonna Taylor Way in the downtown area next to Rosa Parks Circle.[49]

Breonna's name and image would appear on placards, billboards, murals, music videos, movies, and demonstrations around the United States and around the world. In July 2020 the nonprofit Future History Now partnered with the Banneker-Douglass Museum and the Maryland Commission on African American History and Culture to organize a team of volunteers and community residents for the creation of a 7000-square-foot ground mural of Breonna Taylor in Annapolis, Maryland.[50] Her portrait, which first appeared on the cover of *Vanity Fair* magazine, was displayed in the Smithsonian's National Museum of African American History and Culture as part of the exhibition "Reckoning: Protest. Defiance. Resilience."[51] In 2024 Niecy Nash-Betts dedicated her Emmy award to "every Black and Brown woman who has gone unheard yet over-policed, like Glenda Cleveland, Sandra Bland, and Breonna Taylor."[52] The response to her speech was a rousing, emotional, standing ovation.

Breonna's mother, Tamika Parker, reads from her daughter's words in her senior scrapbook. "I was God's blessing to my mother. She brought me into this world as her first child her first baby girl. From this day forward, I was living to please my mother. I feel like I owe her the world".[53] For the mothers, aunts, sisters, cousins, family, friends, and admirers she left behind, we say her name and vociferously proclaim that like the other Black women and women of color who have perished or suffered unjustly at the hands of police, Breonna Taylor's life matters.

Notes

1 *Say Her Name: Breonna Taylor*. S43 E5. An investigative "20/20" by *ABC News* and *Louisville's Courier Journal*. 20 November 2020. https://abc.com/shows/2020/episode-guide/2020-11/20-say-her-name-breonna-taylor

2 Ibid.

3 In homage to *Invisible No More* and author Andrea Ritchie, I refer to Breonna Taylor by her first name as a way of humanizing her.

4 *The Killing of Breonna Taylor* S1 E3 2020. *New York Times* Presents. Lora Moftah and Lizzie Blenk Producers.

5 Callimachi, Rukmini. "Breonna Taylor's Life Was Changing. Then Police Came to Her Door" *New York Times*. 30 August 2020. https://www.nytimes.com/2020/08/30/us/breonna-taylor-police-killing.html#:~:text=Then%20the%20Police%20Came%20to%20Her%20Door.,Credit...&text=An%20ex%2Dboyfriend's%20run%2Dins,she%20tried%20to%20move%20on

6 Ibid.

7 *Say Her Name: Breonna Taylor.*

8 Ibid.

9 *The Killing of Breonna Taylor.*

10 Ibid. In another interview that appears in *Say Her Name* Preonia Flakes describes her relationship with Breonna accordingly: "Instead of being twin sisters, we were twin cousins: Pre and Bre. We always had a bond as kids."

11 Ibid.

12 Ibid.

13 *Say Her Name: Breonna Taylor.*

14 Ibid.

15 Kobin, Billy. "Breonna Taylor's Western High School Teachers Remember a 'Natural-Born Leader'". *Louisville Courier Journal*. 2 October 2020. https://www.courier-journal.com/story/news/local/breonna-taylor/2020/10/01/breonna-taylor-remembered-by-western-high-school-teachers/3589420001/

16 Ibid. Imbedded in the original article, there is a video from the press conference of Breonna's former teachers.

17 Ibid.

18 Ibid.

19 *Say Her Name: Breonna Taylor.*

20 "Breonna Taylor's Life Was Changing."

21 *Say Her Name: Breonna Taylor.*

22 "Breonna Taylor's Western High School Teachers Remember."

23 Ibid.

24 "Breonna Taylor's Life Was Changing."

25 *The Killing of Breonna Taylor.*

26 Ibid.

27 "Breonna Taylor's Life Was Changing."

28 Wolfson, Andrew and Billy Kobin. "Former Louisville Police Officer Pleads Guilty to Lying on Breonna Taylor Search Warrant," *Louisville Courier Journal.* 23 August 2022.

29 *The Killing of Breonna Taylor.*

30 Ibid.

31 Ibid. "It was the first time I had ever fired the weapon outside of the shooting range," Kenneth would later state.

32 *Say Her Name: Breonna Taylor.*

33 Ibid.

34 Ibid.

35 Ibid.

36 Ibid.

37 Ibid.

38 Ibid.

39 Ibid.

40 Ibid. The chilling video of the arrest on the night of the raid shows Kenneth, a young man, scared, crestfallen, and just a twitch away from being shot by any one of the dozens of police officers shouting and pointing their guns at him.

41 Ibid.

42 Ibid.

43 The representative for the LMPD stated in the news conference on the evening of March 13, "This morning we had a critical incident involving one of our officers who was shot and another person at the scene who was killed. I want to say that we are extremely fortunate that our officer ... was not more seriously injured."

44 Ibid.

45 See Lovan, Dylan. "2nd Breonna Taylor Grand Jury Criticizes Proceedings" Associated Press. 22 October 2020 https://www.wsj.com/us-news/law/mistr ial-declared-in-case-against-former-officer-involved-in-breonna-taylor-raid-b8fd2 16a?mod=Searchresults_pos1&page=1.

46 According to a Louisville Courier-Journal article, "Hankison in recent weeks also has been accused of sexual assault by multiple women in viral social media posts. The allegations are similar, saying that he offered intoxicated women a ride home from bars before sexually assaulting them." Costello, Carcy. "Louisville Police Is firing Officer Brett Hankison Involved in Breonna Taylor Shooting". *Louisville Courier Journal.* 19 June 2020. See also Lovan, Dylan. "2nd Breonna Taylor Grand Jury Criticizes Proceedings" Associated Press. 22 October 2020 https://www.wsj.com/ us-news/law/mistrial-declared-in-case-against-former-officer-involved-in-breonna-taylor-raid-b8fd216a?mod=Searchresults_pos1&page=1.

47 Johnson, Krista and Billy Kobin "Fourth Louisville Police Officer Fired in Connection to Raid on Breonna Taylor's Apartment." *Louisville Courier Journal.* 19 August 2022.

48 On November 16, 2023, a US district judge declared a mistrial after the jury failed to reach a consensus on charges filed by the Justice Department that Hutchinson violated Breonna Taylor's civil rights. Three other officers were also indicted at the federal level, with one of them, Goodlett, pleading guilty to falsifying the affidavit. The trials for the two other officers charged is scheduled to begin in 2024 (Calfas,

Jennifer. "Mistrial Declared in Case Against Former Officer Involved in Breonna Taylor Raid". *Wall Street Journal* 16 November 2023).

49 Tunison, John. "Signs Installed in Downtown Grand Rapids for 'Breonna Taylor Way'" *Michigan Live*. https://www.mlive.com/news/grand-rapids/2020/12/signs-installed-in-downtown-grand-rapids-for-breonna-taylor-way.html

50 https://www.futurehistorynow.org/projects/breonna-taylor-mural

51 https://nmaahc.si.edu/about/news/last-chance-view-amy-sheralds-iconic-breonna-taylor-portrait#:~:text=Amy%20Sherald's%20posthumous%20portrait%20of,Vanity%20Fair's%20September%202020%20issue.

52 https://www.nbcnews.com/video/niecy-nash-betts-dedicates-emmy-win-to-breonna-taylor-and-sandra-bland-201970245829

53 *Say Her Name: Breonna Taylor.*

2 Ignored, but Essential: The Relationship of Black Women to the U.S. Political Zeitgeist

Athena M. King

Breonna Taylor, Law Enforcement, and Black Women

Were it not for George Floyd's death at the hands of police officer Derek Chauvin being live streamed in May 2020 during the pandemic, the world may not have learned about Breonna Taylor. People in Louisville, Kentucky knew about the 26-year-old Black woman (emergency room technician) who was shot five times and killed by Louisville police officers who burst into her apartment using a "no knock" warrant, looking for an ex-boyfriend believed to be selling drugs out of her home.[1] Louisville residents learned that there was no ambulance on site with the police; her current boyfriend was armed due to threats from her ex; no lifesaving measures were taken on Breonna's behalf; no drugs were found in her apartment; and her autopsy did not list shooting as her cause of death. Interestingly, the officer who fired the fatal shots – Myles Cosgrove – was not charged or reprimanded for the shooting. However, (former) Detective Brett Hankison fired his weapon but was charged with "wanton endangerment" for potentially *threatening her neighbors* by firing the gun. A woman is shot dead by police, but the only charges stem from the potential threat of her (white) neighbors being shot as well. Why might that have been the case? Black residents in Louisville knew: The life of a Black person – in particular, the life of a Black woman – meant so little to Louisville police that the police lied about her cause of death, no one was charged in her shooting, and her story received little to no coverage outside of Louisville until Floyd's death prompted her family to speak out as well.

Breonna's name has been added to the "Say Her Name" Movement which tells the stories of Black females killed by law enforcement.[2] Since 2015, police have killed nearly 250 women – of which, 48 were Black.[3] Based on the approximate percentage of representation in the country, Black women shot by police (19.2%) represented a higher percentage of those deaths compared to the percentage of Black women in the country (13.9%)[4]. In addition, Black women are generally left out of the conversations regarding police brutality and are oftentimes "collateral damage" if their deaths occur because the police were chasing someone else. To reiterate, the reason Breonna's case came to light was in response to the death of George Floyd at the hands of Milwaukee police officer Derek Chauvin on May 25, 2020, all of which was captured on video on a bystander's phone and broadcast to the rest of the country (and later, the world). *Why might that have been the case?*

In this chapter, I argue that Breonna's murder – and that of other Black women – is indicative of the broader, general lack of concern for what happens to Black women in the United States. More importantly, the same lack of concern for the needs and voices of Black women extends to the political system. Despite the presence of prominent Black women in politics (e.g., Michelle Obama, Kamala Harris, Ketanji Jackson-Brown), the political arena has consistently failed Black women – even though they are the "heart, soul, and backbone" of the Democratic Party. Since the passage of the Voting Rights Act of 1965, a vast majority of Black women are registered Democrats and are the demographic most likely to vote "straight ticket" in every election (Gillespie and Brown 2019). In recent years, Democrats have come to rely on Black women specifically to help win an election – in particular, (former) US Senator Doug Jones in Alabama, Presidents Obama and Biden (in 2008, 2012, and 2020, respectively), and "flipping" the State of Georgia from "red" to "blue" in the 2020 election, courtesy of the "ground campaign" of gubernatorial candidate-turned-political operative Stacey Abrams (Wiltz 2022). In fact, the Democratic Party tends to rely heavily on turnout among Black women voters if they are to have any chance at winning, since the party has seen steady defections of whites (including educated white women) to the Republican Party and supporting Republican candidates for nearly a decade[5].

The party's – and U.S. democracy's – need for Black female participation suggests there would be "positive reciprocity" in which policymaking by Democrats will be designed to accommodate the needs and policy preferences of Black women. To date, only one policy – the CROWN Act – does specifically benefit Black women as it is designed to protect Black women in education and the workplace against discrimination based on Afrocentric hairstyles (e.g., braids, afros, locs, etc.). However, the policy has not been promulgated in all states and has only recently been introduced in Congress for federal consideration[6]. Overall, the political institutions, policymaking in said institutions, and documents which form our government's foundation are not designed to accommodate Black women, and any political "benefits" accrued by Black women were designed with another group in mind.

In this chapter, I address several factors which suggest Black women, while vital to the electoral success of Democrats, have been largely ignored in the political zeitgeist. First, I examine federal electoral policies which should have benefited Black women upon promulgation but did not come to fruition until decades later. I examine voting rights through the lens of the 15th and 19th Amendments and the phenomenon of women's suffrage (particularly through the actions of Sojourner Truth), as the 15th Amendment was designed originally for Black men (and the 19th for white women; as a whole, Black women were largely excluded from the conversation). Black women did not benefit from either – or both – until the passage of the Voting Rights Act of 1965. Next, I look at Black women who made an impact politically but have been relegated to little more than "historical footnotes". I focus on three women – Ida B. Wells-Barnett, Mamie Till (Mobley), and Fannie Lou Hamer – and the roles they played in (a) calling attention to violence against Black people through lynching, and (b) elevating the voice of Black women in the political sphere.

Finally, I focus on factors which contribute to the lack of concern for Black women and their safety/needs at the hands of law enforcement and in the political realm overall. Arguably, stereotypical thinking toward Black women shapes their public and political perceptions in the minds of many non-Black people. The images of Black women as embodiments of the "sapphire", "jezebel", or "mammy" stereotypes continue to be employed everywhere, including the political realm. At the same time, stratification of racial and ethnic groups based on the "Stereotype Content Model"/BIAS map (Cuddy et al. 2008) suggests that Black women rank low in terms of "warmth" and "competence", which renders them undeserving of (and unlikely to receive) positive consideration from the world at large. Because Breonna was single, had multiple boyfriends, and had dated men suspected of criminal activity (drug dealing), she was not afforded a level of respect that otherwise would have been given to a white woman in the eyes of the police. In addition, I address the notion of Black women as stereotypically "loud", "angry", "confrontational", and "masculine"; these stereotypes contribute to law enforcement's perception that Black women, like Black men, are an existential threat. Finally, Black women have been stereotyped as "strong" for so long to the point that, from a medical perspective, they are deemed to have higher pain thresholds and less severe injuries or ailments. As such, even when Breonna lay bleeding to death, law enforcement on the scene did not view her injuries as "serious". In addition, her autopsy report downplayed the role of being shot *five times* in her death. This suggests that in their minds, Louisville police imbued her with preternatural strength and that she must have succumbed to something *other* than bullet wounds. History tells us that Black women's strength is borne of necessity, so Black women have been "strong" historically because they had to be. The notions of "femininity" and "fragility" have never been bestowed on Black women as a group, so it stands to reason that law enforcement members who think of Black women in stereotypical terms would not see Breonna as "an innocent bystander or a victim."

Voting and Black Women: The 15th and 19th Amendments, Women's Suffrage, and the Voting Rights Act

The formal end of slavery in the United States (codified in the 13th Amendment) brought with it the promise of citizenship for Black people; later, the 15th Amendment brought with it the promise of electoral participation. The 15th Amendment gave Black men the right to vote and was used particularly in the South to help Black men register, vote, and elect their own to office at the local, state, and federal levels during Reconstruction.

The basic text of the Amendment implies that this right is extended to all citizens "regardless of race, color, or previous condition of servitude" (U.S. Const. amend. XV, § 1). However, women of all races were denied this opportunity; as such, the push for female suffrage was undertaken by both white and Black women. Unfortunately, the roles of Black women in the suffrage movement were overshadowed by the presence of white female personalities, including Elizabeth Cady Staton, Susan B. Anthony, and Lucretia Mott. Sojourner Truth, former slave and tireless advocate for women's rights, is perhaps the best-known Black woman connected to the movement (Accomando 2003; Humez 1996; Mabee 1988; Painter 1994; Washington 2013). Truth sought to impress upon President Lincoln in 1864 that Black women should be included in all discussions regarding equality – thus, "challenging prevailing notions of racial and gender equality" (womenshistory.org). However, suffrage leaders – and Black men such as Frederick Douglass – did not give serious consideration to the rights of Black women to participate in the political sphere. Douglass' focus was on enfranchising the Black male, which was not terribly unusual given the fact that no women had been given the right to vote (except for states such as Wyoming in 1870). The complicating factor for Black women came with white suffragettes – especially Staton, whose political disagreements with Douglass were born out of the perception that suffrage should be predicated on race *before* gender. As such, white women should receive the right to vote before Black men. In these conversations, it was expected that issues of race and gender in voting rights would preclude Black women from the institution. Sojourner Truth spent much of her time post-slavery advocating for the rights of Black women and at odds with the leading suffragettes of her time (see Accomando 2003; Garland 2005; King 1988; Mabee 1988). In their exchanges, Truth made sure to include the plight of Black women and to argue for their inclusion in the push for women's voting rights. Like Truth, Frances Ellen Watkins Harper was also dedicated to achieving the same rights for Black women; unfortunately, her legacy is even less familiar to the public. However, the one thing the two women had in common was the perception of a "split narrative" where they, as Black women, had to choose in 1869 between advocating for Black, male suffrage (to support the race) and advocating for women's suffrage regardless of race (McDaneld 2015). Both Harper and Truth continued to advocate for both their racial group *and* gender; however, it was Truth who was eventually co-opted by the white suffragettes and allowed to speak and participate in the movement. Despite this "participation", the leaders saw her as a "potential threat" to women's suffrage overall, because the idea of extending voting rights to Black women threatened the probability of any voting rights being established on the national level. Southern states were intransigent in their desire to maintain segregation and keep Blacks in positions of servitude and second-class status; this included extending disenfranchisement indefinitely, if possible.

Eventually, actions by the (white) suffragettes led to the passage of the 19th Amendment. Again, the text of the amendment – "The right of citizens of the United States to vote shall not be denied or abridged by the United States and by any state on account of sex" – suggests inclusion of Black women. Finally, Black women would be afforded the right to vote! Unfortunately, that was not to be the case for many Black women, especially in the South. But why didn't white women fight harder for Black female inclusion in the suffragette movement? Two factors emerged: (1) first, the need to keep Black women at "arm's length" so that Southern states would be more willing to consider women's suffrage legislation if it tacitly excludes Black women (Miller 2015), and (2) the perception of white women toward Black women, which rooted Black women in positions of inferiority and subservience to white women. Perceptions of Black women which exuded strength and independence were antithetical to many white women's thinking – especially Southern women. For Southern women, Black women were viewed most favorably when they embodied the "mammy" stereotype (to be discussed later in the text). Overall, allowing Black women to vote would, in their opinion, be tantamount to establishing parity between Blacks and whites (Miller 2015).

Any chance of Blacks achieving rights similar to whites was soundly rejected in the 1870s with (a) the demise of Reconstruction (and electoral gains made by Black men were reversed through threats of violence), (b) the *Plessy v. Ferguson* decision which established *de jure* segregation in the South, and (c) the attendant practice of "Jim Crow" in the South which entrenched segregation further via state and local laws, customs, and practices[7]. The actions taken by Black women during the Suffragette Movement did not result in universal voting rights for Black women vis-à-vis the 19th Amendment. Instead, it relegated Sojourner Truth to the role of "abolitionist" in the minds of those who know of her, and, unfortunately, rendered the strong, feminist stance of Frances Ellen Watkins Harper to that of a forgotten footnote.

Black women's access to the ballot box was effectively sealed until the passage of the Voting Rights Act of 1965 (VRA). The VRA ensured, finally, the inclusion of Black women in the political sphere. As a result, the percentage of Black women of voting age has increased considerably; according to Census data, the percentage of Black female citizens of voting age increased approximately 31 percent between 2000 and 2017[8].

In addition, the percentage of Black women reporting their political participation (by voting in both presidential and non-presidential years) has remained close to that of white women (within 7 percentage points since the 1980s). The figure below reflects electoral participation of Black women in each decade (from the 1980s to 2020s) compared to other Black men and other racial/ethnic groups (see Figure 2.1).

In addition to voting, registration gave way to Black women seeking and obtaining political office. To date, an estimated 855 Black women have held (or currently hold) office at the local, state, and federal level; of these, 19 have served as a statewide executive (i.e., Lt. Governor, Secretary of State, Attorney General), 50 served (or currently serve) as members of the House of Representatives, but only two served as Senators – sitting Vice President Kamala Harris (D-CA) and Carol Moseley Braun (D-IL, 1993–1998).[9] While these numbers are extremely small given the percentage of Black women in the United States, the number and percentage of Black female officeholders have grown considerably in the 21st century. Regardless of whether they run for office or not, most Black women in the United States tend to support the Democratic Party and its candidates (irrespective of race). Because the Democrats were the party that pushed for passage of the VRA (and Civil

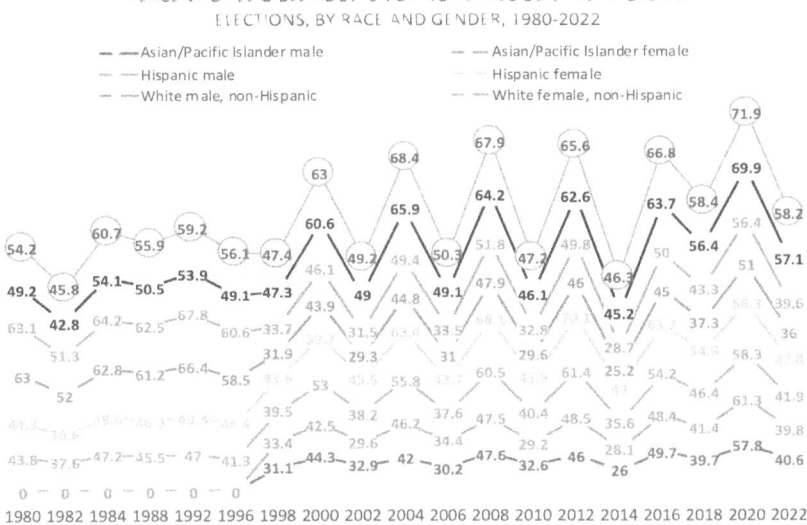

Figure 2.1 Percentage of Adults Voting by Race and Gender in Each Decade, 1980s–2020s

Source: Author's graph compiled using data from Center for American Women and Politics.[10]

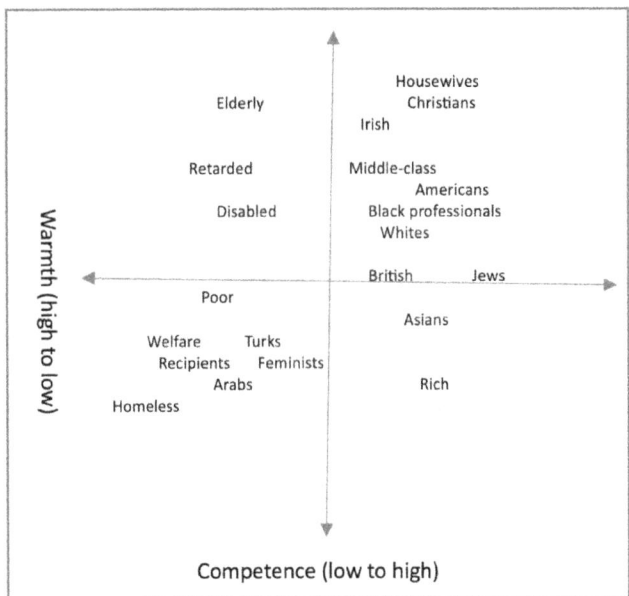

Figure 2.2 Reimagined Stereotype Content Model

Source: The Stereotype Content Model as reimagined by the author with original labels

Rights Act of 1964), they were "rewarded" with Black support, especially from Black women. Since then, Black women have voted in overwhelming numbers for Democratic candidates, and the turnout of Black women has been relied on consistently by Democratic candidates if they are to have any chance at winning (see GA, FL, POTUS elections of 2008–2020). Unfortunately, the Supreme Court decision *Shelby County v. Holder* (2013), which protected Black suffrage in states with histories of disenfranchisement, has made it challenging for Black voters (including Black women) to partici-pate as it removed U.S. Department of Justice oversight of all elections. This decision, coupled with redistricting and Republican-led efforts to hamper minority voting, threatens Black political participation even more.

(Relatively Unknown) Black Female Sociopolitical Pioneers

Black women have always been integral to this country's development; unfortunately, many names are lost to history or are known by some sin-gle, defining characteristic (e.g., "Harriett Tubman freed slaves using the Underground Railroad"). From a sociopolitical (and historical) perspec-tive, there is a perceived lack of emphasis (outside of the Black commu-nity) on the roles of Black women in shaping of public policy and political discourse outside of predominantly Black spaces. When asked to name a few Black women who influenced our history and politics, many students – and members of the public – may mention "contemporary" Black women in politics (i.e., Obama, Harris, Brown-Jackson, Abrams). In this section, I discuss three women whose actions directly shaped politics for Black Americans – and the country as a whole – but have been relegated to "polit-ical footnotes". They include (1) Ida B. Wells-Barnett, whose reporting on lynching called attention to extrajudicial violence committed against Black people (especially in the South); (2) Mamie Till (Mobley), whose 14-year-old son Emmett was the victim of lynching; his story alerted the world to the horrors of lynching and is considered by some to be the catalyst of the Civil Rights Movement; and (3) Fannie Lou Hamer, leader of the Mississippi Democratic Freedom Party and one of the first Black women to argue for Black policy preferences on the national stage (with emphasis on voting and representation within the Democratic party). Individually, each woman – again, not necessarily "household names" – is largely influ-ential in shaping Black politics. More importantly, each woman's actions were overshadowed by mainstream press perceptions of Black women in the United States, and the level of public support each received is consider-ably less than that of many white women (e.g., Gloria Steinem, Geraldine

Ferraro, Hillary Clinton) who made their own demands for policy preferences benefiting women primarily.

Ida B. Wells-Barnett (1862–1931)

Part of the painful legacy of being born Black in America is contending with the history of violence and intimidation committed against the group in the form of lynching. Lynching is defined as "when three or more persons, which constitute a mob, put someone to death extralegally, without court sanction, without legal sanction, and they do it for the purpose of tradition and/or whatever their version of justice is.[11]" The extrajudicial killing of an individual based on the victim's race was the main "tool of terror" used by whites against Black people in the late 19th–mid 20th century, especially in Southern states. Many Blacks could recount a story of someone they knew (or heard about) who were abducted by a group of white men, often tortured and mutilated, then hanged. As a tool of intimidation, the bodies were left to send a message to other Black people: "Commit any kind of infraction (real or imagined), and this could happen to you, too." Estimates of the number of people lynched vary, because the exact number cannot be known (although most settle somewhere between 3,000 and 5,000; the Equal Justice Initiative documents 4,075 lynchings between 1877–1950[12]); however, the prevalence of lynchings was brought to the attention of people outside the South through the writing and reporting of Ida B. Wells-Barnett. She epitomized the actions of Black women in this country: tireless effort which goes largely unnoticed or unappreciated, but important to the overall fabric of America. Wells-Barnett was spurred to action after the deaths of three friends who were lynched in 1892 in Memphis (Tucker 1971), writing anti-lynching pamphlets *Southern Horrors: Lynch Law in All Its Phases* and *A Red Record: Tabulated Statistics and Alleged Causes of Lynchings in the United States, 1892– 1893–1894* (Davis 1995) and co-founding the *Free Speech* newspaper in Memphis (Blaque 2012). Prior to her reporting and writing, the graphic details of lynchings were couched in lurid prose by white, male writers who perpetuated stereotypical notions of Black males as "brutal rapists" and constant threats to white women and used both to justify the torture and death of the condemned men. However, in a vast majority of cases, the Black, male victim had little to no contact with any white woman, let alone one who stepped forward to make an accusation. Rather, white men would frequently (and baselessly) presuppose the existence of some prior assault or insiste that an assault could occur in the future, thus providing pre-emptive protection of white women's perceived "virtue" (Curry 2012; Davis

1995; Giddings 2001; Hamington 2005; Ochiai 1992; Pich 2015; Pinar 2001; Squires 2015). Wells-Barnett challenged these assertions in her writing while advocating for the Black, male victim. At the same time, she used platforms available to her – writing and speeches – to "correct the narrative" regarding lynching. She traveled to Great Britain (England and Scotland) in 1893 to lecture on lynching and apprize Europeans of this peculiar American practice. Her travels were not for pleasure but rather served as "information sessions" to both address lynching and dispel negative perceptions of Black people (especially Black women – see Totten 2008). Wells-Barnett's activities made her the target of the white press, especially white male reporters in the South. One reporter referred to her as a "Black scoundrel"; others are quoted as referring to her as

> notorious negro courtesan, disreputable colored woman, half-cultured hater of all things Southern, saddle-colored Sapphira, intriguing adventuress, strumpet, malicious wanton, paramour to both J.L. Fleming and Taylor Nightingale, unimportant adventuress, and infamous slanderer and traducer. (White 2003: 322)

As such, because Wells-Barnett was stereotypically dismissed by the white press, relatively few whites – particularly in the South – expressed any interest in her work or ending the practice. The influence of the white press encouraged lynching in the South, to the extent that an unofficial, unwritten "lynch law" existed which, according to Wells-Barnett, "It is considered a sufficient excuse and reasonable justification to put a prisoner to death under this 'unwritten law' for the frequently repeated charge that these lynching horrors are necessary to prevent crimes against women[13]." Even whites who saw themselves as "liberal" and "benevolent" had difficulty in accepting Wells-Barnett's narratives. In fact, Wells-Barnett's writing put her at odds with someone she admired – Jane Addams, who made similar arguments to those of white, male reporters regarding reasons for lynching Blacks (Hamington 2005; Townes 1989).

Despite (or perhaps, because of) her actions, Wells-Barnett's influence did not spread far beyond the Black community. Her appeals to the US Congress (along with Presidents McKinley and Wilson) for anti-lynching legislation were largely ignored; however, in 1918 the NAACP supported anti-lynching legislation introduced by Missouri Representative Leonidas Dyer (a white, male, progressive Republican). The bill passed the House but was filibustered in the Senate[14]. An additional bill was introduced in 1935 by New York Democratic Senator Robert F. Wagner and Senator Edward Costigan, who represented Colorado; called the "Costigan-Wagner Bill",

President Roosevelt demurred on supporting it for fear of alienating representatives from the South. Like the Dyer bill, the Costigan-Wagner bill also died in the Senate because of filibuster from Southern representatives[15]. Throughout the remainder of the 20th century, several more anti-lynching bills were introduced, with no successful passage; most recently, H.R. 55 – (the) Emmitt Till Antilynching Act – was signed into law on March 29, 2022 – a century after Wells-Barnett's reporting and activism. 20th-century feminists and scholars sparked a renewed interest in her writings, with similar emphasis on the importance of Wells-Barnett's body of work and legacy regarding reporting and feminism (see Blaque 2012; Boyd 1994; Curry 2012; Giddings 2001; Ochiai 1992; Pich 2015; Pinar 2001; Townes 1989). It is hoped that Wells-Barnett's influence will grow beyond academic circles. She deserves proper credit for both calling the nation's attention to lynching in the late 19th–early 20th century and serving as an influence for women reporters and activists.

Mamie Till-Mobley (1921–2003)

In October 2022, Universal Pictures released the movie *Till*, which introduced much of the world to the story of Mamie Till (later, Mobley). Though critically acclaimed, the movie was not a financial success and has since been made available for online streaming. Regardless, the movie serves as a fictionalized story of a Black mother enduring the pangs of grief for the world to see while exposing them to the horrors of lynching which Wells-Barnett wrote about less than four decades prior.

In August 1955, Mrs. Till sent her 14-year-old son and only child, Emmitt, to Money, Mississippi from Chicago to visit relatives; on August 28, Emmitt was abducted in the middle of the night; three days after that, his mutilated body was found, weighed down by a cotton gin fan tied around his neck. Emmitt's death – and images of his decomposed corpse – brought the horrors of lynching into the mid-20th century for people in the United States and around the world. Though two men – Roy Bryant and J.W. Milam – were charged with murdering the teenager and tried, they were subsequently acquitted by an all-white, male jury. Later, both confessed in a paid magazine interview. Till's murder is seen by some to be the catalyst for the Civil Rights Movement and Mamie Till became the face of "Black female suffering": a mother dealing with the death of a child who was subjected to an extrajudicial killing in an area of the country where separation of the races and relegation of Blacks to permanent second-class status was codified into law, and the ability of whites – especially white men – to inflict harm on Blacks was standard (Harold and DeLuca 2005; Houck 2005; Hudson-Reems 1998; Lawson 2018; Metress 2003; Nash 2018; Onwuachi-Willig 2016; Smith 2015). Though Mrs. Till's grief galvanized many at the time, she is not, arguably, as familiar to the public as she should be. Had she been a white mother, it is likely that her name would not only be remembered but also the death of her child would most likely result in policies designed to prevent this action in the future or provide considerable punishment to people who commit this crime. Today, we have "Amber alerts" and "Polly's Law" – why did it take until 2022 for legislation to be promulgated into law regarding lynching (H.R. 55)? In addition, why is there no additional legislation requiring harsher punishment for the perpetrators if the victim is a child? Why are Black mothers not afforded the same levels of recognition and sympathy as white mothers? Finally, why is Mamie Till remembered mostly by the Black community (2022 movie withstanding)?

It can be argued that Mrs. Till's name does not reverberate across history the way it should because as a Black woman, society dictated she "struggle on her own", and was unworthy of public support and legislation which would have protected her son's life. Many whites in the South gave tacit support to lynching if it meant maintaining "white supremacy". As previously argued, many whites invoked racial stereotypes of Black males to justify lynching. Emmitt was alleged to have "wolf-whistled" at Bryant's wife Carolyn; also, the stereotype of "Black men preying on white women" and robbing them of their "virtue" was the catalyst behind many lynchings. As such, this assumption prompted her brother and husband to abduct the child in the dead of night (Harold and DeLuca 2005; Houck 2005; Lawson 2018; Metress 2003; Nash 2018; Onwuachi-Willig 2016). Though he was only 14 years old, many whites tend to see Black children as "older" or "more mature" than they are[16], [17]; thus, many whites (especially in the South) saw nothing wrong with punishing a Black male – regardless of age – of "sexually intimidating" a white woman. In addition, Black women were expected to "keep their male children in line"; thus, Emmitt's lynching was seen by some as her fault for failing to instill proper manners and etiquette in her son – when in reality, Mrs. Till iterated several times in interviews that she gave Emmitt lessons on how to interact with – or avoid whites in the South, since she was originally from Mississippi herself but moved to Chicago as part of the "Great Migration" (Eichenlaub et al. 2010; Logan et al. 2015; Marks 1985; Price-Spratlen 2008; Tolnay 2003; Tolnay and Beck 1990; Tolnay and Beck 1992; Trotter 2002).

Some whites familiarized themselves with the fact that Mrs. Till's husband (and Emmitt's father) Louis was executed in 1945 by hanging while serving in the Army. Mr. Till was court-martialed and hanged in Italy on July 2, 1945, accused of murdering an Italian woman and raping two others in Civitaveccia[18]. This information was not widely known until after Emmitt's murder; two white Mississippi senators (James Eastland and John C. Stennis) unearthed the information. Southern journalists used this information to justify what was done to the boy. It painted a picture in the minds of white Southerners that Mamie Till perhaps "enabled" the behaviors of her late husband and son, and thus they did not deserve sympathy. (Note that many states had "miscegenation laws" on the books which labeled sex between a Black man and white woman as "rape", so even though Emmitt's father was accused/tried/executed for harming Italian women, journalists and many in the white public gravitated toward his guilt as if the event occurred on American soil.)

Mrs. Till also failed to procure white sympathy in the South due to her perceived "outsider" status; many Blacks in Northeast and Midwestern cities moved there as part of the "Great Migration" (Eichenlaub et al. 2010; Logan et al. 2015; Marks 1985; Price-Spratlen 2008; Tolnay 2003; Tolnay and Beck 1990; Tolnay and Beck 1992; Trotter 2002). While most went in search of greater economic and educational opportunities, many fled due to the perceived threat of lynching. Blacks in the South feared that any misstep could bring a horde of armed white men to their doorstep in the middle of the night and dragging them away to certain death. In fact, the threat of lynching was such that even if the person was not the mob's actual target, they could still be victimized as some lynchings took place because a Black man was in the "wrong place at the wrong time", seen as a "suitable replacement" for the accused. Finally, some Black men were lynched simply for trying to live better lives (e.g., buying a new car, getting a raise/promotion at work). This incensed some whites enough for the "uppity Negro" to be "put in his place". Law enforcement could not be counted on to help, as they were often instigators, participants, or merely willing to turn a blind eye to the event. In any case, the threat of such treatment was enough to force many Blacks northward; once gone, many whites saw them as "traitors" or "agitators" seeking to upset the balance of life in the South. Thus, Mamie Till was seen by some as a "carpetbagger" whose sole purpose was to stir up trouble. In fact, when she learned of Emmitt's disappearance and went to Mississippi, several law enforcement officials tried to convince her that her son was not missing because of kidnapping but ran away on his own. When his body was recovered, they tried to convince her that it was not her son – even though Mrs. Till identified her son's badly decomposed body through a signet ring left to him from his late father (Smith 2008).

While many people know of Emmitt Till, what happened to him, and perhaps have seen the photo of his corpse taken at his viewing (on which Mamie insisted), she herself is not very well-known outside of the Black community. When discussing women as leaders from the 20th century, Mrs. Till is oftentimes ignored or treated as a footnote; however, she should be recognized as an ongoing national symbol against domestic terrorism and violence as well as a woman who lost her entire immediate family to racial violence. Sadly, this was not to be the case for her, and it continues into the 21st century – Black mothers and their grief are often overlooked by the public at large – especially among whites who believe the dead child somehow deserved to lose his – or her – life. Carolyn Bryant, the woman who accused Emmitt of "sexually accosting" her and doomed him to death, was never formally charged with committing a crime. In 2022, the public learned she had been writing a memoir, and had recanted her accusation against Emmitt. She died on April 25, 2023, at the age of 88, never apologizing to Mrs. Till or the Black community for her role in the child's lynching. Black people will remember that in the moments before George Floyd suffocated under Derek Chauvin's knee, he called out for his deceased mother. We can only speculate that Emmitt called out for his as well. Though it did not spare him from death, Mamie Till "heard" her son's cries for help and was spurred to activism in its wake. Unfortunately, the pleas for justice for Black victims continue to be ignored by many whites in this country; as such, Mamie Till deserves to be recognized, remembered, and appreciated in far greater measures.

Fannie Lou Hamer (1917–1977)

It is reasonable to assert that the influence of Black women in the Democratic Party can be traced back to Fannie Lou Hamer (Brooks 2011; Cox 2018; Hamlet 1996; Irons 1998; King 1988; Perlstein 1990; Rouse 2000; Sanders 2015). Beyond her home state (Mississippi) and in a few academic and civil rights circles, Hamer's name and actions have largely been ignored. Born the daughter of sharecroppers in rural Mississippi, Hamer knew the importance of voting and elections to Black people. This was particularly important in Mississippi, in which Black males gained considerable electoral success during Reconstruction, culminating in the election of Hiram Rhodes Revels and Blanche Bruce to the U.S. Senate and dozens more to the Mississippi Senate and House. At the end of Reconstruction, threats of violence – and actual violence – against Black people ensured that Black voting rights in Mississippi would be severely curtailed until the passage of the Voting Rights Act of 1965. However, Mrs. Hamer knew the political winds were shifting and that with civil rights for Blacks guaranteed by the Civil Rights Act of 1964, gaining the right to vote for Blacks (regaining it for Black men) and securing representation for men and women of color was of paramount concern. Hamer's reach in shaping the Democrats goes beyond her role as co-founder of the Mississippi Freedom Democratic Party (MFDP). She was also instrumental in organizing "Freedom Summer", a concentrated effort by activists to fan out across the South to register Blacks to vote, often meeting with resistance and violence from whites. In addition, she co-founded the National Women's Political Caucus, an apparatus used to recruit and train women of all races to run for office. Though Hamer fought for Black suffrage in particular, her work was multiracial, multiethnic, and inclusive in scope; for her, everyone deserved the right to participate in government and have representation in said government (Brooks 2011; Cox 2018; Hamlet 1996; Irons 1998; King 1988; Perlstein 1990; Rouse 2000; Sanders 2015).

So, why is Mrs. Hamer not a household name, even among Black people? First, Hamer presented as a darker-skinned, overweight Black woman with limited education and myriad health concerns. As such, her ascendance to the national political stage was both unexpected and seen as an affront to whites ranging from poll watchers who administered literacy tests (which she passed on the third attempt) and poll taxes (which she paid, eventually), to law enforcement who beat her and other civil rights activists savagely prior to arrest and while incarcerated. Hamer's injuries were such that they caused lifelong health problems. Her greatest exposure – and degree of push-back – came with her attempts to get the MFDP delegates seated at the 1964 Democratic National Convention and President Johnson's literal "silencing" of her during her testimony before the body (Mondale and Ginther 2014; Stern 1990; Walton and Gray 1975; Waltzer 1966). In the eyes of whites, Hamer represented their greatest fear – that white people would be forced to listen not only to someone they deemed racially inferior but who was also a woman. In her attempt to have the MFDP seated alongside the all-white delegation, Hamer exposed the hypocrisy of putative "liberal whites" and their notion of "equality". Vice President Hubert Humphrey was seen as a liberal who supported Black suffrage; however, Humphrey also chose to disrespect Hamer and her delegation by offering a "compromise" of sorts whereby only two members of the MFDP delegated would be seated. More importantly, Humphrey failed to intervene when Hamer's testimony before the convention was preempted by Johnson. Two things account for the preemption: (1) The presence of a Black woman speaking about Black rights before a mostly white, largely conservative audience (with a strong contingent from the South), and (2) Hamer's rhetorical style – coupled with her physical appearance – was being broadcast to a national audience, and Democrats were loath to be associated with a woman who, in their eyes, was the physical embodiment of the "mammy" stereotype (to be discussed in the following section).

Perhaps the most challenging aspect for Hamer – and even larger contributor to her relative obscurity – was the treatment she received at the hands of other Black activists and intellectuals. Because Hamer's formal education ended at the sixth grade and her speaking style utilized what is now referred to as AAVE (African-American Vernacular English), several Black leaders and intellectuals believed that she was not an "adequate" representation of Black people in white "spaces". One could argue, perhaps, that Hamer's level of education, appearance, and speaking style was seen as being unrepresentative of DuBois' "Talented Tenth": After all, the Black founders of the NAACP were light-skinned and well-educated; Martin Luther King, though darker-skinned, was highly educated and eloquent. Plus, the notion of "leadership" was regarded still as the domain of men, and women leaders were predominantly white, middle- to upper-class, and intellectuals.

In essence, Hamer was expected to fail based on skin color, appearance, socioeconomic characteristics, and perceived lack of eloquence. She was not expected to have any such exposure; however, the fact that she achieved was not as well received by Blacks, women, the poor, and other racial/ethnic/socioeconomic groups as it should have been. Despite the challenges before her in and by the public, Hamer continued to fight on behalf of everyone, herself included, despite the toll it took on her health. She died of breast cancer at age 59 in 1977; however, health problems were secondary to what she saw as the biggest obstacle: overcoming centuries of socioeconomic and political disparities for Blacks, women, other groups of color, and the poor. Though she eventually gained accolades and tributes, and her influence on the Democratic Party and women's rights is still felt, the name "Fannie Lou Hamer" does not resonate the way it should across politics – all because she dared to reject her supposed "station in life" and fought on behalf of many – including those who would not have returned the favor were the roles reversed.

(Negative) Black Women Stereotypes and Their Influences on Perception

When the white officers burst into Breonna Taylor's apartment and began firing, they entered expecting to find a Black woman protecting her "criminal" boyfriend. After she was shot, no one came to her immediate aid while the police wasted no time tending to their colleague injured in the crossfire.

Why was this man's health and safety prioritized over Breonna's? Perhaps it is because the officers did not see Breonna as an "innocent victim"; rather, they most likely saw her in terms of a stereotype generally applied to Black women. Historically, Black women have been negatively stereotyped as (1) "sapphires" – loud, angry, pushy, emasculating; (2) "jezebels" – oversexed, duplicitous, perhaps criminally inclined; or (3) "mammies" – overweight, matronly, chaste, harmless, and happy to be in the employ and company of whites. Current stereotypes include the "angry Black woman" – an updated version of "sapphire" who is hostile, aggressive, overbearing, and ill-tempered, and the "welfare queen" – uneducated, unemployed, and lazy, living lavishly off government "handouts" while lying about her inability to work and/or having multiple children and receiving assistance instead of working.

Arguably, the white officers expected to find an unemployed Black woman cohabitating with a known drug dealer boyfriend, both of whom were inclined to resist arrest and should be considered armed and dangerous. We know this was not the case, as Breonna was employed as a full-time emergency room technician, had broken up with the boyfriend/presumed drug dealer, and had no expectations of police breaking down her apartment door in the middle of the night. Her last boyfriend, however, was armed – but primarily to provide defense for Breonna and himself against her ex-boyfriend. In addition, the plight of Black women – and the likelihood of being kidnapped, injured, or killed – is downplayed frequently in the media, especially when juxtaposed against white women.

When a white female goes missing or is severely injured or killed, the media goes to great lengths to humanize her and elicit sympathy for her as a victim while fomenting outrage against the perpetrator. However, it is not unusual for the media to ignore the story when the victim is a Black woman. Arguably, the Louisville police expected no one would care much if a Black woman was injured or killed because of their raid; in fact, Breonna's case remained local until after the George Floyd incident went viral, and Black activists learned of what happened to her. Who is to say whether anyone besides her family, friends, and neighbors would have known anything about her situation had the George Floyd incident not happened? Again, it is a testament to the perceived "invisibility" of Black women and society's inability to see us as lives and experiences to be valued alongside white women.

The Medical Profession and "Strong Black Woman" Trope

Another disturbing trope which may have contributed to Breonna's death is the "strong Black woman". While some may consider being "strong" a compliment, it has the potential to be dismissive. By declaring a Black woman "strong", one may overlook any pain and suffering she is experiencing. Coupled with this notion is the perception that Black women – Black people in general – are less likely to be given proper diagnoses/treatment or receive pain medication; in addition, medical schools taught their students that "Blacks have thicker skin" than other racial groups and are impervious to pain (see Bolnick 2015; Hoffman et al. 2016; Pearson 2015; Stepanikova 2012). As recently as the early 21st century, medical students were taught to believe this. In addition, the history of medicine includes tremendous suffering of Black women at the hands of medical professionals for the sake of medical progress (but with little to no consideration for the patient). For example, experimentation on Black women slaves allowed J. Marion Sims to make history as the "father of gynecology" (Ojanuga 1993; Owens 2017; Savitt 1982; Wasserman 2007). Along with this, Black women have been subjected to unnecessary or unwanted fertility surgeries such as tubal ligation or hysterectomy – dubbed "Mississippi appendectomies" (Barber et al. 2015; Bass 2013; Beal 2008; Fried 2000; Hood 1978; Roberts 2000). Black women are also less likely to receive adequate testing for illness, substandard treatment upon diagnosis, and comparatively less follow-up or aftercare.

Because of the assumptions made about Black women's health, it is reasonable to assume that while Breonna was dying, the police thought her gunshot injuries were not particularly serious; when she died, the cause of death was not listed as gunshot wounds on the death certificate. It must be noted that the concerns of Black women are oftentimes not considered to be an "emergency". The fact that the ambulance was sent away just prior to the door breach and brought back an hour after the shooting indicates that the police considered Breonna's injuries to be a "low-level priority".

Stereotype Content Model and Black Women

To conceptualize stereotypes, Cuddy, Fiske, and Glick (2008), developed the "Stereotype Content Model" (SCM), a typology which maps positive and negative stereotypical groups along dimensions of (a) "competence" (traits which include efficacy, skill, creativity, confidence, and intelligence) and (b) "warmth" (morality, trustworthiness, sincerity, kindness, and friendliness –Cuddy, Fiske and Glick 2008: 63). The author's interpretation of the SCM is shown in figure 2.2 above.

Because stereotypes applied to Black women tend to be negative, the typology suggests Black women stereotyped as "welfare queen" are "LC/ LW" ("low competence/low warmth"); however, Black women with professional jobs (e.g., doctors, lawyers, judges, professors) could be regarded as "HC/HW" ("high competence/high warmth") – which contradicts the "high warmth" designation because of the added stereotype of "being angry". Finally, Black women who are regarded through the "mammy" stereotype – generally thought of as "maternalistic" yet wholly subservient – could be thought of as occupying the space between "LC/HW" and "LC/LW". The "mammy" stereotype is generally seen as an asexual, genial being who is indispensable to white families and cares for them out of love and devotion (which gives her "warmth"), while at the same time having little to no formal education and lacking sophistication (which suggests "incompetence").

Influence of Stereotypical Biases on Assumptions of Guilt

There is a pervasive sentiment in the public (especially among whites) that Blacks who are arrested and injured/killed at the hands of law enforcement must have done something to deserve this treatment. This type of thinking has its roots in slavery, as the "slave patrols" in the South gave way to law enforcement[19]. Also, racialized thinking by whites presents Blacks as "perpetual criminals", so even if the person had not committed or been in commission of a crime at the time they encountered law enforcement, stereotypical thinking of Black people as "criminals" would lead some people to believe the police were justified in their actions. Finally, two laws passed in the 1600s appear to have continued influence on white perceptions of Blacks as criminals: (1) The Virginia law passed in 1669 (and promulgated across the South) made it so that escaped slaves could not fight back against those sent to capture them; more importantly, no one could be charged criminally for killing a slave. And (2) a subsequent law passed in 1672 which allowed any white person to pursue an escaped slave and provided financial remuneration to the owner should the slave die in the process. Together, the two laws rendered slaves powerless to defend themselves; centuries later, it appears those same attitudes are in place regarding law enforcement's perception of Black people. Just as our enslaved ancestors were thought to have committed a crime (by trying to escape bondage) and were at the mercy of slave patrols (or any white person), Blacks today are often assumed to have committed some sort of crime, and the extreme measures law enforcement takes to subdue Black suspects are seen as "justifiable" by them and those who support them. Many surviving suspects (or families of deceased suspects) will sue the officers and department to compensate for their loss. In some instances, law enforcement may be subjected to racial sensitivity training or updated police procedures (e.g., abolishment of "no-knock" warrants, and changes in how suspects are apprehended or detained). Some police departments even seek to hire more police officers of color or engage in community outreach. What the public is less likely to see is law enforcement accepting culpability for their actions since "qualified immunity" allows them to engage in behavior without consequences; rarely does a member of law enforcement get charged for violence against a suspect, especially a Black one. Rarer still is the likelihood of trial/conviction/incarceration of law enforcement for the death of a Black suspect. The police responsible for the death of George Floyd have received this treatment; the officers connected to Breonna's murder were charged with civil rights violations in August 2022, but as of this writing, no state criminal charges have yet to be filed, and Myles Cosgrove – the officer who fired the fatal shots – was hired by the Carroll County (KY) Sheriff's Department in April 2023[20]. Regardless of future actions and outcomes, Breonna's family – and the Black community – seek two specific things: a sincere apology from law enforcement admitting its culpability, along with a comprehensive plan to prevent such occurrences in the future.

Conclusion

Perhaps a bit of justice will come to Breonna Taylor's family after all; on August 4, 2022, the four officers responsible for her murder were federally charged with violations of her civil rights, including (1) unlawful conspiracy, (2) unconstitutional use of force, and (3) obstruction.[21] The officers – Joshua Jaynes, Brett Hankison, Kelly Goodlet, and Kyle Meany – conspired to falsify the affidavit used to obtain the search warrant, giving them permission to conduct the raid which resulted in Breonna's death. Hankison had been charged in state court earlier but was acquitted; Cosgrove fired the shot that killed Breonna and was fired, but interestingly did not receive federal charges. It is hoped that like the George Floyd case, the officers responsible will be brought to justice in some fashion; however, true justice remains elusive since the officer whose bullet ended Breonna's life has been acquitted in state court (and has a new job in another county). Nevertheless, Breonna and her family deserve justice. Perhaps for once, the life of a Black woman will matter; it is hoped that even though the political system has failed to respond to the policy preferences of Black women, and that Black women have been relegated to the fringes of political discourse and action (except when needed at election time), this case will provide the impetus for the political system to finally recognize the role Black women play in it, that we have had leadership that should be better understood and celebrated, and that we are much, much more than stereotypes.

What does it mean to be a Black woman in 21st-century America? For Black women, the notions of "freedom" and "liberty" exist largely in the abstract: As a group, America does not love them – and it never has. The end of slavery in 1865 held the promise that Black women will be treated as citizens, equal to that of white women (at least). While we know that white women were also treated as second-class citizens, white women have been able to rely on race to occupy higher social and economic positioning than Black women as well as being credited with the aesthetic to which all women, regardless of race, are expected to attain if they wish to be accepted in society. Black women in the United States know that despite the strides they have continued to make in the 21st century – especially in terms of income, educational/occupational attainment, status in politics, sports, entertainment, business, etc. – they reside in a country that does. . .not. . .love. . .them. The story of Breonna Taylor's death, along with the historical (mis)treatment of Black women in the United States across centuries and perpetuation of negative stereotypes against Black women, serves as daily reminders that the life of a Black woman is severely undervalued. If this country intends to live up to the promises of "freedom" and "liberty" as espoused in the Declaration of Independence, Black women must be made part of those promises.

Notes

1 Oppel, Richard A. Jr., Derrick Bryson Taylor and Nicholas Bogel-Burroughs "What to Know About Breonna Taylor's Death." https://www.nytimes.com/article/breonna-taylor-police.html?name=styln-breonna-taylor&region=TOP _BANNER&block=storyline_menu_recirc&action=click&pgtype=Article&vari ant=show&is_new=false (Accessed August 21, 2022).
2 #SayHerName. African-American Policy Forum website. https://www.aapf.org/say hername (Accessed July 27, 2022).
3 "Nearly 250 Women Have Been Fatally Shot by Police Since 2015". https://www. washingtonpost.com/graphics/2020/investigations/police-shootings-women/ (Accessed June 30, 2022).
4 "Quick Take: Women of Color in the U.S." February 1, 2023. Catalyst: Workplaces That Work for Women. https://www.catalyst.org/research/women-of-color-in-the-united-states/
5 Igielnik, Ruth. August 18, 2020. "Men and women in the U.S. continue to differ in voter turnout rate, party identification". Pew Research website, https://www.pewr esearch.org/fact-tank/2020/08/18/men-and-women-in-the-u-s-continue-to-dif fer-in-voter-turnout-rate-party-identification/ (Accessed July 24, 2022).
6 Tannenbaum, Emily. July 27, 2022. "Here's Every State That Has Passed the CROWN Act." Glamour Magazine website, https://www.glamour.com/story/the-crown-act-banning-hair-discrimination (Accessed July 30, 2022).
7 *Plessy v. Ferguson*, 163 U.S. 537 (1896).

8 Steven Ruggles, Sarah Flood, Matthew Sobek, Danika Brockman, Grace Cooper, Stephanie Richards, and Megan Schouweiler. IPUMS USA: Version 13.0 [dataset]. Minneapolis, MN: IPUMS, 2023. https://doi.org/10.18128/D010.V13.0

9 "Women Elected Officials by Race and Ethnicity." Rutgers University Center for American Women and Politics. https://cawpdata.rutgers.edu/women-elected-officials/race-ethnicity?race_ethnicity%5B%5D=Black%2FAfrican+American&current=2&yearend_filter=All&items_per_page=50

10 Center for American Women and Politics. "Gender Differences in Voter Turnout" Proportion of Eligible Adult Population Who Reported Voting by Race (Presidential and Non-presidential Years, 1978-2022). https://cawp.rutgers.edu/facts/voters/gender-differences-voter-turnout#NPGR

11 "The Origins of Lynching Culture in the United States." Facing History and Ourselves website, https://www.facinghistory.org/resource-library/video/origins-lynching-culture-united-states

12 "Lynching in America: Confronting the Legacy of Racial Terror." Equal Justice Initiative website, https://eji.org/reports/lynching-in-america/ (Accessed July 23, 2022).

13 Wells, Ida B. "Lynch Law in America – January 1990." Iowa State University Archives of Women's Political Communication website, https://awpc.cattcenter.iastate.edu/2017/03/21/lynch-law-in-america-january-1900/#:~:text=It%20is%20considered%20a%20sufficient,to%20prevent%20crimes%20against%20women. (Accessed July 30, 2022).

14 "Dyer Anti-Lynching Bill". NAACP website, https://naacp.org/find-resources/history-explained/legislative-milestones/dyer-anti-lynching-bill (Accessed July 19, 2022).

15 "Costigan-Wagner Anti-Lynching Bill". NAACP website, https://naacp.org/find-resources/history-explained/legislative-milestones/costigan-wagner-bill (Accessed July 19, 2022).

16 "Black Boys Viewed as Older, Less Innocent Than Whites, Research Finds." American Psychiatric Association website, https://www.apa.org/news/press/releases/2014/03/Black-boys-older (Accessed July 28, 2022).

17 Shapiro, T. Rees. June 27, 2017. "Study: Black girls viewed as 'less innocent' than white girls." Washington Post website, https://www.washingtonpost.com/local/education/study-Black-girls-viewed-as-less-innocent-than-white-girls/2017/06/27/3fbedc32-5ae1-11e7-a9f6-7c3296387341_story.html (Accessed July 28, 2022).

18 Fan, Ryan. November 5, 2021. "Emmitt Till's Father Died For the Same Reason as His Son." Medium website, https://medium.com/frame-of-reference/emmett-tills-father-died-for-the-same-reason-as-his-son-fe6dc7dc451e

19 "The Origins of Modern-Day Policing". NAACP Website, https://naacp.org/find-resources/history-explained/origins-modern-day-policing (Accessed July 13, 2022).

20 Williams, Kevin and Nicholas Bogel-Burroughs. April 24, 2023. "Sheriff's Office in Rural Kentucky Hires Detective Who Killed Breonna Taylor." https://www.nytimes.com/2023/04/24/us/breonna-taylor-police-officer-kentucky.html (Accessed May 15, 2023).

21 Bogel-Burroughs, Nicholas. "Federal Officials Charge Four Officers in Breonna Taylor Raid." https://www.nytimes.com/2022/08/04/us/breonna-taylor-officers-charged.html (Accessed August 8, 2022).

Bibliography

Accomando, Christina. "Demanding a Voice among the Pettifoggers: Sojourner Truth as Legal Actor." *MELUS* 28, no. 1 (2003): 61–86. https://doi.org/10.2307/3595246.

African-American Policy Forum. #SayHerName. website. https://www.aapf.org/sayhername (Accessed July 27, 2022)

Barber, Jennifer S., Jennifer Eckerman Yarger, and Heather H. Gatny. "Black-White Differences in Attitudes Related to Pregnancy among Young Women." *Demography* 52, no. 3 (2015): 751–86.

Bass, Loretta E. "Living in the American South and the Likelihood of Having a Tubal Sterilization." *Sociological Focus* 46, no. 1 (2013): 47–67.

Beal, Frances M. "Double Jeopardy: To Be Black and Female." *Meridians* 8, no. 2 (2008): 166–76.

"Black Boys Viewed as Older, Less Innocent Than Whites, Research Finds." American Psychiatric Association website, https://www.apa.org/news/press/releases/2014/03/Black-boys-older (Accessed July 28, 2022).

Blaque, Ellesia. "Black Ink: Writing Black Power with the Words of David Walker, Ida B. Wells, and Malcolm X." Counterpoints 406 (2012): 5–18.

Bogel-Burroughs, Nicholas. "Federal Officials Charge Four Officers in Breonna Taylor Raid." https://www.nytimes.com/2022/08/04/us/breonna-taylor-officers-charged.html (Accessed August 8, 2022)

Bolnick, Deborah A. "Combating Racial Health Disparities through Medical Education: The Need for Anthropological and Genetic Perspectives in Medical Training." *Human Biology* 87, no. 4 (2015): 361–71. https://doi.org/10.13110/humanbiology.87.4.0361.

Boyd, Melba Joyce. "Canon Configuration for Ida B. Wells-Barnett." *The Black Scholar* 24, no. 1 (1994): 8–13.

Brooks, Maegan Parker. "Oppositional Ethos: Fannie Lou Hamer and the Vernacular Persona." *Rhetoric and Public Affairs* 14, no. 3 (2011): 511–48.

Brown, Nadia, and Kira Hudson Banks. "Black Women's Agenda Setting in the Maryland State Legislature." *Journal of African American Studies* 18, no. 2 (2014): 164–80.

Celeste, Manoucheka. "'What Now?': The Wailing Black Woman, Grief, and Difference." *Black Camera* 9, no. 2 (2018): 110–31. https://doi.org/10.2979/Blackcamera.9.2.08.

Cox, Julia. "Never a Wasted Hum: The Freedom Singing of Fannie Lou Hamer." *Women's Studies Quarterly* 46, no. 3 & 4 (2018): 139–57.

"Costigan-Wagner Anti-Lynching Bill". NAACP website, https://naacp.org/find-resources/history-explained/legislative-milestones/costigan-wagner-bill (Accessed July 19, 2022).

Cuddy, Amy J. C., Susan T. Fiske, and Peter Glick. "Warmth and Competence as Universal Dimensions of Social Perception: The Stereotype Content Model and the BIAS Map." Advances in Experimental Social Psychology, 40: 61–149. Academic Press, 2008. https://doi.org/10.1016/S0065-2601(07)00002-0.

Curry. "The Fortune of Wells: Ida B. Wells-Barnett's Use of T. Thomas Fortune's Philosophy of Social Agitation as a Prolegomenon to Militant Civil Rights Activism." *Transactions of the Charles S. Peirce Society* 48, no. 4 (2012): 456. https://doi.org/10.2979/trancharpeirsoc.48.4.456.

Davis, Simone W. "The 'Weak Race' and the Winchester: Political Voices in the Pamphlets of Ida B. Wells-Barnett." *Legacy* 12, no. 2 (1995): 77–97.

"Dyer Anti-Lynching Bill". NAACP website, https://naacp.org/find-resources/history-explained/legislative-milestones/dyer-anti-lynching-bill (Accessed July 19, 2022).

Eichenlaub, Suzanne C., Stweart E. Tolnay, and J. Trent Alexander. "Moving Out but Not Up: Economic Outcomes in the Great Migration." *American Sociological Review* 75, no. 1 (2010): 101–25.

Fan, Ryan. November 5, 2021. "Emmitt Till's Father Died for the Same Reason as His Son." Medium website, https://medium.com/frame-of-reference/emmett-tills-father-died-for-the-same-reason-as-his-son-fe6dc7dc451e

Fiske, Susan T., Amy J. C. Cuddy, Peter Glick, and Jun Xu. "A Model of (Often Mixed) Stereotype Content: Competence and Warmth Respectively Follow from Perceived Status and Competition." Journal of Personality and Social Psychology 82, no. 6 (June 2002): 878–902. https://doi.org/10.1037/0022-3514.82.6.878.

Fried, Marlene Gerber. "Abortion in the United States: Barriers to Access." *Health and Human Rights* 4, no. 2 (2000): 174–94. https://doi.org/10.2307/4065200.

Garland, Libby. "'Irrespective of Race, Color or Sex:' Susan B. Anthony and the New York State Constitutional Convention of 1867." *OAH Magazine of History* 19, no. 2 (2005): 61–64.

Giddings, Paula. "Missing in Action Ida B. Wells, the NAACP, and the Historical Record." *Meridians* 1, no. 2 (2001): 1–17.

Gillespie, Andra, and Nadia E. Brown. "#BlackGirlMagic Demystified: Black Women as Voters, Partisans and Political Actors." *Phylon (1960-)* 56, no. 2 (2019): 37–58.

Hamington, Maurice. "Public Pragmatism: Jane Addams and Ida B. Wells on Lynching." *The Journal of Speculative Philosophy* 19, no. 2 (2005): 167–74.

Hamlet, Janice D. "Fannie Lou Hamer: The Unquenchable Spirit of the Civil Rights Movement." *Journal of Black Studies* 26, no. 5 (1996): 560–76.

Harold, Christine, and Kevin Michael DeLuca. "Behold the Corpse: Violent Images and the Case of Emmett Till." *Rhetoric and Public Affairs* 8, no. 2 (2005): 263–86.

Hoffman, Kelly M., Sophie Trawalter, Jordan R. Axt, and M. Norman Oliver. "Racial Bias in Pain Assessment and Treatment Recommendations, and False Beliefs about Biological Differences between Blacks and Whites." *Proceedings of the National Academy of Sciences of the United States of America* 113, no. 16 (2016): 4296–301.

Hood, Elizabeth F. "Black Women, White Women: Separate Paths to Liberation." *The Black Scholar* 9, no. 7 (1978): 45–56.

Houck, Davis W. "Killing Emmett." *Rhetoric and Public Affairs* 8, no. 2 (2005): 225–62.

Hudson-Weems, Clenora. "Resurrecting Emmett Till: The Catalyst of the Modern Civil Rights Movement." *Journal of Black Studies* 29, no. 2 (1998): 179–88.

Humez, Jean M. "Reading 'The Narrative of Sojourner Truth' as a Collaborative Text." *Frontiers: A Journal of Women Studies* 16, no. 1 (1996): 29–52. https://doi.org/10.2307/3346921.

Igielnik, Ruth. August 18, 2020. "Men and Women in the U.S. Continue to Differ in Voter Turnout Rate, Party Identification". Pew Research website, https://www.pewresearch.org/fact-tank/2020/08/18/men-and-women-in-the-u-s-continue-to-differ-in-voter-turnout-rate-party-identification/ (Accessed July 24, 2022)

Irons, Jenny. "The Shaping of Activist Recruitment and Participation: A Study of Women in the Mississippi Civil Rights Movement." *Gender and Society* 12, no. 6 (1998): 692–709.

King, Deborah K. "Multiple Jeopardy, Multiple Consciousness: The Context of a Black Feminist Ideology." *Signs* 14, no. 1 (1988): 42–72.

Lawson, Erica S. "Bereaved Black Mothers and Maternal Activism in the Racial State." *Feminist Studies* 44, no. 3 (2018): 713–35. https://doi.org/10.15767/feministstudies.44.3.0713.

Logan, John R., Weiwei Zhang, Richard Turner, and Allison Shertzer. "Creating the Black Ghetto: Black Residential Patterns before and during the Great Migration." *The Annals of the American Academy of Political and Social Science* 660 (2015): 18–35.

"Lynching in America: Confronting the Legacy of Racial Terror." Equal Justice Initiative website, https://eji.org/reports/lynching-in-america/ (Accessed July 23, 2022)

Mabee, Carleton. "Sojourner Truth and President Lincoln." *The New England Quarterly* 61, no. 4 (1988): 519–29. https://doi.org/10.2307/365943.

Mabee, Carleton. "Sojourner Truth, Bold Prophet: Why Did She Never Learn to Read?" *New York History* 69, no. 1 (1988): 55–77.

Marks, Carole. "Black Workers and the Great Migration North." *Phylon (1960-)* 46, no. 2 (1985): 148–61. https://doi.org/10.2307/274413.

McDaneld, Jen. "Harper, Historiography, and the Race/Gender Opposition in Feminism." *Signs* 40, no. 2 (2015): 393–415. https://doi.org/10.1086/678147.

Metress, Christopher. "'No Justice, No Peace': The Figure of Emmett Till in African American Literature." *MELUS* 28, no. 1 (2003): 87–103. https://doi.org/10.2307/3595247.

Miller, Joe C. "Never a Fight of Woman against Man: What Textbooks Don't Say about Women's Suffrage." *The History Teacher* 48, no. 3 (2015): 437–82.

Mondale, Walter, and Morgan Ginther. "The Mississippi Delegation Debate at the 1964 Democratic National Convention: An Interview with Former Vice President Walter Mondale." *Southern Cultures* 20, no. 4 (2014): 106–15.

Nash, Jennifer C. "The Political Life of Black Motherhood." *Feminist Studies* 44, no. 3 (2018): 699–712. https://doi.org/10.15767/feministstudies.44.3.0699.

"Nearly 250 Women Have Been Fatally Shot by Police Since 2015". https://www.
washingtonpost.com/graphics/2020/investigations/police-shootings-women/
(Accessed June 30, 2022)

Ochiai, Akiko. "Ida B. Wells and Her Crusade for Justice: An African American Woman's
Testimonial Autobiography." *Soundings: An Interdisciplinary Journal* 75, no. 2/3
(1992): 365–81.

Ojanuga, Durrenda. "The Medical Ethics of the 'Father of Gynaecology', Dr. J. Marion
Sims." *Journal of Medical Ethics* 19, no. 1 (1993): 28–31.

Onwuachi-Willig, Angela. "The Trauma of the Routine: Lessons on Cultural Trauma
from the Emmett Till Verdict." *Sociological Theory* 34, no. 4 (2016): 335–57.

Oppel, Richard A. Jr., Derrick Bryson Taylor and Nicholas Bogel-Burroughs.
"What to Know About Breonna Taylor's Death." https://www.nytimes.com/
article/breonna-taylor-police.html?name=styln-breonna-taylor&region=TOP
_BANNER&block=storyline_menu_recirc&action=click&pgtype=Article&vari
ant=show&is_new=false (Accessed August 21, 2022).

"The Origins of Lynching Culture in the United States." Facing History and Ourselves
website, https://www.facinghistory.org/resource-library/video/origins-lynching-
culture-united-states (Accessed July 23, 2022)

"The Origins of Modern-Day Policing". NAACP website, https://naacp.org/find-resour
ces/history-explained/origins-modern-day-policing (Accessed July 13, 2022).

Owens, Deirdre Cooper. "Black Women's Experiences in Slavery and Medicine." In
Medical Bondage, 42–72. Race, Gender, and the Origins of American Gynecology.
University of Georgia Press, 2017. https://doi.org/10.2307/j.ctt1pwt69x.7.

Owens, Deirdre Cooper. "Contested Relations: Slavery, Sex, and Medicine." In *Medical
Bondage*, 73–88. Race, Gender, and the Origins of American Gynecology. University
of Georgia Press, 2017. https://doi.org/10.2307/j.ctt1pwt69x.8.

Owens, Deirdre Cooper. "Historical Black Superbodies and the Medical Gaze." In
Medical Bondage, 108–22. Race, Gender, and the Origins of American Gynecology.
University of Georgia Press, 2017. https://doi.org/10.2307/j.ctt1pwt69x.10.

Painter, Nell Irvin. "Representing Truth: Sojourner Truth's Knowing and Becoming
Known." *The Journal of American History* 81, no. 2 (1994): 461–92. https://doi.
org/10.2307/2081168.

Pearson, Rachel. "Racial Bias in Medicine." *Scientific American* 313, no. 5 (2015): 14–16.

Perlstein, Daniel. "Teaching Freedom: SNCC and the Creation of the Mississippi
Freedom Schools." *History of Education Quarterly* 30, no. 3 (1990): 297–324.
https://doi.org/10.2307/368691.

Pich, Hollie. "Various, Beautiful, and Terrible: The Life and Legacy of Ida B. Wells-
Barnett." *Australasian Journal of American Studies* 34, no. 2 (2015): 59–74.

Pinar, William F. "Black Protest and the Emergence of Ida B. Wells." *Counterpoints* 163
(2001): 419–86.

Plessy v. Ferguson, 163 U.S. 537 (1896).

Price-Spratlen, Townsand. "Urban Destination Selection among African Americans during the 1950s Great Migration." *Social Science History* 32, no. 3 (2008): 437–69.

"Quick Take: Women of Color in the U.S." February 1, 2023. Catalyst: Workplaces That Work for Women. https://www.catalyst.org/research/women-of-color-in-the-united-states/

Ritter, E. Jay. "Sojourner Truth." *Negro History Bulletin* 26, no. 8 (1963): 254–255

Roberts, Dorothy. "Black Women and the Pill." *Family Planning Perspectives* 32, no. 2 (2000): 92–93. https://doi.org/10.2307/2648220.

Rouse, Jacqueline A. "Examination of Black Female Grass Roots Leaders in Mississippi during the 1960s: Annie Devine, Fannie Lou Hamer and Annie Rankin." *Negro History Bulletin* 63, no. 1/4 (2000): 23–30.

Ruggles, Steven, Sarah Flood, Matthew Sobek, Danika Brockman, Grace Cooper, Stephanie Richards, and Megan Schouweiler. IPUMS USA: Version 13.0 [dataset]. Minneapolis, MN: IPUMS, 2023. https://doi.org/10.18128/D010.V13.0.

Sanders, Crystal R. "More Than Cookies and Crayons: Head Start and African American Empowerment in Mississippi, 1965–1968." *The Journal of African American History* 100, no. 4 (October 2015): 586–609. https://doi.org/10.5323/jafriamerhist.100.4.0586.

Savitt, Todd L. "The Use of Blacks for Medical Experimentation and Demonstration in the Old South." *The Journal of Southern History* 48, no. 3 (1982): 331–48. https://doi.org/10.2307/2207450.

Shapiro, T. Rees. June 27, 2017. "Study: Black girls viewed as 'less innocent' than white girls." Washington Post website, https://www.washingtonpost.com/local/education/study-Black-girls-viewed-as-less-innocent-than-white-girls/2017/06/27/3fbedc32-5ae1-11e7-a9f6-7c3296387341_story.html (Accessed July 28, 2022).

Smith, Shawn Michelle. "The Afterimages of Emmett Till." *American Art* 29, no. 1 (March 2015): 22–27. https://doi.org/10.1086/681653.

Smith, Valerie. "Emmett Till's Ring." *Women's Studies Quarterly* 36, no. 1/2 (2008): 151–61.

Squires, David. "Outlawry: Ida B. Wells and Lynch Law." *American Quarterly* 67, no. 1 (2015): 141–63.

Stepanikova, Irena. "Racial-Ethnic Biases, Time Pressure, and Medical Decisions." *Journal of Health and Social Behavior* 53, no. 3 (2012): 329–43.

Stern, Mark. "Lyndon Johnson and the Democrats' Civil Rights Strategy." *Humboldt Journal of Social Relations* 16, no. 1 (1990): 1–29.

Strings, Sabrina. "Obese Black Women as 'Social Dead Weight': Reinventing the 'Diseased Black Woman.'" *Signs* 41, no. 1 (2015): 107–30. https://doi.org/10.1086/681773.

Tannenbaum, Emily. July 27, 2022. "Here's Every State That Has Passed the CROWN Act." Glamour Magazine website, https://www.glamour.com/story/the-crown-act-banning-hair-discrimination (Accessed July 30, 2022)

Tolnay, Stewart E. "The African American 'Great Migration' and Beyond." *Annual Review of Sociology* 29 (2003): 209–32.

Tolnay, Stewart E., and E. M. Beck. "Black Flight: Lethal Violence and the Great Migration, 1900-1930." *Social Science History* 14, no. 3 (1990): 347–70. https://doi.org/10.2307/1171355.

Tolnay, Stewart E., and E. M. Beck. "Racial Violence and Black Migration in the American South, 1910 to 1930." *American Sociological Review* 57, no. 1 (1992): 103–16. https://doi.org/10.2307/2096147.

Totten, Gary. "Embodying Segregation: Ida B. Wells and the Cultural Work of Travel." *African American Review* 42, no. 1 (2008): 47–60.

Townes, Emilie M. "Black Women and Social Evil: Ida B. Wells-Barnett's Social and Moral Perspectives as Resources for a Contemporary Afro-Feminist Social Ethic." *NWSA Journal* 1, no. 3 (1989): 568–69.

Trotter, Joe William. "The Great Migration." *OAH Magazine of History* 17, no. 1 (2002): 31–33.

Tucker, David M. "Miss Ida B. Wells and Memphis Lynching." *Phylon (1960-)* 32, no. 2 (1971): 112–22. https://doi.org/10.2307/273997.

Walton, Hanes, and C. Vernon Gray. "Black Politics at the National Republican and Democratic Conventions, 1868-1972." *Phylon (1960-)* 36, no. 3 (1975): 269–78. https://doi.org/10.2307/274392.

Waltzer, Herbert. "In the Magic Lantern: Television Coverage of the 1964 National Conventions." *The Public Opinion Quarterly* 30, no. 1 (1966): 33–53.

Washington, Margaret. "Going 'Where They Dare Not Follow': Race, Religion, and Sojourner Truth's Early Interracial Reform." *The Journal of African American History* 98, no. 1 (2013): 48–71. https://doi.org/10.5323/jafriamerhist.98.1.0048.

Wasserman, J., M. A. Flannery, and J. M. Clair. "Raising the Ivory Tower: The Production of Knowledge and Distrust of Medicine among African Americans." *Journal of Medical Ethics* 33, no. 3 (2007): 177–80.

Wells, Ida B. "Lynch Law in America – January 1990." Iowa State University Archives of Women's Political Communication website, https://awpc.cattcenter.iastate.edu/2017/03/21/lynch-law-in-america-january-1900/#:~:text=It%20is%20conside red%20a%20sufficient,to%20prevent%20crimes%20against%20women. (Accessed July 30, 2022)

White, Lisa A. "The 'Saddle-Colored Sapphira' Versus The 'Slimy Rattlesnake': The Rhetorical Melee of Ida B. Wells and Edward Carmack On the Subject of Lynching." *Tennessee Historical Quarterly* 62, no. 4 (2003): 310–31.

Williams, Kevin and Nicholas Bogel-Burroughs. April 24, 2023. "Sheriff's Office in Rural Kentucky Hires Detective Who Killed Breonna Taylor." https://www.nytimes.com/2023/04/24/us/breonna-taylor-police-officer-kentucky.html (Accessed May 15, 2023)

Wiltz, Kyler. "'Who Runs the World? Girls!' A Case Study on the Role That Stacey Abrams Has Played in Changing the African American Political Voice and American Political Realm as a Whole," n.d., 19. (2022)

"Women Elected Officials by Race and Ethnicity." Rutgers University Center for American Women and Politics. https://cawpdata.rutgers.edu/women-elected-officials/race-ethnicity?race_ethnicity%5B%5D=Black%2FAfrican+American&current=2&yearend_filter=All&items_per_page=50

3 Total War: The Justification of Lynching Black Women

AARON TREADWELL

> By and by up springs a woman,
> Rushes boldly to the front;
> Shouting, "I will board the vessel,
> And for justice I will hunt."
>
> – Abraham Kendric[1]

Introduction

On September 29, 1885, Harriet Finch was lynched in Chatham County, North Carolina. Her reported offense was murder, and her day in court was never had. Lynchings are illegal executions conducted publicly by three or more assailants.[2] This definition asserts lynching as a crime since the assailants did not have the legal right to prosecute; and yet, those who lynched were seldom persecuted and were often reported as "hands of the unknown." The practice of lynching in the United States had become so prevalent in the 19th and 20th centuries that monikers of the act have become common jargon. Some phrases include practicing "judge lynch" and exercising "vigilante justice." These particular terms express the commonality of lynching practiced in the United States and its unwarranted support amongst the public.

Lynching culture in American history has frequently received review as a male-on-male phenomenon; this narrative often depicts white men as the attackers and Black men as the victims. However, revisionist history has been telling a more inclusive story, which includes the lynching spectacle targeting Black women.[3] At least seventy-four African American females were lynched in the long-Nadir Era of race relations (1877–1930), and many of their murders included abnormal ceremonies compared to the aforementioned male-on-male attacks.[4] Many of these catastrophes include acts of sexual abuse, which exposes an intricate dynamic often overlooked in lynching culture. *Judge Lynch*, especially when transgressed against Black women, was more than an attempt to punish wrongdoings, but as a psychological and physical tool that sought to strip one's gender and humanity. By raping and hanging a Black woman in the nude, African Americans of the day were forced into racial castes that included a denial of femininity. In order to comprehend the events that led to the death of Breonna Taylor, this chapter will expose the nation's tradition of publicly executing Black women and how it sought to strip their femininity. Psychological reverberations from Black female lynchings should be recognized as a horror equal to male counterparts and a unique tradition that continues to impact the Black psyche. In addition, the gruesome treatment attached to Black female lynching spectacles exhibits a dual-stripping of Blackness during this specific event. Black women were not just stripped of their humanity in death, but onlookers were reminded of their inability to attain "true femininity."

The horrors of these events have caused generational reverberations identified by psychologists as P.T.S.S. (post-traumatic slave syndrome).[5] Many historical lynch reports have erroneously described Black women only as companions of the lynched instead of acute victims. By overlooking the experiences of Black women, many of the future violent acts against Black women will not receive their proper contextualization. For example, many male-on-male lynchings were enacted in the name of vigilante justice to punish a supposed criminal. These acts would eventually create a social narrative of Black criminality. In contrast, the lynching of Black women in the same era included persons convicted of crimes and those associated with convicted men, resulting in a culture that not only dignified the graphic abuse of a Black woman in public but also the condemnation of her humanity based on her surroundings (Black men).

Analysis of the lynching activities in the long-Nadir Era exhibits five white women being lynched, compared to seventy-four Black women.[6] It is common that social and racial communities disproportionally enact violence on themselves (i.e., white-on-white crime, Black-on-Black crime, etc.). That said, the Nadir Era tradition of lynching did not follow this standard. Black women were targeted with lynching crimes by only white males, and there was a ratio of 1 to 15 compared to their white female counterparts.[7] This ratio exhibits the willingness of Americans in the Nadir Era to treat Black women in a way that was unique to the standards of their society. Statistical analysis also exposes a historical trend that Black women were often lynched for relationships and not actual crimes. Twenty-six Black women are listed in the

OSF lynching database as an "accessory to murder," "complicit in murder," or of "relation to the murderer," which exhibits the danger thrust amongst the entire African American community.[8]

The arguments presented above expose two haunting correlations. First, being a Black woman in the long-Nadir Era made one fifteen times more likely to be lynched. By so doing, this tradition exhibits the historical tradition of Black women not receiving equal access to the judicial system. Simply put, Black women were considered fifteen times less deserving of their Fifth Amendment rights. Second, 35% of lynched Black women were killed for living with or being in close relation to a Black man.[9] This point indicates the totality in which violence was enacted upon the Black family and reinforces the necessity to include women in racial violence research. When examining the intricacies of Black female lynchings, this chapter will explain why exploring racial violence in American history without mentioning Black women is an incomplete study. By so doing, a study on Black female lynching will expose why Breonna Taylor was caught in a historical "total (race) war" that has been commonplace within the United States.

Theorizing Complicity

During the Nadir Era, a Black woman's social surroundings resulted in thirty-five lynchings, and the inner workings of this statistic were due to racism's desire to redefine womanhood during the Nadir Era.[10] As mentioned earlier, the system is historically known as the "cult of true womanhood," and it would impact white and Black persons. The experiences of white women, especially those privileged within the system, included physical protection, social control of their sexuality (miscegenation), protection from hard domestic labor, and the establishment of eugenic beauty standards (an elevation of value based on white phenotype).[11] In contrast, Black women were plagued by this ideology and ultimately received a juxtaposition within its practice. The polarization included a public acceptance of physical punishment, a tradition of white male sexual abuse, a standard placement in domestic and demeaning labor forces, and a denigrated status of beauty due to their phenotype. The culmination of these trends amongst Black women allowed them to receive heinous treatment compared to white women, which included experiences as visceral as those received by Black men.

The cult of true womanhood was one Victorian-based concept utilized in the Nadir Era.[12] The "Southern Belle" was another concept used to diagnose the inner workings of true femininity and a hierarchy used to define womanhood. The norms within this concept included the "quality" of one's hair, the color and softness of one's skin, one's ability to be absent from manual labor, and one's ability to dress in fine Victorian clothing. Access to these attributes warranted protection in the name of white supremacy, and those juxtaposed were permanently (racial caste) blocked from deserving protections.[13] Hence, Blackness and femininity had become an ideological contradiction.

These forms of ideological control sought to restrict the maneuverability of womanhood, creating a hierarchy of womanhood and supplying justification for male constraint over women. For the white male, white womanhood's constraints were connected to their "softness," which justified protection. In contrast, Black women were itemized as not needing such protections, and she was objectified as lacking true "femininity." Lacking femininity, as mentioned above, impacted public and private treatment and even equated to receiving treatment equal to that of a man. Female lynching is but one of the appropriate examples.

Domestic workers, sharecroppers, and other remedial workers were often identified as the antithesis of the cult of true womanhood based on their proximity to white femininity. Such positioning forced Black women of the Nadir Era into a racial caste that received mental and physical denigration. Symbolic depictions of Black women as "mammies, pickaninnies, jezebels, and sapphires" advanced the "treat them like men" sentiments and became justifications for Black women "lacking" true womanhood. This ideological system also negated white guilt if persons were to transgress against a Black woman.

The ideological components of the cult of true womanhood also stripped Black women from owning their sexual identity by stereotyping them in non-normative extremes. Some Black women were described as masculine, emphasizing their mistreatment (or anti-white protection). When Black women were put to work with Black male counterparts, this experience would often result in them being described as having male physiques that could take the "wear and tear" of a man.[14] These stereotypes would even evolve to clinicians arguing that Black women could bear children without pain due to tough and manly genetics.[15] Black women would also be ideologically targeted with internal stereotypes, including a belief that they had extremely high libidos. These typecasts socially identified Black women as over-sexualized persons who could never be raped and instead temptresses for white men. Known as "sapphires," these stereotypes often described Black women as lacking the restraint of true womanhood.[16]

Being denigrated to a lower tier of femininity haunted Black women in the Nadir Era psychologically and physically, including the public's comfortability in using demeaning epithets toward Black women, sexually assaulting

Black women, and lynching Black women without public remorse. Whenever sexual violence was enacted against Black women in the long-Nadir Era, due to their racial-caste identification and lack of "femininity," repercussions were seldomly reinforced. According to one freedwoman, "in those days you didn't 'rape' (Black women). You just took what you wanted from the woman."[17] The process of stripping humanity and sexuality during slavery has received significant research, whereas the stripping of Black femininity during the Gilded Age must continue to be examined. If slavery stripped the humanity from African Americans and lynching stripped away femininity, comprehending why seventy-four Black women hung on a rope becomes a logical progression toward the Breonna Taylor murder.

The Rituals Used Against Black Women

As white terrorists exercised "judge lynch" to protect the "cult of true womanhood" from Black men raping them, coincidently, many Black female victims were "mob-raped before being executed" by white men.[18] Marie Scott, a teenager at the time of her lynching, was allegedly raped or involved in a nonconsensual relationship at the time of her death. Reports were soon released that Scott was a prostitute intended to justify her sexual concourse. Lemuel Peace, the alleged white perpetrator, was said to have been killed by Scott during a sexual transaction. There is no evidence from Scott supporting or negating this claim, and her defense was ignored due to the assumption that she was a predatorial sex worker.[19]

   In response to her alleged crime, the public decided to enact vigilante justice against her. Some reports identify as many as 1,000 persons storming the Wagoner City jail and "dragging" Scott from her prison cell. On the Casaver Avenue and Main Street intersection, she would be lynched right in front of Stockton's grocery store. Reports of this lynching also described a "gang rape" prior to the lynching. Instead of condemning these heinous acts, public papers justified Scott's sexual abuse by advertising her supposed drug use, prostitution, and gambling in the local media. The *Tulsa Star* described Scott as part of a "red light" district, and other journals identified her as a member of a local Black prostitution house. This particular establishment was said to be "run by Black women" and was targeting white men in a predatory way. In comparison, white-owned sex houses were not deemed as dangerous.[20]

   Alma Houze and her sister **Maggie Houze** also endured sexual torture. They were lynched in 1918 for allegedly murdering their employer. This unnamed man had an abusive history with both women and at the time of the lynching, both sisters were pregnant with his child. The women argued that they acted in self-defense but never had their time in court. They were publicly lynched after a torturous gang rape.[21]

Laura Nelson endured sexual abuse prior to her lynching in 1911 in Okfuskee County, Oklahoma. Nelson, who also went by Mary, got into a dispute with local Sheriff Loney over an accusation that her husband stole from a butcher. After conducting an illegal search of the Nelson residence, Loney found no evidence but refused to end the interrogation. Instead, it was reported that he decided to arrest Mary and her son, L.D., for criminal suspension. Nevertheless, Sheriff Loney never made it to the police station. Loney was found dead after the attempted arrest, and Mary and L.D. soon became suspects on the run. There are conflicting reports of the incident, but Mary testified when caught that she shot the sheriff in self-defense. L.D. also took credit for shooting the sheriff and argued that the sheriff was attempting to attack his mother sexually.[22]

Both Mary and L.D. were eventually arrested and charged with the murder of Sheriff Loney and were booked in the Okfuskee County Jail in Okema. Mary's husband was also arrested for burglary, leaving the entire family behind bars. When rumors spread in the community of an attempted family jail escape, a lynch mob took Mary and her son from the Okfuskee County jail. It traversed several miles outside the city to Yarbrough's Crossing. It was at this location that both persons were sexually tortured. L.D. was castrated in public, while Mary was gang raped. Both mother and son were then hanged and shot by a firing squad as they hung from the North Canadian River bridge.

Charlotte Morris, in 1896 was not documented as being raped prior to her lynching, but her case did expose sexual control as part of her trauma. Her alleged crime was miscegenation, and her documented form of death was arson and gunshots. Documents state that Morris became a target when she started a business rivalry with a local white saloonkeeper, and she "started to sell cakes and coffee and lunch to the men who worked with [her husband], and as Johnnie Gassener only sold whisky and beer, and a little other stuff."[23] When the community attacked Ms. Morris, her house was set on fire twice near the Westwego Wharf of the Texas and Pacific Railway Company.[24] According to records, the second fire caused the interracial couple to flee their boat, leaving them to be met by a barrage of gunshots. When the Morris family's remains were retrieved, it was said that one of the bodies "had been decapitated," although there is no mention of who was beheaded.[25] The event had a witness: the couple's 12-year-old son, Patrick Morris Jr. His testimony was not held up in court due to his race, and nobody was charged for this crime, even as a national story.[26]

Alongside female lynching and sexual torturing, there was also the practice of Black women being targeted for their proximity to Black men. In 1915, **Cordella Stevenson** was kidnapped by terrorists in front of her husband, raped, and then hanged naked in public. These actions were in response to her son's alleged role in arson. It should be noted that instead of attacking her son or her husband, Arch Stevens, Cordella's murderers decided to attack only her. This questionable decision exposes the frequency with which Black women are used as social pawns in the battle of intimidation. It also exposes how women were often strategically attacked due to their accessibility.[27]

Contextualization

In the early 20th century, the NAACP (National Association for the Advancement of Colored People) fought diligently to pass anti-lynching legislation in the United States. The goal was to pass a federal law that would define lynching as a federal hate crime while educating America about its tumultuous history of racial-caste violence. The NAACP would release a report in the 1920s, *Thirty Years of Lynching in the United States, 1889–1919*, to encourage congressional action and would soon attach itself to Representative "Dyer's" Bill, H.R. 11279 on April 18, 1918.

Dyer's Bill sought to "protect citizens of the United States against lynching in default of protection by the States." It would charge lynch mobs with capital murder in federal court, fine persons between $5,000 and $10,000, and those monies would be paid to the victim's immediate family. Jail time was included in this bill, and this supported the establishment of a fair courtroom proceeding.[28]

On January 26, 1922, a Republican-controlled chamber passed Dyer's Bill 231 to 119, whereas the highly influenced southern Senate overturned the bill. Its consideration would be continued to be stalled until it was ultimately killed in the 1920s by the "indifference of its friends and the strategy of its enemies."[29] Fast forward 100 years, and in 2022, the Senate passed an anti-lynching bill titled the Emmett Till Anti-Lynching Act. Till's lynching, which took place in 1955 Mississippi, happened over thirty years after Dyer's Bill introduction and finely exhibited an *Alea iacta est*, or the "die has been cast" attitude toward lynching in the nation. Suppose it took 4,000 persons to be lynched prior to Till in order for Americans to identify the horrors of racial-caste violence, and over sixty-seven years after his death to pass legislation on racial-caste violence. In that case, the psychological cleansing of the nation has exposed itself as a slow process decades behind.

Part of the "die" metaphor in the United States includes the psychological acceptance of Black female terrorism and the utilization of such violence for total war juvenile justice. Taylor's murder was acted upon similarly to the 20th century lynchings mentioned above. The raid on the Taylor household was botched and cited as wanton endangerment, as the officers willingly ignored their civil rights. They lied about a search warrant and the use of deadly force.[30] Just as vigilante justice raids operated during the Nadir, the Louisville officers also took advantage of the systematic racist legislation of their time, which included the allowance of "no-knock warrants" in the city. By so doing, inner-city and predominately Black communities would be stripped of their fourth amendment rights, which protected them from unreasonable searches and seizures by the government. Just as lynch mobs illegally burst into holding cells to take the lives of Black persons, police officers broke into the Taylor house and shot her five times.

By analyzing the closeness of the two events, racial-caste violence has exposed itself as an ideological norm within America that has yet to be exterminated. Even with the passing of the Emmett Till Anti-Lynching Act, the erasures of Critical Race Theory within society's learning spaces allowed heinous traditions and customs to be misidentified as one-off incidents. Instead, by identifying the cultural norms of racial-caste violence within this nation, researchers may properly enhance their ability to curtail America's ultimate sin.

Notes

1 Abraham Kendric, *Indianapolis Freeman*, 1895.
2 Amy Wood, *Lynching and Spectacle: Witnessing Racial Violence in America, 1890–1940*.
3 Michael J. Pfeifer, *The Roots of Rough Justice Origins of American Lynching*.
4 Seguin, Charles, and Rigby, David. United States National Lynching Data, 1883–1941. Catalog no. 2833. Ithaca, NY: Cornell University. Cornell Center for Social Sciences | Research Support. Charlottesville, VA: Center for Open Science [distributor]. 2023-5-1. Version 1. https://doi.org/10.6077/fwrd-k930.
5 Joy a Degruy, *Post Traumatic Slave Syndrome: America's Legacy of Enduring Injury and Healing*, Joy Degruy Publications Inc; Revised ed. edition (September 11, 2017).
6 OSF Database.
7 Seguin, C., and Rigby, D. (2019). National Crimes: A New National Data Set of Lynchings in the United States, 1883 to 1941. Socius, 5. https://doi.org/10.1177/2378023119841780
8 Ibid.
9 Seguin, C., and Rigby, D. (2019). National Crimes: A New National Data Set of Lynchings in the United States, 1883 to 1941. Socius, 5. https://doi.org/10.1177/2378023119841780.

10 Ibid.

11 Barbara Welter. "The Cult of True Womanhood: 1820–1860." *American Quarterly* 18, no. 2 (1966): 151–74. https://doi.org/10.2307/2711179.

12 Catherine Clinton, "Reconstructing Freedom" in *Divided Houses: Gender and the Civil War*, ed. Catherine Clinton and Nina Silber (New York: Oxford University Press), 311.

13 Welter. The Cult of True Womanhood.

14 Keisha Goode and Barbara Katz Rothman. "African-American Midwifery, a History and a Lament." *The American Journal of Economics and Sociology* 76, no. 1 (2017): 74–76. http://www.jstor.org/stable/45129363.

15 Ibid.

16 J. Celeste Walley-Jean. "Debunking the Myth of the 'Angry Black Woman': An Exploration of Anger in Young African American Women." *Black Women, Gender + Families* 3, no. 2 (2009): 70–71. https://www.jstor.org/stable/10.5406/blacwomegendfami.3.2.0068.

17 Tera Hunter, *To 'Joy My Freedom: Southern Black Women's Lives and Labors after the Civil War* (Cambridge: Harvard University Press, 1997), 34.

18 Frank Shay, *Judge Lynch: His First Hundred Years* (New York: Ives).

19 Maria Delongoria (2006). "Stranger Fruit: The Lynching of Black Women The Cases of Rosa Richardson and Maria Scott." Dissertation University of Missouri-Columbia.

20 *Sista's Swung Too; Tulsa Star,* 25 April 1912; *Coweta Star,* 2 April 1914; *Tulsa Star,* 4 April 1914; *Wagoner County Record,* 2 April 1914.

21 *House papers.*

22 Clark, p. 96; This account of the lynching was compiled from the following sources: the Daily Oklahoma, 31 March 1914; the Independent, 9 April 1914; Coweta Star, 2 April 1914; Coweta Times, 2 April 1914; Morris News, 9 April 1914; Muskogee Phoenix, 3 April 1914; Tulsa Daily World, 3 March 1914; Tulsa Democrat, 1 April 1914; Tulsa Evening Star, 4 April 1914; Tulsa Star, 4 April 1914; Wagoner County Courier, 2 April 1914; Wagoner County Record, 2 April 1914; the Tuskegee News Clippings File, Lynching-1914, Microfilm Collection, Reel 221; Clark's Lynching in Oklahoma; and Johnnie P. Stevenson, interviewed by Maria DeLongoria, Oklahoma City, Oklahoma, 28 April 2005. Stevenson authored a fictional account of the lynching.

23 Richmond Planet, January 25, 1896.

24 Lauren Davis *Masters Thesis*

25 Delongoria (2006) "Stranger Fruit.

26 Ibid.

27 Chicago Defender, December 18, 1915.

28 *Congressional Record*, House, 65th Cong., 2nd sess. (May 7, 1918): 6177.

29 Zangrando, *The NAACP Crusade against Lynching, 1909–1950*: 69.

30 Bogel-Burroughs, Nicholas. "What Is 'Wanton Endangerment,' the Charge in the Breonna Taylor Case?" *The New York Times*, September 23, 2020, https://www.nytimes.com/2020/09/23/us/wanton-endangerment.html.

4 Witch Hunts, Lynchings, and No-Knock Raids upon the Black Female Body: White American Mores, Social Order, and Safety

BISOLA A. WALD

Introduction

> If any female feels she need anything beyond herself to legitimate and validate her existence, she is already giving away her power to be self-defining, her agency. (hooks 2014)

This chapter is grounded within the self-defining power of Black women across the histories and borders of Black Africa, who remain as our shared mother, and of all Black lives. The Dahomey women (1600s–1890s) of present-day Benin, West Africa, were famed as intellectual strategists and warriors who protected their community and ensured its continued prosperity. Queen Nzinga Mbande (c. 1583–1663) of the Mbundu tribe in present-day Angola spent decades defending her people from Portugal's colonial encroachment. Despite their attempt to capture her, she remained with her people and peacefully died in her old age. Queen Nanny (c. 1685–c. 1750), though kidnapped from her home in Ghana into enslavement in Jamaica, trained other captives in guerrilla warfare, ultimately freeing some eight hundred enslaved people. Queen Yaa Asantewaa (c. 1840–1921) of the Ashanti Empire reclaimed her homeland, laying siege to British forces until her capture and exile. Stories of African women as mothers, wives, intellectuals, diplomats, engineers, inventors, rulers, and warriors stretch across Pan-African history and cannot be defined, understood, nor contained within the Eurocentric logic of whiteness and womanhood.

As a descendent of Africa and a daughter of these Pan-African Sister-elders, I claim that creation resounds the legitimacy of the Pan-African woman and validates her critical role in the existence and protection of Black life. All human life was birthed from the divine interconnection/transformation that had taken place within her. As her children, we self-define and create our paths because her teachings of freedom and self-determination are written on our hearts and inscribed on our souls. In employing her power to birth humankind, she did not give away her power. That power, which legitimizes itself along with our existence, continues to validate our collective right to live in partnership with one another and with creation. Since the beginning, to herself the Black woman bears witness, for nothing beyond her can neither legitimize nor validate her testimony.

With this truth, I stand in solidarity with the testimonies of the living (Anjanette Young, 2019, Darnella Frazier[1] and her 9-year-old cousin, 2020, Diamond Reynolds[2] and her 4-year-old daughter, 2016, Alayna Albrecht-Payton,[3] 2021, Karissa Hill,[4] 2020, Piaget Crenshaw,[5] 2014) and of the taken (Mary Black, 1692, Jennie Steer, 1903, four young girls[6] named Addie Mae Collins, Cynthia Wesley, Carole Robertson, and Denise McNair, 1963, also Eula Love,[7] 1979, Eleanor Bumpers,[8] 1984, Mary Mitchell,[9] 1991, 7-year-old Aiyana Mo'Nay Stanley-Jones,[10] 2010, Atatiana Jefferson,[11] 2019, Janisha Fonville,[12] 2015, Michelle Cusseaux,[13] 2014, Gabriella Nevarez,[14] 2014, Tanisha Anderson,[15] 2014, Breonna Taylor, 2020). We commit to saying their names, asserting their mattering, and remembering their stories (see endnotes).

The violence that has desecrated their humanity and the aggression and traumas we continually endure remain passed over as insignificant by white supremacist hetero-patriarchal politics, legislation, and hegemonic institutionalized culture. Even if we are left alive to tell our stories of the atrocities and indignations that occur in the margins, dominance cannot or will not listen past the media attention of trending hashtags. Our Black womanhood, even our girlhood, is rendered invisible and simultaneously a clear and present danger. America repeats what it has told our ancestors for generations: their violence and our trauma are ours alone to bear, and the expectation remains that we will bear them quietly. However, Mother Africa, who willed our ancestors to speak, resist, and live, implores us now to open our mouths. We who will not tolerate the omission of what we saw and what we heard and experienced, this disruptive resound, is a tribute to you. Sister Breonna Taylor, I say your name with the shared breath that our Dark Mother has given us. I say your name.

This essay decenters the moral scapegoating of the "few bad apples" dominant narratives. It aims to explore the ideological and social construction of the binarism of the Black pagan and the white (and moral) colonizer

(Paglia 96). This binarism undermines our consciousness while justifying the demoralization and criminalizing of Black individuals and communities as a necessary source of white sociocultural purging. Therefore, I explicate the historical and traditional characteristics of white systemic terrorism by exposing the relationship between the European and Early Colonial American witch hunts (Jones), how its colonial and imperial desire to control and discipline the Black body has remained constant despite our multicultural context (McLaren 91), and its presence within our current circumstance – modern-day state-sanctioned witch hunts enacted upon Black communities. I assert that these witch hunts, as ritualistic now as they were in the American past, are performed under three main pretenses: morality, safety, and social order. Similar to the witch hunts legitimized by European and Colonial American moral and political systems, the present-day hunting and execution of Black women reflect unscrupulous and ideological domination rooted at the intersection of white supremacy and misogyny.

The Taken Black Lives

Breonna Taylor (taken in 2020)

Breonna Taylor was born in Grand Rapids, Michigan, on June 5, 1993. Raised by Tamika Palmer (her mother) and Trory Herrod, she graduated from Western High School in Louisville, attended the University of Kentucky, and soon became an Emergency Medical Technician and Practicing Registered Nurse. On March 13, 2020, her life was abruptly and violently taken by Louisville police officers while she was sleeping in her apartment.

On March 13, 2020, Louisville Metro Police Department (LMPD) Detective Brett Hankison, Sgt. Jonathan Mattingly and Officer Myles Cosgrove broke down Taylor's apartment door, fully armed and wearing plain clothing. Upon hearing what he assumed was a home invasion, Kenneth Walker, Breonna's boyfriend, armed himself and approached the door. As the intruders broke into the home with weapons drawn, Walker fired one shot in self-defense. Subsequently, LMPD officers opened fire, killing Taylor by firing five bullets into her body. Despite being licensed and registered to own the firearm he used to protect the home from plain-clothed and fully armed intruders, Walker was initially arrested for attempted homicide but later released.

The LMPD failed to accurately report the events surrounding the fatal intrusion, initially stating that Taylor did not suffer any injuries. Moreover, the No-Knock Warrant prepared by Detectives Cosgrove and Jaynes and executed by Hankison, Mattingly, and Cosgrove proved to be unnecessary because their suspect, Jamarcus Glover, did not reside at the residence and had been apprehended by officers earlier that morning 10 miles from Taylor's home.

Tamika Palmer filed a wrongful death lawsuit, and during the proceedings and the aftermath of the investigation, LMPD Police Chief Steve Conrad retired, Detective Hankison was terminated, the officers who prepared the search warrant were also terminated, and Kentucky issued a law to limit, but not entirely ban, the future use of No-Knock Warrants. Detective Hankison was charged with wanton endangerment of neighboring residents when he recklessly shot fire into Taylor's home, yet was not charged for her death. However, on August 23, 2022, Detective Kelly Goodlett came forward and pleaded guilty to conspiracy to mislead, falsify information, and obstruct justice. She explained how she and another detective met in a garage to construct the stories they later gave the public.

Ms. Taylor left behind her partner, Kenneth Walker, her mother, Tamika Palmer, her mother's partner, Trory Herrod, and her little sister Ju'niyah Palmer. She will be sorely missed by her family, friends, work colleagues, patients, and various community members. With no criminal involvement, Sister Breonna was taken at age 26 by law enforcement officers who invaded her home while she was sleeping (Castello and Duvall).

The Preamble to the U.S. Constitution

> We, the People of the United States, in Order to form a more perfect Union, establish Justice, ensure domestic tranquility, provide for the common defense, promote the general welfare, and secure the Blessings of Liberty to ourselves and our Posterity, do ordain and establish this Constitution for the United States of America. (The United States Constitution)

Justice and domestic tranquility may be inscribed within the preamble of the U.S. Constitution, but their claims did not maintain the tranquility of Breonna's home on March 13, 2020. Moreover, their ideals did not produce justice in the aftermath of her death. Instead, promises of justice and domestic tranquility were undermined by our nation's dominant and distorted claims of morality, safety, and social order, which serve to rationalize policies and practices that are irrational, dehumanizing, and destructive.

Establishing justice and assurance of tranquility may be inscribed within the Constitution. However, individuals and communities in the margins have historically and traditionally held the United States accountable to its constitutional commitments. This labor has disproportionately burdened those systematically marginalized due to intersectional social identities. In a closer look at the events surrounding Breonna's death, the undermining of justice and domestic terrorism rather than domestic tranquility during and after her death are evident.

The events during and after Breonna's death do not reflect these social mores and commitments of justice, domestic tranquility, liberty, or general welfare. However, these esteemed values and practices are given prominence within the U.S. Constitution. Within early U.S. documents, such as the Constitution, justice is centered as essential to the foundation and beliefs undergirding American life.

However, a closer look at the definition and underpinnings of the concept of "justice" and "just" elucidates salient social assumptions and agreements. Justice is defined as "the maintenance or administration of what is just, especially by the impartial adjustment of conflicting claims or the assignment of merited rewards or punishments" (Merriam-Webster). Moreover, within the same source, "just" is defined as "conforming to fact, reason, a standard of correctness; or to what is morally upright or good." Therefore, to contextualize or administer justice within a place and time, there are assumed mores that inform and bind customary beliefs and practices shaping the guidelines used to evaluate and judge individuals and groups.

To assist in this inquiry, I interrogate the inherent contradictions of dominant ideologies, which are stitched together by three significant notions within the U.S. context: morality, safety, and social order. Moments from now, I will share stories of my sisters – of our ancestors. Despite the actions of systemic domination to demonize (morality), criminalize (public safety), and control or kill (social order) them, their personhood remains. These three cords stitch together this chapter; however, it is up to you to discover them and, hopefully, interrogate them. These cords serve to stitch together justifications surrounding accounts of state-sanctioned violence (too many to list here fully).

Nevertheless, these discursive cords are weak threads that undermine any legitimacy, and that rather unhinge the whole damn thing. These cords of morality, public safety, and social order claim to be true to their nature, but when applied to an American history that fails to see itself honestly, we see a reflection of ideas, practices, and outcomes that are quite the opposite. These three false commitments weave deceptive discourses meant to demonize, criminalize, and control, even to the point of murder. These guises produce material consequences that disproportionately burden Black lives, families, and communities.

I will not (or will try not to) labor to persuade you of the value of Black lives. They already hold inherent value gifted to them by our Dark Mother.

I need not persuade you of their humanity. Instead, in the (re)tellings we share, you will see their humanity and your own through the (re)embodiments of Black life, death, and survivorship. Moreover, as you and I sit here together, as we honor Sister Breonna in conversation, I do not plan to reduce my rage, disgust, or hurt in the circumstances she endured.

In the same way that I approach this moment with you, I invite you to feel, to listen, to pause my words *even in mid-sentence*, to breathe, to feel again, and to come back to our conversation – you, Breonna, and me. Attend to your body, spirit, and emotions by allowing them to respond to how power and subjugation enter a space. Suddenly, sweet moments are forced to shift away from what might have been moral, safe, and orderly just minutes or seconds before. Notice these cords as guises and observe their contradictions and question the ways in which they betray and undermine themselves.

Let's talk first about our Sister.

Mary Black (Taken in 1692)

On July 1, 1692, Sister Mary Black, an enslaved woman of African descent, was accused of performing witchcraft in Salem Village, Massachusetts. She, and at least two other enslaved women, Candy and Tituba, were accused of using magic to harm a group of white adolescent girls who had recently become "afflicted." When summoned and questioned by Reverend Samuel Parris, Mary insisted on her innocence. Nevertheless, she was imprisoned from April 21, 1692, to January 1693. Her trial began during the last month of her confinement, and with no continued testimonies against her, the case was dismissed, and she was released back to her enslaver (Hoffman).

Mary's case was a part of the Salem Witch Trials (1692–1693), a time of moral panic and mass hysteria around divination and superstition. About 200 individuals were accused in the aftermath, and many were hung or burned at the stake. The mass accusations and killing of many lives reflected an early colonial obsession with morality and spirituality. It also provides an example of America's early indulgences in manipulating moral precepts and spiritual authority for public character defamation and personal and sociopolitical gain.

Sister Breonna...

I see important fragments of your story woven within that of Sister Mary Black. Although Mary lived through the accusations she endured while bearing the burdens of white supremacy, patriarchy, and enslavement, her examination and confinement were further rationalized by pretenses of moral superiority and judgment. What released her from imprisonment was not an acknowledgment of the right, the good, or innocence that characterized her testimony but the chang-ing will of the European colonists who had lost interest or motivation towards her trial. Notions of wholesome American moral beliefs and legal practices con-tinually offer immunity from criminal liability to law enforcement officers in the same way that these notions offered immunity to the law enforcement offi-cers who avoided judicial consequences for taking your life. Although Detective Hankison, who shot through your body, was indicted for wanton endangerment, he was not charged with endangering you.

Moreover, even though no drugs or money associated with illegal activity were found in your home, your character and worth were still publicly scruti-nized under the gaze of a criminal justice system and dominant society that assumes its moral superiority and assigns moral deficits to marginalized com-munities. Under these pretenses of moral standards and judgments, early colo-nial America first attempted to control society and secure its place within it. The pretense of morality, along with its assumed standards and rights of judgment, continue to rationalize the reckless and unnecessary use of no-knock warrants, increasing from 3,000 (1981) to 60,0000–70,000 (Kraska, 2010) along with the racialized and disproportionate targeting of a "suspected subject population" comprised of 42% Black individuals. These figures are extremely significant, being Black and African Americans comprised only 12.3% of the United States population in 2010. (U.S. Census Bureau)

Jennie Steer (Taken in 1903)

On July 27, 1903, *The Cincinnati Enquirer* read, "News has reached here that Jennie Steer, who gave poison in a glass of lemonade to beautiful sixteen-year-old Elizabeth Dolan, caused a frightful death, was lynched by an infu-riated mob about sundown last night. The lynching occurred on the Beard plantation, near where the woman's crime was committed."

Although Jennie, a Black woman, maintained her innocence, the report suggested that, because of her arrest "for deliberately poisoning a young girl," she had also likely murdered her white employer whose death she had reported months prior. The report concludes by stating that "there is no apparent sympathy for the negress… among the law-abiding blacks of that section." Not only do these final words suggest a solidarity of consent regard-ing Jennie's perceived negative character and insignificance, but it also alludes to her social expendability within the Black community.

The white mob may never have discovered how the child had become sick to death. However, in their communal and ritualist purge upon the Black body, they assumed that the ambiguity of the tragic death of a child could be soothed by nothing else but the reestablishment of social disorder as they knew it. They feared the foreign body, the Black body, as much as one might fear the powerlessness, uncertainty, and emotional pain of loss. The common characteristics of social order are structured and patterned practices. In U.S. capitalism and society, social order offers relational regulation and customs of power and hierarchy. The death of a white child, of any child, painfully unsettles family systems and relationships. These painful feelings are heightened in a society that physically captures, enslaves, and domesticates dark bodies that they fear in an attempt to rationalize a tragic death and reconcile a perceived fear toward racial outsiders. Their murderous rage served to reestablish hierarchical structures of power and social order. What they could not reconcile within their bodies, they were hell-bent on reconciling outside their bodies, specifically through Sister Jennie Steer's body.

Sister Breonna. . .

I see specific reflections of your story mirrored in that of Sister Jennie Steers. Like you, her execution turned up no criminal evidence beyond what was crafted in the imaginations of an irrational and infuriated mob of vigilantes who effectively curtailed any opportunity for true justice. Like her, those who assumed moral superiority over her were committed to their humanity and notions of a good/bad binary. This ideology centers on white people's values, interpretations, and experiences and uses racializing beliefs to justify disparate treatment and practices. The white bodies, motivated by racial bias and hatred and experiencing the pain and ambiguity of the unexpected death of a white child in their community, looked to soothe themselves through false vindication. Seeking an object upon which to execute their justice, they internalized false notions of their inherent righteousness and judicial authority while legitimizing their violent ritual by purging the hate, the pain, and the irrational through a foreign body. Despite Sister Jennie's inherent worth and humanity, pretenses of morality and social order forced her torture and death to be an example – a balm for the cognitive dissonance that has plagued White America for generations.

The officers who took your life later learned that who they were looking for was apprehended moments earlier across town. However, in the impetus of the raid, as officers of the law, they believed that their work in your apartment was to bring back into alignment with the social order, activities and contrabands assumed to be in your home that undermined and threatened that order. This forceful reestablishment of power hierarchies fails to address the social disorder we have all inherited. Through white ideologies and commitments enshrined by racializing beliefs and practices, corporal punishment on Black bodies is feigned as justifiable.

The officers in your death may not have been struggling to reconcile the trauma of a white community unexpectedly losing a white child; however, the work of Menakem (59–62) explains how the white body harbors racialized trauma that has become decontextualized from the historical roots of gender and ethnic violence first among Europeans and then extended to nonwhite groups. White America continues to control the movement of nonwhite bodies while unable to control their own white racialized fears of the past and present nor honestly explain the disparities that implicate their ancestors and most esteemed leaders, systems, and traditions.

I assert that those most committed to white ideological pretenses of mores, social order, and safety who prioritize whiteness as normative thought and standard will continue to enforce, regulate, and unscrupulously judge through racialized lenses that fail to reconcile their consciousness with their reality. Ironically, regardless of racial identity, however strongly shaped by it, many of those most committed to these White American ideologies saturate law enforcement, military, and government positions. Moreover, these racialized lenses undermine our U.S. Constitution just as the initial writers of the Constitution so effectively evaded justice in their own time.

The Living Black Lives

In order to acknowledge our full humanity, I challenge progressive U.S. interests that espouse Black lives when they are dead while failing to recognize the humanity of the Black lives who currently reside in their schools, churches, places of work, and communities. I assert that the voices of Black women who have lived through these invasive and often fatal European/White American racialized purgings should be heard as clearly and urgently as the voices of our taken Black Sisters. Our lives and names matter before our deaths popularize them into hashtags, murals, posters, T-shirts, or political discourses. Although symbols, gestures, and organizing around our collective struggle and human solidarity across backgrounds are invaluable and necessary, valuing our lives as Black people cannot remain suspended in white progressive consciousness. Recognizing our truths means valuing our knowledge, experiences, and humanity. At the same time, we live as worthy of mattering even before the potential to mobilize a posthumous movement, protest, or hashtag after we are gone.

With this undeniable truth, similar to Sister Breonna's story, I explore the modern no-knock and quick-knock warrants that invaded the lives of Black women who are still alive, housing the truth and the trauma they experienced.

To analyze this persistent and violent phenomenon, I take a close look at the experience of Sister Anjanette.

Anjanette Young (2019 Survivor)

A Chicago-area social worker named Anjanette Young was winding down from a day's work in her apartment in Chicago, Illinois. As she proceeded to undress in the safety of her apartment, twelve white male police officers abruptly broke down her front door and entered her home while she stood naked. For up to forty-five minutes, she pleaded to be covered up, stating that they were in the wrong house and demanding to know what was happening. Later, Sister Anjanette reported feeling invisible as the officers ignored her cries and tears and willfully left her physically unprotected and sexually exposed. During the initial days and months after the sexual injustice and trauma that she experienced, the city of Chicago and the police department dismissed her attorney's request for accountability. Moreover, the city attempted to block video content and information that was critical in exposing the misconduct of the officers.

The following are the words of Sister Anjanette as she reflects on the night of terror:

> One of the biggest issues with the night of the incident is I felt like they didn't see me. So that night, they didn't see me. I yelled, I cried, I made requests and they never responded to me. And when they did respond to me, it was like, "You need to calm down." They never heard me when I was crying out to them, "Can I please put some clothes on?" They didn't hear me when I said over 43 times, "You have the wrong place." They continued to do what they did in standing right in my presence but totally ignoring me. So no, they didn't see me and then I continued to feel like I was not seen by the city. (Young et al. 135)

Although the Chicago police department and mayor's office assumed their sexual and psychological violence and trauma was hers alone to bear, Sister Anjanette refused the expectation that she would bear it quietly. Today, she is using her knowledge, experience, background in social work, and her community to work for justice through collaborative efforts that acknowledge the voices and nurture healing among women, girls, and men whose traumatic experiences have been forced in the margins due to paradigms of power and privilege.

Sister Breonna...
  I see specific reflections of your story mirrored in that of Sister Anjanette Young. Like you, her safety appeared to be the furthest concern from the task law

enforcement perceived for themselves. Her psychological and physical safety were not prioritized in the raid of her home. She reported overwhelming fear and trauma experienced through the sexual violence happening to her as the twelve white men invaded her home. Though unarmed, she had little reason to doubt that any movement on her part would have cost her life.

As in your story, Sister Anjanette's life was secondary to the well-being of armed officers. Political discourse stemming from former U.S. President Ronald Reagan's "war on drugs" indeed created a war – a domestic war between local and federal law enforcement and Black humanity fatally taken and forever traumatized in their own homes. No-knock and quick-knock warrants continue legitimizing White American practices rooted in white supremacy, patriarchy, and anti-Blackness. The "war on drugs" continues to materialize dark bodies as nothing more than casualties of that war. Despite the common phrase among law enforcement units to "protect and serve," many officers most effectively protect their own racialized fears that center their humanity and power at the expense of human casualties – at the desecration of domestic tranquility. As in your case and that of Sister Anjanette, and in a similar fashion to the unethical recklessness of law enforcement, governing and judicial bodies serve themselves by protecting their powerful constituents, their reputations, and their reelection agendas with little concern as to how their concealment of facts, abuse of power, and compliance with injustice undermines our U.S. Constitution and American life.

No-Knock and Quick-Knock Raids

No-knock and quick-knock warrants have increased to 60,000–70,000 in 2010 compared to 3,000 in 1981 (Kraska). In the case of SWAT team raids where no-knock and quick-knock entries are most routine, the ACLU (2014) reported that 50 percent of these raids are against Black Americans. Kraska believes that no-knock and quick-knock raids, also called dynamic entries, appeal to Public Protection Units (specialized law enforcement teams) due to financial benefits. After testifying to the U.S. Senate, Kraska was met with the following statement by a high-ranking SWAT team member: "You know why SWAT took off don't you? It's because of civil asset forfeiture.[16] We were generating a ton of new revenue for our departments" (Kraska). Kraska (153) further reports that almost all police departments have adopted this practice of civic asset forfeiture, and "it has proven to be highly lucrative, with many PDs supplementing their annual operating budgets by as much as 60 percent (Ingraham, 2015)." It is no irony that white and dominant agencies of authority encounter Black bodies and destroy Black lives, all while accumulating wealth for themselves and their institutions.

Moreover, as conversations of antiracism have progressed, so has the white political imagination in its use of the law to support the continuation of racialized misogynistic witch hunts using No-Knock Warrants. However, white perceptions of moral law, safety, and social order did not need No-Knock Warrants when they murdered young Emmitt Till in Mississippi in 1955. From the colonial days of the 1500s through the Emancipation Proclamation (1863), the Reconstruction Era (1865–1877), the Civil Rights Movements, and in recent news, violent irrationalities of white fears and mores did not need a No-Knock Warrant as law enforcement and self-appointed citizens of the law seeking "justice and domestic tranquility" punished dark and foreign bodies. Historically and traditionally, these "moral" agents forced bodies deemed as "other" to bear the cross of a white ideological consciousness that attempted to legitimize an irreconcilable cognitive dissonance.

Today, as we continue to see the acquittal of law enforcement officers, we also continue to witness the local and federal judicial systems' attempts to legitimize historically false ideologies and irreconcilable cognitive dissonance in the testimonies of officers and White Americans who "feared for their lives" without the physical evidence that might justify those fears (Crutchfield et al.). Moreover, much like ancient Greek myths about witches who flee upon seeing their own mirrored reflections, when viral recordings of the events in question challenge the testimonies of officers, false, inaccurate, or missing content within police reports serve to ensure that pertinent information flees the public eye. In conscious and unconscious attempts to evade accountability and undermine racial justice, this distorted consciousness assumes moral and judicial superiority while making excuses for its immoral and incongruent reality. Similar to executions in early U.S. history as the enactments of socio-cultural and moral purges, the United States fails to acknowledge its ongoing participation in the ritualistic purging of bodies of "undesirable" truths. These purgings, as debased and irrational as they were in the American past of witch hunts and lynchings, are disproportionately enacted in Black homes and on the Black body.

Warrants that sanction dehumanizing home invasions by police and vigilantes committed to current systems of oppression can perpetuate a deeply rooted historical tradition characterized by white men and their allies breaking the Black home and desecrating Black life. These violations are not isolated events but are rather traumatic reverberations on the Black psyche, particularly of Black women and girls. Progressive racism has allowed whiteness to further normalize their heinous actions under pretenses of morality, safety, and social order. These white assaults on Black homes and families leave Black women and girls dead or traumatized as they are left with testimonies that are often concealed, dismissed, or invalidated. In the margins of Black female life, behind the already pervasive backdrop of patriarchy and oppression, white systems of misogyny and racism indulge a familiar form of cultural and spiritual purging at the intersections of racial genocide and gendercide. Located at these intersections, we find Breonna Taylor and all of our Sisters, both living and taken.

Conclusion and Implications

This chapter offers implications for a conceptual shift in our understanding of present policies and practices by orienting them in their historical and traditional context. We must understand how paradigms of power are contextualized within geopolitical and historical space and time. Current power dynamics have inherited their ideas, structures, and functions from ideologies and practices rooted in history. Policymakers within institutions and systems must understand the historical ideologies and practices that inform their current ideas, structures, and functions. Institutions, systems, and society must account for racial disparities as evidence of racism rather than perceived deficits among social groups, which further legitimize the gaping dissonance between our American beliefs and our actual practices.

Moreover, institutions that serve and govern society must welcome accountability from the public as fundamental to the U.S. Constitution while accepting the consequences for subverting this accountability. In solidarity with our collective humanity, racially and critically conscious White Americans must interrogate dominant notions of mores, social order, and safety within discourses in their families, schools, social and professional networks, and political affiliations. In our interpersonal interactions, to dismantle and heal divisive barriers of race, ethnicity, gender, sexuality, ability, etc., we must engage the invitation to self-reflect using the question posed by Sister Anjanette Young. White and dominant U.S. society must engage in a Sankofa experience to understand how white terror, conceived in the past, persists in modern-day forms. Contrary to whitewashed historical retellings, pillaging the lives of the children of Africa did not cease with the end of slavery. It continues invading Black life and separating Black families in various areas. The continued differential treatment of human life reflects an ideological and cultural deficit practiced among dominant societies. In regard to the twelve white male officers who invaded her home and traumatized her sexually, psychologically, and emotionally, we join our voices with that of Sister Anjanette when she demands, "What in *you* did not allow you to treat me as a *human*?"

Breonna – Thank you for your Light. Thank you for the Power that your Story forever holds. I am grateful for the Rest, Freedom, and Joy I know is now yours. When my voice is silenced, and my mattering is rendered invisible, I remember Your Name and speak it aloud. When my Children and my Community are lied to in the hopes that we might forget the Beauty and Brilliance of our Histories, it is then that I will draw from our Creator, our People, and You – our Sister and our Ancestor.

Notes

A Tribute to Our/My Sisters: Both the Living and the Taken

1 Darnella Frazier and her 9-year-old cousin, 2020. She is one of the living who filmed the murder of George Floyd by Minneapolis, Minnesota police officer Derek Chauvin. At age 17, she and her young cousin suffered the trauma of watching Chauvin take Floyd's life by restricting his ability to breathe for nearly ten minutes while he remained restrained and unarmed, begging for his life.

2 Diamond Reynolds and her 4-year-old daughter, 2016. She and her daughter are two of the living who witnessed a Minnesota police officer shoot and kill her fiancé, Philando Castile, while being wrongfully detained. Upon the officer's request for his identification, Castile reached to retrieve it and was shot.

3 Alayna Albrecht-Payton, 2021. As she sat in the passenger's seat, she was one of the living who witnessed the killing of her boyfriend, Daunte Wright, by a Brooklyn Center, Minnesota police officer. The officer reported that she had intended to draw her Taser when she instead drew and used her firearm.

4 Karissa Hill, 2020. She is one of the living who survived the killing of her father, Andre Hill, by Columbus, Ohio police as he entered a neighbor's garage with a Christmas present. After shooting him, officers did not assist him for over five minutes. They rolled his body over to secure his handcuffs after he had passed.

5 Piaget Crenshaw, 2014. She is one of the living who filmed Ferguson, Missouri police as they left 18-year-old Micheal Brown's body dead in the street for four hours after shooting him six times immediately after he turned to face them unarmed and with his hands in the air.

6 Addie Mae Collins (age 14), Cynthia Wesley (age 14), Carole Robertson (age 14), and Denise McNair (age 11), 1963. These four young girls were killed by a bomb planted by a Ku Klux Klan member. At the time of the explosion, the girls were in the basement ladies' room preparing for Sunday service at 16th Street Baptist Church in Birmingham, Alabama.

7 Eula Love, 1979. She was shot and killed by Los Angeles Police Department officers months after she and her young daughters survived the loss of her husband. The police were requested by the gas company servicemen who were unable to collect a $22.09 payment from her.

8 Eleanor Bumpers, 1984. She was an elderly, mentally ill woman who was shot and killed by New York Police Department officers enforcing an eviction due to an overdue rental payment of $98.65.

9 Mary Mitchell, 1991. She was shot and killed by a Bronx, New York police officer after allegedly threatening him with his own nightstick. Police had been called in for a domestic dispute. The district Attorney General's office found that there was no need for the officer to fire in self-defense when faced with only a nightstick.

10 Aiyana Mo'Nay Stanley-Jones, 2010. She was 7 years old when she was shot and killed by a Detroit, Michigan police officer during an apartment raid targeting a suspect who lived on another floor.

11 Atatiana Jefferson, 2019. She was shot and killed in her home by a police officer in Fort Wayne, Texas, who was called due to a neighbor's concern that the front door was open. Her 8-year-old nephew witnessed her death.

12 Janisha Fonville, 2015. She was shot by Charlotte, North Caorlina police while holding a knife. Rather than de-escalating the situation using protocol and training, they shot her at point-blank range in the chest and stomach.

13 Michelle Cusseaux, 2014. Suffering from bipolar disorder and schizophrenia, she called a behavioral health provider for assistance. The provider perceived a threat and contacted the Phoenix, Arizona police. After she refused to open the door to the officers, she was shot at point-blank range in the chest and killed while holding a hammer.

14 Gabriella Nevarez, 2014. She was shot and killed by Citrus Heights, California police during a vehicle pursuit. She suffered from bipolar disorder and had taken her grandmother's vehicle.

15 Tanisha Anderson, 2014. Suffering from bipolar disorder and in a nightgown, she stopped breathing after being slammed to the pavement, handcuffed, and restrained by Cleveland, Ohio police. The family had called for mental health assistance and were surprised when police arrived rather than an ambulance.

16 This comment regarding how *civic asset forfeiture* creates increased incentives for officers and departments to raid communities is highly relevant within a racial capitalist society driven by the accumulation of power and property and the practice of racialization as a means to extract that labor and property from a socially constructed and systemically subjugated class (Robinson 2). Naming the quite prominent intersection of race, capitalism, and differential power as it pertains to the disproportionate targeting of Black individuals and neighborhoods, it is important to note that whether or not a suspect has been charged or convicted of a crime, law enforcement officers still have the legal right to enact civic asset forfeiture, seizing assets and properties belonging to civilians. It is not ironic that white and dominant authority agencies encounter Black bodies and enter Black homes and communities, taking Black assets to be absorbed into the systems that embody whiteness and colonial terror.

Bibliography

Andre, Emmanuel. "Chicago Police Video of Anjanette Young Should Shock America. It Doesn't Shock Chicago." *NBC News*, 22 December 2020, https://www.nbcn ews.com/think/opinion/ncludi-police-video-anjanette-young-should-shock-amer ica-it-doesn-ncna1252123 Accessed 30 January 2022.

Boyer, Paul and Stephen Nissenbaum. "The Salem Witchcraft Papers: Verbatim Transcriptions of the Court Records." *Salem Witch Trials Documentary Archive and Transcription Project*, 1977, https://web.archive.org/web/20150226233445/http://salem.lib.virginia.edu/texts/tei/swp. Accessed 30 January 2022.

Costello, Darcy and Tessa Duvall. "Minute by Minute: What Happened the Night Louisville Police Fatally Shot Breonna Taylor." *Louisville Courier Journal*, 15 May 2020, https://www.usatoday.com/story/news/nation/2020/05/15/minute-minute-account-breonna-taylor-fatal-shooting-louisville-police/5196867002/. Accessed 30 January 2022.

Crenshaw, Kimberlé W., et al. "Say Her Name: Resisting Police Brutality against Black Women." (2015). https://scholarship.law.columbia.edu/faculty_scholarship/3226

Crutchfield, Jandel, Amy Fisher, and Sarah L. Webb. "Colorism and Police Killings." *Western Journal of Black Studies* 41 (2017).

Davis, Henrietta Vinton. "Black Women Who Were Lynched in America." *NEOGRIOT*. 1 August 2008, https://kalamu.posthaven.com/history-black-women-who-were-lynched-in-ameri. Accessed 30 January 2022.

Donaghue, Erin. "No Charges in Death of Breonna Taylor; Officer Indicted for Endangering Neighbors." *CBS News*, 23 September 2020, https://www.cbsnews.com/news/breonna-taylor-decision-louisville-police-wanton-endangerment-grand-jury/. Accessed 30 January 2022.

Dunham, Roger G., Geoffrey P. Alpert, and Kyle D. McLean. *Critical Issues in Policing: Contemporary Readings*. Waveland Press, 2020.

Ezell, Margaret JM. "Looking Glass Histories." *Journal of British Studies* 43.3 (2004): 317–338.

Foner, Eric. *A Short History of Reconstruction [Updated Edition]*. Harper Collins, 2015.

Grieco, Elizabeth M., and Rachel C. Cassidy. *Overview of Race and Hispanic Origin, 2000*. Vol. 8. No. 2. US Department of Commerce, Economics and Statistics Administration, US Census Bureau, 2001.

Hoffmann, Jonah. "Remembering Candy and Mary Black." *Salem Witch Museum*, 18 February 2022, https://salemwitchmuseum.com/2022/02/18/remembering-candy-and-mary-black/. Accessed 30 January 2022.

hooks, bell. *Feminism Is for Everybody*. 2nd ed. London, England: Routledge. 2014.

Hwang, Junghyun. "Rupturing Salem, Reconsidering Subjectivity: Tituba, the Witch of Infinity in Maryse Condé's I, Tituba, Black Witch of Salem." *American Studies in Scandinavia* 51.1 (2019): 43–59.

Ingraham, C. "Law Enforcement Took More Stuff from People Than Burglars Did Last Year" *Washington Post*, 23 Nov. 2015.

Jones, Adam. *Case Study: The European Witch-Hunts, C. 1450–1750 and Witch-Hunts Today*. Gendercide Watch, 2002.

Kappeler, Victor E., and Peter B. Kraska. "Normalising Police Militarisation, Living in Denial." *Policing and Society* 25.3 (2015): 268–275.

Kraska, Peter B., and Louis J. Cubellis. "Militarizing Mayberry and Beyond: Making Sense of American Paramilitary Policing." *Justice Quarterly* 14.4 (1997): 607–629.

Kraska, Peter B. "Questioning the Militarization of US Police: Critical versus Advocacy Scholarship." *Policing and Society: An International Journal* 9.2 (1999): 141–155.

Kraska, Peter B. "Militarization and Policing—Its Relevance to 21st Century Police." *Policing: a Journal of Policy and Practice* 1.4 (2007): 501–513.

Kraska, Peter B., and Shannon Williams. "The Material Reality of State Violence: The Case of Police Militarization." *The Routledge International Handbook of Violence Studies*. Routledge, 2018. 145–159.

Lartey, Jamiles, and Sam Morris. "Pain and Terror: America's History of Racism. How White Americans Used Lynchings to Terrorize and Control Black People." *The Guardian*, 26 April 2018. https://www.theguardian.com/us-news/2018/apr/26/lynchings-memorial-us-south-montgomery-alabama. Accessed 30 January 2022.

Last, Anne M. "July 25, 1903: Jennie Steer (The Cincinnati Enquirer)." *Strange Fruit and Spanish Moss*, 25 July 2014, https://strangefruitandspanishmoss.blogspot.com/2014/07/ncl-25-1903-jennie-steer.html. Accessed 30 January 2022.

Martin, Jordan. "Breonna Taylor: Transforming a Hashtag into Defunding the Police." *J. Crim. L. & Criminology* 111 (2021): 995.

McLaren, Peter. "Chapter III: White Terror and Oppositional Agency: Towards a Critical Multiculturalism." *Counterpoints* 4 (1995): 87–124.

Menakem, Resmaa. *My Grandmother's Hands: Racialized Trauma and the Pathway to Mending Our Hearts and Bodies*. Penguin UK, 2021.

Merriam-Webster, ed. *Merriam-Webster's Collegiate Dictionary*. Merriam-Webster, 2004.

Newsweek. *The Lesson of Salem*, 31 August 1992, https://web.archive.org/web/20161027123146/http://gnauss.hrsbteachers.ednet.ns.ca/sites/gnauss.hrsbteachers.ednet.ns.ca/files/documents/The%20Lesson%20of%20Salem.pdf. Accessed 30 January 2022.

Nielsen, Euell. "Breonna Taylor (1993–2020)." *Blackpast*, 16 July 2020, https://Www.Blackpast.Org/African-American-History/People-African-American-History/Breonna-Taylor-1993-2020/. Accessed 30 January 2022.

Norwood, Candice. "The War on Drugs Gave Rise to 'No Knock' Warrants. Breonna Taylor's Death Could End Them." *PBS NewsHour*, 12 June 2020, https://www.pbs.org/newshour/politics/the-war-on-drugs-gave-rise-to-no-knock-warrants-breonna-taylors-death-could-end-them. Accessed 30 January 2022.

Office of Public Affairs. Former Louisville, Kentucky, Police Detective Pleads Guilty to a Federal Crime Related to the Death of Breonna Taylor. Department of Justice, 23 August 2022, https://www.justice.gov/opa/pr/former-louisville-kentucky-police-detective-pleads-guilty-federal-crime-related-death-breonna. Accessed 31 August 2022.

Paglia, Camille. " 'Black' Pagan or White Colonizer?" *Outlaw Culture: Resisting Representations*, edited by bell hooks, Routledge, 2006, 96–105.

Piccoli, Sean. "No-Knock Raids Statistics: 5 Eye-Opening Facts, Figures on No-Knock Warrants." Newsmax, 19 June 2015, https://www.newsmax.com/FastFeatu res/no-knock-raids-SWAT-facts-figures/2015/06/19/id/651434/. Accessed 30 January 2022.

Pitchon, Allie. "Female Warriors Who Led African Empires and Armies." *A & E Television Networks, LLC*, 20 September 2022, https://www.history.com/news/ncl udi-female-warriors. Accessed 1 March 2023.

Pruitt, Sarah. "Salem Witch Trials: Who Were the Main Accusers?" *A & E Television Networks, LLC*, 27 Sep. 2021, https://www.history.com/news/salem-witch-tri als-accusers. Accessed 13 May 2023.

Ray, Benjamin C. *Satan and Salem: The Witch-Hunt Crisis of 1692*. University of Virginia Press, 2015.

Robinson, Cedric J. "Black Marxism: The Making of the Black Radical Tradition. 1983." *Chapel Hill: U of North Carolina P* (2000).

Sack, Kevin. "Door-Busting Drug Raids Leave a Trail of Blood." *The New York Times, 18 Mar. 2017*, https://www.nytimes.com/interactive/2017/03/18/us/forced-entry-warrant-drug-raid.html. Accessed 20 March 2022.

Taylor, Mildred Europa. "Known as the Black Witches of Salem, These Women Caused Massive Hysteria in a U.S. Town in the 1690s." *Face 2 Face Africa*, 7 Aug. 2018, https:// face2faceafrica.com/article/known-as-the-black-witches-of-salem-these-women-cau sed-massive-hysteria-in-a-u-s-town-in-the-1690s. Accessed 30 January 2022.

The United States Constitution. *National Constitution Center*, 2023, https://constitutio ncenter.org/the-constitution/full-text. Accessed 30 January 2022.

Tillet, Salamishah. *Sites of Slavery: Citizenship and Racial Democracy in the Post-Civil Rights Imagination*. Duke University Press, 2012.

Wright, Simeon, and Herb Boyd. *Simeon's Story: An Eyewitness Account of the Kidnapping of Emmett Till*. Chicago Review Press, 2010.

Young, Anjanette, et al. "# IamHer: Anjanette Young Speaks Truth to Power." *Affilia* 36.2 (2021): 129–139.

Zack, Naomi. *White Privilege and Black Rights: The Injustice of US Police Racial Profiling and Homicide*. Rowman & Littlefield, 2015.

Part II Summer of 2020 and Beyond: Centering Black Women

5 Breathe and Grieve: Reconciled Voices of Black Women Teachers in Critical Movements

Julia A. Lynch

> . . .for those of us
> Who are imprinted with fear
> like a faint line in the center of our foreheads
> learning to be afraid with our mother's milk
> for by this weapon
> this illusion of some safety to be found
> the heavy-footed hope to silence us
> For all of us
> this instant and this triumph
> We were never meant to survive. . .
>
> – Audre Lorde

At daybreak, I awake from my sleep and hear the voices of my loved ones who have passed on to glory say to this young soul, "Rise, fight, sprinkle, dance, then fight some more." As I wash my face with the tears of my soul, I think about what it means to others to be a Black woman in America. Then, what it means to me? For me, we are the strength of the Earth, the love of humankind, and the healing of all humanity. I am bruised by how white folks have thrown me away, but the spirit of my ancestors carries me. To the *others*, I may presumably be a monetized token of little to no value unless used for profit. I have been used and squeezed like a lemon until my wrinkled fabric was of no more use. Hung to dry for the recycled purpose of perpetuating another vicious cycle of trauma, thrown away like trash because of the use-lessness seen in my beautiful Black skin, *wounded-*

Tracing the Black woman through traumatic experiences is crucial to help understand her contextually. It also allows us to understand how to heal the land. To center the voices of Black women centers humankind and bridges communities. I breathe deeply, inhaling the bruising of society's whimpered white tones and exhaling the power to speak back into those voices. I muster up the strength to continue the pursuit of completeness for my Black sistas, but it is not without grief. I will mention grief as a thread in this poetic narrative chapter to describe the pursuit of healing and Black women teachers' (BWTs) journey of confronting whiteness, Eurocentric mindsets, and dominant culture. Grief is long-standing, deeply painful, traumatic, silencing, and personal. Gloria Anzaldúa speaks to this personal journey of self-actualization, noting that to step into the transformative power of "risking the personal," we develop a critical *conocimiento* and open ourselves up to alternative ways of knowing that destabilize the dominant Westernized epistemologies. How does one suffer through grief? Through loss, survivors' remorse, or post-traumatic stress? And the anger? This chapter performs the soulful stages of Black women teachers living in rural N.C., whose identities and voices speak across the historical narrative portraits of being a Black woman. The BWTs were given names or phrases that they felt best summarized their story.

As to not get lost in this journey, I offer a navigating path to enter this chapter. This poetic narrative uses the word "disease" metaphorically to imagine how whiteness can be seen as a terminally ill diagnosis with BWTs. Yet, they rebuke the diagnosis by speaking against whiteness and providing a healing-centered story of their beings. The stages of this disease, misdiagnosis, mistreatment, and healing, are built around the ideologies concerning whiteness and are threaded with grief.

I pray I see tomorrow

> I ain't the girl you think
> I should be
> Fair skin wanna be
> Nawl, I ain't hu
> I ain't too loud, but I can be
>   Don't Push Me
> You see my hair is perfect, kinky or straight
> Looking in the mirror, trying to see what I can create
> Do I wear it up? Do I wear it down? One thing for sure it CAN'T be braided or out
> in a puff
> Ugh...
> I just hate being the girl you think I should be
> When my eyes open tomorrow and the Sun cracks the sky
> I'll be sure to be the Black woman God made me to be
> Whatever the weather, whatever the season

Whatever the job, whatever the reason
I'll wake up and be the Black girl God made me
Today just ain't the day
Grief-

Whiteness as Disease

Existing in white spaces can threaten the Black woman's identity, ways of knowing and being, and spirit. The culture of whiteness seeps into every corner of our educational systems and can be hard to name without a critical consciousness. It is not racism or white privilege alone, but a complexity of inequities that Ibram X Kendi states "is as visible as the law, or as hidden as our private thoughts" (22).

Whiteness shows up historically in education as a disease attempting to drain the life out of organizations, leaders, teachers, and students. I remember when I was teaching at a rural school in the south, and I was walking my kindergarteners down the hallway with my instructional assistant. A few students were chatting it up using AAVE (African American Vernacular English) in the hallway, and my assistant looked at them and said, "Hey, *we* don't speak that stuff in here. *We* [white folks] speak English." White folks have always desired power over any ethically sustaining teaching practice, and whiteness weaponized demonstrates a sense of entitlement, anger, a need for retaliation, feigned fear, and white fragility. All of which are harmful to teachers and students of color.

This disease was something that the BWTs have highlighted. "Life ain't been no crystal stair"[1] notes how being compared to her white counterparts affected her ability to see herself and her effectiveness as a Black woman teacher. She states, *"I was teaching to perform and to fit this white mold of what they [white teachers] thought a good teacher should be, and I would lose every time."* School systems, institutions of higher learning, and the wider society perpetuate cycles of racism by upholding deficit narratives of Black communities, normalizing Anti-Blackness ideologies that sustain the culture of whiteness and devalue Black identity. Black women constantly grapple with societal constraints of identity acceptance, sometimes resulting in a dysconscious state of identity. One may justify inequities that maintain the status quo even if it harms one's cultural identity. Joyce E. King helps us conceptualize the ideas of dysconsciousness, noting, "[D]ysconsciousness is an uncritical habit of mind (including perceptions, attitudes, assumptions, and beliefs) that justifies inequity and exploitation by accepting the existing order of things as given" (135). A dysconscious identity, similar to dysconscious

racism, is not the absence of consciousness but an impaired way of thinking about how stereotypes and racial myths distort one's own sense of self.
BWTs working in the rural southeastern part of the United States note this
in-betweenness below:

The Walls Are Gray

> I awake and look myself in the mirror,
> Lost in stereotypes, in anti-Blackness, and lost
> in the duality of my identities,

".. I've been perceived as a white girl that was trapped in a black girl's body.
I guess because I can talk as if I'm educated. I've been told, 'You don't talk like
them' when I'm in a professional setting. Or 'You don't sound like me!' when
I'm with other black teachers" (Evolving)[2]

"...to be able to go back and forth (between identities) at this point is absolutely
necessary. ".(Inside Edition)[3]

".. it's so funny because when I talk to my friends on the phone, and they hear me
talking to a white colleague, they like, 'Oh, you so fake.' And I say no, I'm being
adaptable...I can be professional, and I can be ratchet...I know how to turn it
(ratchet side) on and off" (I'm B!ack and I'm proud)[4]

When we awaken our private thoughts, we then disrupt law, policy, normalcy,
and deficit perspectives – all of which perpetuate the cycle of colonization, hege-
mony, bigotry, and the – isms.

As we name, then examine the issues with the power of whiteness, we
begin to understand that the culture of whiteness in a white-dominated educational system creates spaces where issues of race, racism, white supremacy,
and the complexity of inequities may reinforce the status quo without critical
consciousness.

(Mis)diagnosis

The history of Black women in America portrays images considered less favor-
able because of systemic racism dating back to viewpoints on African women
when white folks visited Africa before slavery. This context is necessary for
understanding how we have gotten to the cost of Black life and the murder of
Breonna Taylor, enslaved and counted as worthless, voiceless, invisible, and

sexual property. Black women in the United States have never been given a fair opportunity for freedom. Black women were raped by their enslavers, and when they tried to defend themselves, courts ruled in favor of their owners, citing Blacks, particularly Black women, had no rights and would be considered equal to cattle and stock. However, here we are trying to turn the blame onto the Black woman, her promiscuity, and ghetto fabulous lifestyle, that uses the welfare system as a crutch.

There are endarkened spaces in our silent histories that are invisibly present because oppressive systems have sublimely uninvited them. A space occupied within a BWT's pedagogy speaks to name-calling and invisibility. The histories of our experiences are interdependent on contextualized circumstances of oppressive circumstances, family, education, location, and social movements.

Contextualization is fluid and able to change shape over time. As BWTs experience life and oppression, and throughout time, their teaching practices, beliefs, and truths may also change, making it hard to measure and define what teacher effectiveness and good teaching may look like in a BWT (Gay 1994). Therefore, research that centers on the lived experiences of Black women teachers in rural North Carolina brings insight into how those experiences may constrain or facilitate the success of Black women teachers. To be Black and a woman, then a teacher reaches into the voices that may suffer in oppression but gleams in the hope that as the Black woman teacher *becomes*, her narratives note what crucibles constrained or facilitated her success.

(Mis)treatment

When we are diagnosed with the disease of whiteness, Black women are victimized exponentially, and their identity is used as tools against such weaponized systems. Did Sandra Bland ever have a chance when the police pulled her over? I often wonder if grief killed my sista, Sandra. She was hurt by a murderous system that was supposed to protect her and frustrated that her invisibly present voice was only white noise and static to those who listened. The screams of her soul must have wept feverishly.

Grief..
I wonder, while Breonna Taylor slept in her home, did her profile that the police read aid them in their aggressiveness to storm in and murder her? Which pieces of her did they choose to ignore that created an uncontested knock that proceeded in murder? Did she not deserve a life free from death-from

grief-

Historically, enslaved Black women, seen only as property, had the same treatment plan – a plan used to build concrete slabs of systemic racism that portrays Black women as incomplete.

Black women have been at the start of any revolutionary act of freedom for others yet are continuously mistreated by oppressive systems that deem them incapable decision-makers, aggressive communicators, and sexually promiscuous – bonnet-wearing women who use the welfare system as a reason not to work. These mistreated identities are carried with each Black woman wherever she goes. I remember the media used Michelle Obama's facial expressions during the presidential campaign as a fraudulent identity hack to discredit her and incite fear into white folks. Fear, mainly white fear, is dangerous for Black folks. Black women teachers grappled with that same white gaze yet are always a pillar of cultural sustainability within their communities.

Given the retrospective historical analysis of the BWTs and their needed presence, they are seemingly invisibly present in American schools. Despite reports of the effectiveness of BWTs in the classroom, Pole's 1999 study revealed that Black teachers are not respected in their positions by students or colleagues. The findings showed that most white students do not respect the teachings of Black teachers because the students thought of them as less knowledgeable, and colleagues discredit experience as knowledge. BWT's credibility, intellectualism, and teaching methods have always been questioned by their white female and male counterparts.

Black women teachers are employed at hard-to-staff schools and may receive low wages but do not leave the profession (Ingersoll and May). In Richard M. Ingersoll and Henry May's extensive quantitative study on the recruitment and retention of minority teachers, they found that minority teachers leave the field because of a lack of voice and teacher autonomy, which raises concern about how the teaching practices of BWTs are viewed and voiced in schools. The people making education reform decisions have no experience in the classroom. Stereotypes produce a lack of voice, and teacher education programs contribute to the BWT's invisibility. White supremacy processes within teacher education programs (TEP), educational pipeline, and organizational conditions affect BWTs. It has become common today to dismiss white supremacy discussions in TEPs and classrooms even if there is evidence that the racial power of whiteness guides the activity and interactions of teacher educators. U.S. teacher education programs consistently tell teachers what to see and not to see and what is and is not reasonable (Hayes, et al., 2013). Gloria Ladson-Billings provided an example in her discussion on how white faculty facilitate readings and field experiences without addressing racial power structures. To put it bluntly, when considering the national consciousness of racism escalating in our current social conditions, all of the participants in a teacher education program must be invested in creating culturally responsive teachers and future leaders. Highlighted below is the poetic narrative of a BWT-Silent Revolutionist[5] who speaks to the (mis)diagnosis and (mis)treatment facilitated by the disease of whiteness yet resists the diagnosis by choosing to be reconciled with her grief to awaken her healing.

Silent Revolutionist

Born a slave—
to the chained forces of my abandonment,
"my mother was a heroin addict, and my father an alcoholic."
Philly streets called me, books called me too...—someone loose the chains! A juvenile delinquent, working with juveniles in the same court systems that sentenced me to —chains, but good grades and college enslaved me,
"street girl in order to fit in, the smart goody two shoes in magnet classes" Chains got me...feeling like a slave.
Is the struggle in dual identity a struggle for freedom?

II
Reconciling with my past-
a Black woman-teacher, I became.
Freedom? More like Free-ish, but... at least the chains..well
"I am constantly told I'm controversial and that I need to consult with the white teachers in my building about African American issues as B!ack women!"
Proven intelligence with a sight for equity, a heart for relationships... commune-unity and spirituality. "I am a m-other, it's hard for me to leave. I want my students to go-on"
I develop curriculum, I am living curriculum...Evolving, Emerging..

III
"My prayers have become words, I don't know if they are going unanswered. Am I praying
faithless prayers?"
Lord, deliver me from the chains of my past that anchor me down like a

ship
Lord, is this era of racial injustice for my brothers and sisters ever going to end, Lord, if you are listening...

Trayvon
Freddie
Breonna

Michael
George
Elijah...
I imagine a day when the chains fall off, when the tears stop flowing when the deaths stop
coming. The private deaths...trapped in the minds of those who hate us.

FREEDOM.
Until then,
My intelligence meets my advocacy...My boldness will be like the Sun... pushing away his darkness. Changed,
I am the ancestors, I am Change.

Reconciled Healing

At sunset, when I close my eyes on this side of grief, my soul finds rest in knowing that I am immune to the petri-dish illness America created for me. Black women teachers locate the endarkened space of healing, where they speak back to their oppressors and challenge systems, racial myths, and inequities. Cynthia B. Dillard (2012) conceptualizes this healing, noting that this third space, in between being and becoming, is where the dysconscious identity can no longer reside. Dillard calls Black women teachers out of this distortion, noting:

> Our [Black people] ways of knowing and being have traveled throughout the African Diaspora and continue to live in Black American culture. Sometimes we are able to understand and acknowledge these links. Sometimes we even choose not, have not, or both. But to understand the long struggles for freedom, Black identity, and education that are worthy of Black people, we must (re) member that we come from those who chose to survive the horrors and atrocities from slavery to "freedom" and back again. (Dillard, 11)

The Black women teachers in this narrative began to acknowledge the power of their resistance as a form of healing and challenged the constraints of whiteness. Their collective voices highlighted in the poetic narrative demonstrate this dynamic shift of power:

Reconciled Healing

There are two powers,
The culture of whiteness when given....power... Can occupy in a BWT's space "...my school is majority Black and brown students, and language is certainly a barrier... things get lost in translation and parents just don't understand us and teachers misunderstand parents..." (Inside Edition)

"...testing is necessary..." (Evolving)
"...I mean I believe in the Black Lives Matter movement....but I feel like everybody's lives matter like everybody's life is important. I feel bad for singling out just the Black community" (Catch 22⁶)
....

We choose

To shift The Power

BE IT RESOLVED that moving forward:

BWTs will awaken their critical consciousness to whiteness,
love across differences, challenge the status quo, decolonize our thoughts, and access a liberating pedagogy that challenges existing structures of power for another stay of execution-

"where we don't have to conform" (Inside Edition)
and we "are united as one with cultures to stand up for what's right" (Evolving)
"to be there for our children" (I'm B!ack and I'm Proud)
and teach "not just content but an integration of life lessons" (Life aint been no crystal stair)

so that,
BWTs and their students live fully and deeply (hooks, 1994; Freire, 2018).

Whereas,
"a shift in society's way of thinking, from the historical approach where basically B!lack lives have been seen as expendable to where
our culture
our contributions
our potential
our resources are embraced and taught the same way as white culture,
yeah
a
total
shift" (Silent Revolutionist)

It is within this power that BWTs become whole-listic And
Free

With a justice-oriented lens that re-imagines culturally responsive pedagogy as a hope of sustained freedom and justice for all-who dare.

Resist the struggles of oppression
"We were a needs-based family...my momma made too much to get any assistance and not enough for us to eat" (Evolving)
"...I am a single mother to a B!ack boy" (Inside Edition)
"....other folks knew I was poor before I did..." (Life for me ain't be no crystal stair)

Resist stereotypes
"...I stand for who I am. Even though I feel I've been put in a box. I am a proud B!ack woman, and I want to represent who I am" (Evolving)

Resist the anti-Black rhetoric,
Resist the single-story narratives, Resist the normality of cultural assumptions,

THEN...
RE-emerge and RE-Exist to become reconciled with those experiences

BWTs (re)exist as free

Toward Freedom for Her

The Black woman in the classroom creates a community of cultural wealth and sustainability built on love, not domination. Durryle N. Brooks seeks a more reconceptualized definition of love using Cornell West and Martin Luther King combined, theorizing that this act of love is resistance because it requires us to affirm ourselves despite the many ways that society has systematically oppressed us, as evidenced by chattel slavery, women's oppression, queer oppression, concentration camps, and indigenous slaughter (108). Black women teachers push against those oppressive systems by fostering relationships within their communities, practicing other mothering, and building critical relatable pedagogy to sustain their culture.

Kneeling to say my prayers, I ask God for total healing and vengeance simultaneously because such is love! I pray the prayers of my ancestors, the freedom prayers, the soul-*full* prayers, the redemptive prayers. When I close my eyes, my soul gets teary again, listening to how whiteness fraudulently steals my sistas identity, so much so that she becomes a hostile victim of murder: a lasting hashtag, a billboard, a media story.

A prayer for tomorrow
Now I lay me down to sleep,
I am Breonna Taylor
And she is-
me,
Black women are creators of the universe
Microcosmic webs of starry nights,
Yet cursed-
A community of nations, a soul at peace
Because I know the fight for my sista
Means a fight for humanity
I am my sista's keeper, but am I keeping my sista?
At daybreak or when night falls-
wake me up in the morning.

Notes

1 Black woman teacher, Elementary Education, master's degree, 10 years of experience.
2 Black woman teacher, Elementary Education, master's degree, 9 years of experience.
3 Black woman teacher, Elementary Education, bachelor's degree, 4 years of experience.
4 Black woman teacher, Librarian, master's degree, 6 years of experience.
5 Black woman teacher, Special Education, master's degree, 6 years of experience.
6 Black woman teacher, Special Education, master's degree, 5 years of experience.

Bibliography

Anderson, James D. *The Education of Blacks in the South, 1860–1935*. U of North Carolina P, 2010.

Anzaldúa, Gloria, and AnaLouise Keating. *This Bridge We Call Home: Radical Visions for Transformation*. Routledge, 2013.

Brooks, Durryle N. "(Re)conceptualizing Love: Moving Towards a Critical Theory of Love in Education for Social Justice." *Journal of Critical Thought and Praxis*, vol. 6, no. 3, 2017.

Dillard, Cynthia B. *Learning to (Re)member the Things We've Learned to Forget: Endarkened Feminisms, Spirituality, & the Sacred Nature of (Re)search & Teaching*. Black Studies and Critical Thinking, 2012.

Freire, Paulo. *Pedagogy of the Oppressed*. 1972.

Gay, Geneva. *At the Essence of Learning: Multicultural Education*. 1994.

Griffin, Ada G, and Michelle Parkerson. *A Litany for Survival: The Life and Work of Audre Lorde*. New York, NY: Third World Newsreel, 1996.

Hayes, Cleveland, et al. "Toward a Lesser Shade of White." *Constructing Knowledge*, 2013, pp. 1–16.

Ingersoll, Richard M., and Henry May. "The Minority Teacher Shortage: Fact or Fable?" *Phi Delta Kappan*, vol. 93, no. 1, 2011, pp. 62–65.

Kendi, Ibram X. *How to Be an Antiracist*. One World, 2019.

King, Joyce E. "Dysconscious Racism: Ideology, Identity, and the Miseducation of Teachers." *The Journal of Negro Education*, vol. 60, no. 2, 1991, p. 133.

Ladson-Billings, Gloria. "Teaching in Dangerous Times: Culturally Relevant Approaches to Teacher Assessment." *The Journal of Negro Education*, vol. 67, no. 3, 1998, p. 255.

Ladson-Billings, Gloria. *Beyond the Big House: African American Educators on Teacher Education*. Teachers College P, 2005.

Lorde, Audre. "A Litany of Survival." *The Black Unicorn: Poems*, 31–32. New York: Norton, 1978.

Omolade, Barbara. *The Rising Song of African American Women*. Psychology P, 1994.

Pole, Christopher. "Black Teachers Giving Voice: Choosing and Experiencing Teaching." *Teacher Development*, vol. 3, no. 3, 1999, pp. 313–328.

Sprull. *Chocolate Cakes and Icing.* PhD dissertation.

Walker, Vanessa S. "African American Teaching in the South: 1940–1960." *American Educational Research Journal*, vol. 38, no. 4, 2001, pp. 751–779.

Yancy, George. *Look, A White!: Philosophical Essays on Whiteness.* Temple UP, 2012.

6 *Social Workers Must Stay in the Room: The Experiences of a Black Woman Scholar Prior to and Beyond the 2020 Summer of Racial Reckoning*

Tiffany Lane

I honor the life of Breonna Taylor, who police officers killed in March of 2020. She is an ancestor amongst many ancestors who have been ridiculed, beaten, toured, disregarded, and murdered in the United States by police and other organized systems of oppression.

Why can't we discuss these inhumane acts in our profession without labeling it a "diversity" topic at an anti-oppressive seminar? It is not a matter of embracing diversity but addressing hate, racism, sexism, elitism, classism, biases, and discrimination.

How can we ignore senseless killings and the horrific treatment of Black women?

Why is this ok to disregard people who proclaim that their lives matter?

It is not ok! As a helping profession, let us call it what it is so we can be a part of societal change.

Respect

I pay homage to so many women and ancestors who paved the way for me to have the audacity to center myself and other Black women in spaces not designed for us to survive and thrive. I have taught at two predominately white institutions (PWI) as a tenure track faculty member for much of my academic career in social work. I worked with one Black woman faculty colleague on the tenure track in my academic department at both institutions.

Black women comprise approximately three percent of university and college faculty in the higher education system (Autumn). In the face of the disproportionality, Black women have made remarkable contributions to the Academy in diverse disciplines, which are no easy tasks. Research has suggested that African American women (at predominantly white institutions) are more likely to be isolated, experience imposter syndrome, be overlooked for leadership positions, and endure microaggressions by students and colleagues (Woldai).

The disturbing experiences of Black women in higher education institutions, coupled with overarching blatant societal ills of racism and police brutality, can tax Black women. Profound Black women scholars, such as Patricia Collins, Lois Benjamin, Stephanie Y. Evans, and Gerda Lerner, have published writings about the systematic issues and successes of Black women in the U.S. institutions of higher education and other systems. These mentioned scholars and many more serve as a footing to center on Black women's experiences. Some would argue these texts validate a Black woman's power, resistance, and sheer existence of mattering in a historically racist and sexist institution in the United States; despite this, Black women persist in academia.

Indeed, Black women have persevered and made a mark in U.S. culture and are at the forefront of many social, cultural, and political affairs centered on the mattering of Black women's plight for equity, respect, and, as Solange Knowles illustrates in her 2016 album, "A Seat at the Table." The aftermath of Breonna Taylor's murder, coupled with the inception of the Black Lives Matter movement, has brought to light the social work that "social justice[1]" professionals need to do to address racial disparities.

Social work organizations and schools of social work have since made public antiracist statements and hosted live and virtual conferences and summits to address racial inequalities. These platforms have provided opportunities for Black women scholars to voice the demand for gender and racial justice, and advocacy for Breonna Taylor and other Black people murdered by police and vigilantes. Drawing from the Black women activists and scholars as a source of agency for critical conversations in the social work profession and beyond, I reflect on my experiences, position, and understanding of the social work profession concerning racial and gender justice matters.

As a Black woman in social work education, I have faced racial and gender obstacles in academia and still teach about racial and related social problems that have directly impacted my life – what a heavy task. Thus, I crave written and recorded accounts of the experiences, successes, and endurance strategies of Black women in their personal and professional lives. It is a form of self-care and support as I navigate my profession and the Academy. I have conflicting views about the social work profession, mostly centered on social workers' lack of collectiveness and support of the national leadership to center an action-oriented plan to address racial disparities that intersect with various social problems in the United States. While the Social Work mission is "to enhance human well-being and help meet the basic human needs of all people, with particular attention to the needs and empowerment of people who are vulnerable, oppressed, and living in poverty" (NASW), racism and race relations are often relegated or placed in a "diversity" category instead of a form of oppression that should be addressed on a larger scale. The conflicting reactions and silence of some social workers to Black men and women being killed by police officers and vigilantes warranted my uneasiness with the social work profession; however, it is not the first time I questioned the profession's collective purpose.

Reflections

During my undergraduate social work education (at a Predominately White University), I was aware of the lack of class discussions and assignments centered on marginalized groups in the United States, particularly racial and ethnic populations. While we were required to take a race relations course, a great class, I did not experience an intersecting perspective on social and racial issues throughout my learning, despite all the social and racial ills happening in the world. Many issues, such as police brutality, the disproportionate numbers of Black children and families in the child welfare system, and the increased number of Black men incarcerated, were pertinent to our profession and could inform our practice as social workers. During various classes, I would share my thoughts and feelings about issues prevalent in the news or articles I read addressing institutional racism, poverty, and crime. I expressed my concerns about the lack of discussions about societal issues plaguing some Black and Latino communities, the groups we mainly worked with as social work interns. I did not want only to write papers about these various topics; I wanted to engage in critical conversations and connect them to what I was learning regarding the social work profession's mission.

The silent Resistance to my discourse from my peers about such matters in class, as an undergrad student, felt isolating; however, I kept thinking about the profession's mission and my commitment to the betterment of underserved communities. My dedication was rooted in my experiences growing up in what is referenced as an underserved but beautiful community. And so I kept voicing my opinions and challenging the lack of discussions about oppressed groups. I could tell when some of my classmates figuratively "*left the room*"; because there was a lack of engagement and interest when topics around race and gender were at the forefront of a discussion.

While we were encouraged to engage in "inclusive" class discussions, the topic would be coaxed to focus on all racial and ethnic groups through a diversity lens. Diversity is good; however, some groups, such as Black people in the United States, experienced and are still experiencing exacerbated and explicit institutional racism and oppression more than other races. These disparities are documented in the criminal justice, child welfare, and public school systems. So, why not discuss these societal problems? Why not center Black people for a few classes? Especially given that social workers are more likely connected to and employed by these systems and purportedly change agents. How do we get to the foundation of the intersections of racial disparities and systematic oppression if we do not acknowledge the unique past and current experiences of the racial and ethnic groups in the United States? I was frustrated then and presently by the lack of awareness of how some marginalized groups are sidelined and clumped together in conversations related to diversity and inclusion. Racial and ethnic groups are not all the same; historical events inform systematic racism and discriminatory practices that we see today, particularly concerning police brutality and the overrepresentation of nonwhite people in social services systems. Austin Channing quotes in her blog, "I am wholly uninterested in a conversation about unity that is not rooted in the unrelenting pursuit of racial justice." I share her sentiments and realize this stance was rooted in my spirit before I could intellectualize the importance of social and racial justice in the United States.

So undoubtedly, I made some assumptions about people in the social work profession. The main one was that *all* social workers, regardless of race, gender, class, sexual orientation, religion/spirituality, ethnicity, and ability, shared similar views about societal issues related to poverty and equity. Regardless of one's practice and research agenda, *all* social workers wanted to address social problems that threatened the enhancement of human well-being and the disempowerment of people who are vulnerable, oppressed, and marginalized. Why do I assume this? Welp, because it is the mission of social work. The reality that some people consider themselves social workers and have no regard for the historical and current social, gender, and racial injustices in the United States is baffling and distasteful. How can we address issues of racism, sexism, forms of phobias, and oppression with folks like these in the mix? "If we do not know how to meaningfully talk about racism, our actions will move in misleading directions." Angela Y. Davis' (88) words declare my concerns centered on the direction of racial justice in social work.

The societal reaction to Breonna Taylor's assassination triggered many Black women who shared experiences of racism, marginalization, and blatant disrespect. Many social workers' initial muted and passive responses regarding the murders of George Floyd and Breonna Taylor were alarming for many Black social work practitioners, educators, and allies. While I am fully aware of social workers who diligently focus on addressing intersectional forms of social injustices, there still is a tug-of-war in the profession to center racial justice, and the recent acts of police brutality illuminated this unease and tussle. The National Association of Social Workers president, Dr. Mildred Joyner (an African American woman), released a statement titled, "Racism is America's Human Stain: Black Lives Matter." Dr. Joyner notes that "racism is America's human stain" while further highlighting that the protests of the murders of George Floyd, Ahmaud Arbery, and Breonna Taylor were illicitly interrupted by police and others against the Black Lives Matter movement. She further notes:

> Racial injustice is why there are protests throughout our nation and around the globe.
>
> Black lives matter!
>
> Social justice is a core social work value: it demands that, as practitioners, social workers uphold their code of ethics and take deliberate actions so justice and equity exist in all communities. Social workers who understand the history of why brown and black people are unsafe in their own country can work to dismantle oppressive institutional policies and practices. In order to advocate for vulnerable groups, you must understand the centuries of inequalities that exist in this country.

I understood Dr. Joyner's words as a plea to social workers to advocate and practice social justice, and it was validating and liberating. We should be change agents of institutional racism. While many supported the statements, I was unsurprised at many "social workers" who had issues with the president of NASW's position about the horrific events. The reactions were eye-opening. The most familiar responses were social media posts that dismissed the prominent racial issues (police killing Black people on camera) and endorsed their social justice issues as a point of concern, such as gender rights, which is a valid social justice issue. Still, it seemed like a tactic to deflect the fact that police officers killed Black people. Some even argued that "all lives matter." These reactions made me consider my undergraduate experiences figuratively, noting that my peers and now colleagues "left the room." Some social workers' anti-reactions may have stemmed from the mattering and centering of "Blackness" mirrored by some of the country's reactions, which is problematic and conflicts with social work values and ethics. An

African American woman leader (Dr. Joyner) released the call to action, so the passive and aggressive responses to her call to action felt like a personal attack on all Black women.

Patricia Collins (46) notes that oppressed groups' stances are repressed because self-defined stances can fuel Resistance. I felt the Resistance. While many Black Social Work Scholars like myself saw the senseless murders as a time to stand for justice and fulfill the social work code of ethics, many felt it was sidelined. There were statements of solitary but few action-oriented advocacy efforts from social workers to address these hate crimes. Countless social workers questioned the profession's lack of interest and response to support communities in crisis and racial injustices. For some social work educators and practitioners, particularly Black women, the effects of Breonna's murder were intense feelings of grief, betrayal, and frustration because of the lack of collectiveness among social workers. The events left me heartbroken for the victims' families and society's inadequate attention and accountability toward law enforcement who senselessly killed Black women. I felt powerless at times and livid; however, I was willing to use my voice to discuss what many people frame as "uncomfortable" conversations.

> The truth is that Angry Black Women are looked upon as entities to be contained, as inconvenient citizens who keep on talking about their rights while refusing to do their duty and smile at everyone. (Brittney Cooper, 3)

Experiences of inclusiveness and avoidance on matters of race, gender, and class inequity have been part of my journey in social work. Following George Floyd's murder, I found myself angry and disgusted. I am unapologetic about my deep-seated beliefs and experiences to save face for any organization and profession; it is toxic and does no justice to the horrific acts of Black people. I tap into Brittney Cooper's profound words that note, "[R]eal radicalism implores us to tell the whole ugly truth, even when it is inconvenient. To own the hurt and the pain. To own our shit, too. To think about it systemically and collectively, but never to diminish the importance of the trauma." (270) I am committed to action-oriented advocacy and support policy reform that attack forms of institutional racism, sexism, and other isms, such as acts of violence toward the late Breonna Taylor and Sandra Bland.

At several points in my career, I have had reservations about leaning into my activism beyond my community and the classroom and academic department settings, primarily in academia, as there were few communal and what I would call "safe" supports in the predominately white spaces. At the time of George Floyd's death, life in the Academy was overwhelming. For some, the pressures of tenure and promotion can be overwhelming, coupled with life, the unique experience of working at a predominantly white institution and processing racism in a society that habitually ignores justice and protection for Black people killed by police and vigilantes. Regardless of my regular experiences with isms and secondary trauma from media outlets highlighting police shootings of Black people, as a professor, I am supposed to engage students and colleagues in conversations centered on hate crimes, isms, and social justice. Navigating white-centered higher education spaces feels like a cumbersome task, largely because the ideas of race and injustices are not prioritized in that overarching higher education system, the one mainly of PWIs. In my experience, it is not even a priority in *some* social work programs, which is heartbreaking. I have described it as a battle of the systems, so while social work education is under the umbrella of higher education institutions, these systems have dissonant values, priorities, and approaches to acknowledging and addressing societal concerns that impact diverse groups, which can be challenging for professors whose research, service, and teaching are unapologetically framed from a racial, environmental, and social justice perspective.

Sense of Agency

I get angry about things, then go on and work.
– Toni Morrison

As a Black woman, I have strategized a plan to uphold my research and activist commitment to racial and social justice within predominantly white spaces that may not see the value of my work. Despite my weary days due to continuous news media of racial killings, mass shootings, and a broken political system, I infuse racial and societal issues in all the courses I teach and my scholarship. It is emotionally exhausting and has affected my mental health over the years, mostly in spaces where colleagues and students question my agenda to do social justice work, push back, or are silent in spaces that necessitate racial and social justice conversations and solutions. But I persist.

NPR defines the summer of racial reckoning as a new movement of rallies that spotlight the murders of George Floyd, Breonna Taylor, and Ahmaud Arbery and the desire for justice (Chang et al.). My sense of agency and joy was ignited a few years before the 2020 summer of racial reckoning and is still lit. The movement is making the United States face the racism of its past and present. A sense of agency is an attitude of control over actions and aftermaths and a feeling of confidence. My agency was inspired by my graduate school experience at a Historically Black University in the school of social work, whose curriculum focused on Black lives, Black issues, and

Black solutions globally. My time at this institution was the best time for learning, and for the first time in my academic career, my identity was centered. I needed the knowledge and experience in the program. It was an act of self-love and afforded me a chance to understand the complexities of the U.S. social systems and their impact on Black communities and other marginalized racial and ethnic groups. While the inception of the Black Lives Matter movement was not yet public, I graduated from two HBCUs (Schools of Social Work) that instilled in me that Black social and political agendas matter. We were prepared to bring attention to and contest systems (including social welfare policies) that conflict with that truth.

Black women who engage in social justice work more than often have a tribe of supporters and therapists, which is a genuine act of self-love to ensure we remain mentally well-balanced and retain our joy. Austin Channing Brown affirms that Black women have a chance to rethink social justice work when she analyzes Toi Derricotte's poem titled "Joy is an Act of Resistance." Austin's words of empowerment proclaim that Black women embrace joy while pursuing racial and social justice. Dr. Patricia Collins offers a historical lens on how to rethink Black women's activism and reminds us of the legacy of U.S. Black women's struggle to ensure group survival to combat racial and class oppression. I honor our history and am dedicated to our group's survival and self-definition as Black women engaged in activism. A significant part of my support in academia and social justice work has been on the shoulders of other Black women from all walks of life. I have sought uplift through friends, mentors, profound scholars' writings, and activists, who have helped me find and keep joy and a sense of agency.

Michelle Alexander's book, *The New Jim Crow: Mass Incarceration in the Age of Color Blindness,* gave me agency years after completing my bachelor's and master's degrees. Michelle details the revival of the US caste system and boldly underscores how the African American community is institutionalized in prisons, stuck in a parallel social space, and denied fundamental human rights. Her work is powerful and sets the foundation to examine all acts of injustice in the United States and their impact on marginalized groups. It is more potent than any text focused on social and racial justice I had read in my bachelor's and master's programs. In times of Resistance, we must reflect on how oppressive systems have impacted society and the structures we exist in today. Michelle's book helps one understand the necessity for factual Black histories, movements such as Black Lives Matter, constant local and federal social policy reforms (at times, I have little faith), and my passion for community development. I join with groups whose missions seek racial and social liberation, engage in collective work and responsibility in the Black community, consider historic racial and social systems of oppression as adversaries, and seek to uplift (community and social development activities) and preserve Black culture.

I have become aware of our (Black women) social position(s) with matters of sociopolitical power and oppression and found a voice that will tell our stories without conventional stereotypes and perspectives. Dr. Particia Collins's work underlines the complexities of Black women's standpoint in society regarding oppression and power and the importance of self-definition. In this profound excerpt, she describes how some social situations shaped her social justice: "I was neither blindly trying to change Society nor dispassionately studying it. Rather, I was actively engaged in trying to foster social justice, using the power of ideas as my weapon of choice."(15) Her lived work inspired my ideas and methods of working toward social justice through scholarship and community dialogue that centers on the lives of Black people. She and many other notable Black feminists and womanists have inspired me to resist homogenous narratives of Black women and record and tell our diverse stories.

People are often surprised by my admiration for Ms. Nina Simone, but she is a Black woman activist. May she rest well with the ancestors. Nina's words and actions captivated people across all racial and ethnic lines. She used her artist's platforms to push a racial justice agenda and centered herself, a Black Woman, and Black stories. She was a racial activist off stage with an insistent tactic for racial justice. Ms. Simone embraced an Afrocentric perspective and style of dress that was beautiful, authentic, and liberating. She constructed pieces of work highlighting four Black women's painful experiences by unfolding their physical features, views on how others see them, and how they are treated. It is an emotional story that exposes our stories. Her most notable act of protest was the formation of the song Mississippi Goddam. The song is in response to the horrendous acts of violence toward Black people in the South, particularly the killing of the activist Medgar Evers in Jackson, Mississippi, and the bombing of the church in Alabama, which killed four young girls in 1963. The song illustrates her frustration and tolerance of the killing and hurt of Black people fighting for their civil rights. Ms. Simone's boldness is impeccable and brilliant. Her storytelling about racial inequalities inspires my work and unapologetic nerve to discuss issues that plague Black women and the Black community. I am liberated to voice my disgust with police brutality and intersectional societal problems that plague some Black people.

I started this narrative with an act of reverence to Breonna Taylor and my ancestors as a testimony that, indeed, Black Lives Matter. Despite my shared and valid concerns about the profession, I will continue to use my voice for racial and social justice in social work and beyond, to challenge social workers to "stay in the room," and to engage in collective dialogue that centers on societal change. Channeling Ms.Nina Simone's energy and boldness to continue to confront racial and gender violence is an act of self-valuation. I am honored to be "filled up" with the knowledge and actions of amazing Black women, which has been helpful in me realizing my scholarly and activist agenda.

Black women in the United States have a lineage of strength and perseverance despite countless omissions to our existence and contributions to this country. The attention to the survival and protection of Black women is essential. We are presently living in a time where a Black woman can be shot and killed in her home by a system that is supposed to protect and serve, and a Black woman is pulled over by a cop and arrested (it is still not clear why she was arrested) and then found dead in her jail cell. We are in an era where Black women are questioned about their hairstyle choices and level of competence in the workplace. We need one another to tell and validate our stories, and demand justice. While the emphasis on this account has drawn from who I would call iconic Black women, who showed me ways to be a Black woman in this white world, I am surrounded by immeasurable Black women, and we embrace and elevate one another. My mother, the late Almatine Salters-Coleman, was my greatest teacher. As Black women, we lead, acknowledge, love, teach, mother, auntie, and sister-girl one another to preserve our legacy and significance. Onward. "The way to right wrongs is to turn the light of truth upon them." – Ida B. Wells.

Note

1 Social justice is a core social work value in the NASW (2021) Code of Ethics that decrees social workers should challenge injustices through social change efforts so that vulnerable and oppressed individuals and groups can access needed information and receive equitable services, resources, and fairness of opportunity in society.

Bibliography

Alexander, Michelle. *The New Jim Crow Mass Incarceration in the Age of Colorblindness.* New Press, 2012.

Autumn A. Arnett, (EDU). "Black Women Academics Share Secrets to Success of Navigating the Academy." *Diverse*, November 6, 2019, https://www.diverseeducat ion.com/demographics/ncludi-american/article/15105725/black-women-academ ics-share-secrets-to-success-of-navigating-the-academy.

Brown, Austin Channing. "Joy as Resistance." *Joy As Resistance – by Austin Channing Brown*, Wild Holy & Free, February 9, 2021, https://austinchanning.substack. com/p/joy-as-resistance.

Chang, Ailsa, et al. "Summer of Racial Reckoning." *NPR*, August 16, 2020, https://www. npr.org/2020/08/16/902179773/summer-of-racial-reckoning-the-match-lit.

Child Welfare Information Gateway. "Child Welfare Practice to Address Racial Disproportionality and Disparity." *Child Welfare Practice to Address Racial Disproportionality and Disparity*, 2021, https://www.childwelfare.gov/pubs/issue-briefs/racial-disproportionality/.

Collins, Patricia Hill. *Black Feminist Thought: Knowledge, Consciousness, and the Politics of Empowerment*. Routledge, 2009.

Collins, Patricia Hill. "Looking Back, Moving Ahead." *Gender & Society*, vol. 26, no. 1, 2012, pp. 14–22. https://doi.org/10.1177/0891243211434766.

Cooper, Brittney C. *Eloquent Rage: A Black Feminist Discovers Her Superpower*. Picador, 2019.

Davis, Angela Y. *Freedom Is a Constant Struggle: Ferguson, Palestine, and the Foundations of a Movement*. Edited by Frank Barat, Haymarket Books, 2016.

Joyner, Mildred. "Racism Is America's Human Stain; Black Lives Matter by Mildred 'MIT' Joyner." *Social Workers & Allies Against Solitary Confinement: SWASC*, 2021, https://socialworkersasc.org/racism-is-americas-human-stain-black-lives-matter-by-mildred-mit-joyner.

National Association of Social Workers. Read the Code of Ethics, 2021, https:// www.socialworkers.org/About/Ethics/Code-of-Ethics/Code-of-Ethics-English Accessed May 1. 2023.

Nellis, Ashley. "The Color of Justice: Racial and Ethnic Disparity in State Prisons." *The Sentencing Project*, November 1, 2021, https://www.sentencingproject.org/publi cations/color-of-justice-racial-and-ethnic-disparity-in-state-prisons/.

Wells, Ida. "The Way to Right Wrong is to Turn the Light of Truth upon Them," Quote used for Aderstise for the Lecture Series on Lynching, 1892.

Woldai, Leah. "Black Women in Higher Education: A Reflection on Inequity and Injustice." *The Emory Wheel*, February 12, 2021, https://emorywheel.com/ black-women-in-higher-education-a-reflection-on-inequity-and-injustice/.

7 The afroamor *in the 2020 Writings of Yolanda Arroyo Pizarro:* Afrofeministamente *and Other Reaffirmations of a People*

EMMANUEL HARRIS II

One might be challenged to find Black joy amid the 2020 Summer of Reckoning. Nevertheless, the Louisville writer and activist Tracey Michae'l Lewis-Giggetts set out to do just that with her June 2020 Washington Post article "Dancing in the Rain". That article spawned the book *Black Joy: Stories of Resistance, Resilience and Restoration* (2022) a few years later in which she more fully expands on the importance and indeed the need for Black joy and Black self-love. Upon presenting her work, she identifies some of the peculiarities of what makes joy (more permanent) as opposed to happiness (a temporary emotion) so special to people of African descent, to the point of being a form of resistance to the systematic oppression and the thousands of microaggressions we experience daily.[1] Lewis-Giggetts describes a state of mind that is far from monolithic and that connects the ancestors and the cultural experiences and expressions of Black people: "As the scholar Dr. Yaba Blay once said, 'The idea of Black joy as a liberation strategy is an honor to our ancestors'" (xxiv) and consequently it connects our successes as well as our traumas. She continues, "[T]he experiences of the descendants of African people (the enslaved, particularly) are convoluted at best and therefore our joy is ever intertwined with our struggle; ever integrated with the trauma wielded against us." (xxv) The descendants and the Diaspora in the Spanish Americas also constitute active agents in the literary expression of Black realities including joy.

The cultural contributions in literature of Afro-Latinas – women of African descent in the Spanish, French, and Portuguese-speaking

Americas – are plentiful. Within this very collection, we find a wonderfully enlightening, writing example by the Afro-Uruguayan poet Cristina Cabral. Using the year of the Breonna Taylor tragedy 2020 as a chronothematical point of departure, in Spanish letters we also see in 2020 the English translation of the groundbreaking edited volume by Inés María Martiatu et al, Afrocubanas: *History, Thought, and Cultural Practices*.[2] And in Puerto Rico, there is the prolific and prize-worthy publication by Yolanda Arroyo Pizarro, *Afrofeministamente* [Afrofeministly], saturated with Black love and joy. This chapter takes a critical approach to *Afrofeministamente*, contextualizes it with other texts by the author, and perhaps most importantly for the edited volume, provides a literary and scholarly understanding of its significance under the umbrella of the 2020 Summer of Reckoning and beyond.

Yolanda Arroyo Pizarro (1968) is a writer, activist, blogger, and scholar, and she describes the collection of poems *Afrofeministamente* – one of her most unabashedly Black-affirming, antiracist, works – as a "Una herramienta de afrodescubrimiento, afroautoestima y afroempoderamiento para adolecentes y tode (sic) adultx que necesite estos versos de AfroResistencia." [A tool of Afrodiscovery, Afroself-esteem, Afro-empowerment for adolescents and all adults who need these verses of AfroResistance. [3]] Her themes reaffirming and celebrating Blackness, however, can be observed building in assertiveness and clarity along the trajectory of her writings.

Among others, we could include the following: *Los documentados* [The Documented Ones] (2005) *Las negras* [The Black Women] (2016), *Pelo bueno* [Good Hair] (2018), *Las caras lindas* [The Pretty Faces] (2016) as well as her blogs in Boreales. Arroyo Pizarro's writings encompass particularly poignant and informative meanings about Black lives. She identifies and underscores the importance and beauty of Black people and Black women, especially as feminists, activists, and humanists who have played a major, positive role in the social, political, historical, psychological, and economic landscape of Puerto Rico, the Caribbean, and the Americas. Not only can we use *Afrofeministamente* to better understand her previous works, but the affirmations the book provides also bear profound social significance when considering the 2020 Summer of Reckoning and beyond. Though published the same year as these events, the collection makes no reference to the killings of Breonna Taylor, Ahmaud Arbery, or George Floyd. With the amount of time a book publication requires, there is no way the author could have anticipated the specifics of the social and health-related upheaval of 2020 to include them in a book-length, literary publication of the same year. However, the ideological, social, and cultural foundations have been long since in place throughout Puerto Rico and the Americas to analyze, contextualize, and critique.

Yolanda Arroyo Pizarro begins her collection of poetry *Afrofeministamente* with an epigraph from the Boricua scholar and writer Marie Ramos Rosados: "The history of the Black man and the Black woman is the history of all of the Puerto Ricans." (6) It continues, "[t]hey have taught us to deny all the African contributions that exist in Puerto Rican culture." The celebration of Blackness or more specifically the full splendor of Black women resonates in Arroyo Pizarro's work. Indeed, a growing chorus of contemporary voices has centered Black women's experiences in the Western world, such as the iconic Toni Morrison, Maya Angelou, the late, great bell hooks as well as more recently Brittany Cooper, Austin Channing Brown, Isabel Wilkerson, and Nikole Hannah-Jones among many others. In Hispanic letters, the examples are numerous though still underrepresented when taking into consideration the literary production of the region.

Whereas bell hooks succinctly posits in *Feminist Theory* that feminism is a movement to end sexist oppression (26), she also states in *Black Looks* that loving Blackness is a form of political resistance (9), similar indeed to what Lewis-Giggetts mentioned earlier. Therefore, we can use hooks' words to create a definition of Arroyo Pizarro's *Afrofeministamente*: a movement to end sexist oppression in which loving Blackness forms a foundation of political resistance.

In *Afrofeministamente*, the author presents poems and a few essays accentuating the lives and livelihood of African-ancestored people in all their glory. The cover of the book shows the head and shoulders of a smiling, dark brown-skinned, woman with African face-markings, wearing a headscarf of purple and green African prints. This vivid example of her color, markings, and headwear takes center stage in the poems contained within. Likewise, included throughout the text we see Julio Garcia's hybrid illustrations of enhanced photos of Black youth in traditional African vestments and settings. The section headings also tell a story in and of themselves: Afronanas [Afrolullabies], Afroreparación [Afroreparations], Afroconocernos [Afroselfawareness], Afrotodopoderoso [Afroallpowerful], Afrolibertá [Afrofreedom], and Afrofeministamente. Wherein the literary and artistic at times give way to the sociopolitical, the representations in the texts coupled with the images constitute acts of political resistance, self-affirmation, and *afroamor* or Afrolove.

Nevertheless, pervasive, polymorphic messages convey to those of us who are of African descent or possessing Black features that we are somehow less desirable, unclean, repulsive, or marginalized and this mindset unfortunately inundates our world. hooks states the following:

> Without a way to name our pain, we are also without the words to articulate our pleasure. Indeed, a fundamental task of black critical thinkers has been the struggle to break with the hegemonic modes of seeing, thinking and being that block our capacity to see ourselves oppositionally, to imagine, describe, and invent ourselves in ways that are liberatory. Without this, how can we challenge and invite non-black allies and friends to dare to look at us differently, to dare to break their colonizing gaze? (*Black Looks* 2)

Later hooks adds, "Loving blackness as political resistance transforms our ways of looking and being, and thus creates the conditions necessary for us to move against the forces of domination and death and reclaim black life." (*Black Looks* 21) The very act of inclusion or representation in *Afrofeministamente* brings to the forefront the perspectives and realities of people of African descent.

The celebration of Black esthetics becomes increasingly emphatic from the opening pages, with some of the most vivid pronouncements taking place in reference to Black people's hair and physical attributes. In "Ay ay ay mi Negrita Linda" [Ay, Ay, Ay, My Beautiful Black Girl] we read: "miren a la negrita con su afrito/ miren los rollitos de la nena negra/ esos ricitos lindos y bonitos/ ese montón de lacitos/ ella es mi amor juliaburgesino/ ay ay ay que mi nena es linda/ y pura negra." (22) [Look at the Black girl with her little afro/ look at the curls of the Black child/ the beautiful and pretty locks/ that bundle of ribbons/ she is my Julia de Burgos love/ Ay, ay, ay, my girl is pretty/ and purely Black.] One might be reminded of Toni Morrison's *The Blues Eye* with the 11-year-old Pecola's anxieties, or in Morrison's *Song of Solomon* when the character Hagar pronounces near the text's finale, "'Mama ... Why don't he like my hair'" (315). Also in *Afrofeministamente* we observe what could be a response to such inquiries in "La Afrodiva era mi Abuela" [The Afrodiva was my Grandmother]:

> Yo amo y me afroamor/ mi afroidentidad es sublime e importante/mi afrointelecto viene de las divinidades/ de la sabiduría de las tatarabuelas/ de los juegos de aldea/ de la afrosororidad en tribu/ mi reconocimiento de los ancestros/ y su recuerdo es primordial/ amo mi melanina/ ese color de piel maravilloso/ esa pigmentación de dermis extraordinaria/ el hermoso color café con leche/ el asombroso color carmelo/ ese portentoso color sepia/ somos Altezas de piel canela/ reyes y reinas Ashanti, yoruba/ carabalí (29)
>
>   [I love and I Afrolove me/ My Afroidentity is sublime and important/ my Afrointellect comes from the divinities/ from the knowledge of the great-grandmothers/ from the village games/ from the tribal Afro sorority/ my acknowledgement of the ancestors/ and their memory is primordial/ I love my melanin/ that wonderful complexion/ that extraordinary skin pigmentation/ the beautiful color of café con leche/ the astounding caramel color/ the

threatening sepia color/ we are cinnamon-skinned Royalty/ kings and queens of the Ashanti, Yoruba/ Carabalí]

Centering Blackness or Afrocentricity gives rise to self-love and *afroamor* [Afrolove].

Such centering of Blackness lends itself well to Molefi Kete Asante's definition of Afrocentricity, which he provides in a book by the same name:

Afrocentricity is a mode of thought and action in which the centrality of African interests, values, and perspectives predominate. In regards to theory, it is the placing of African people in the center of any analysis of African phenomena … In terms of action and behavior, it is a devotion to the idea that what is in the best interest of African consciousness is at the heart of ethical behavior. Finally, Afrocentricity seeks to enshrine the idea that blackness itself is a trope of ethics. Thus, to be black is to be against all forms of oppression, racism, classism, homophobia, patriarchy, child abuse, pedophilia and white racial domination. (2)

The centering of Blackness in Puerto Rican histories becomes the focus as leaders, activists, writers, and many others are listed in the Arroyo Pizarro's "Las Negras de mi Kínder" [The Black Woman at My Kindergarten] in which the teacher affirms that her students will learn and know African-ancestored luminaries (a list which I have edited for the sake of brevity): "A las niñas de mi kinder les enseñamos/quién es Angelamaría Dávila. . . Julia de Burgos … Mayra Santos Febres. . . / les decimos qué hicieron/ y que hacen/ las Grandes Negras que son/ y que fueron" (37) [We teach the girls at my kindergarten/ who is Angelamaría Dávila … Julia de Burgos … Mayra Santos Febres . . ./ We tell them what they did/ and what they do/ The Esteemed Black Women they are/ and they were]. bell hooks might refer to such actions as teaching to transgress.

In the book, *Teaching to Transgress*, hooks outlines how certain pedagogical practices that incorporate the perspectives of Black folks constitute a form of transgression. Similar transgressive teachers come to life in Arroyo Pizarro's poem "Maestra Celestina". The verses contained capture the voice of a young, Black, girl who admires her teacher, the historical figure, Celestina Cordero: "Yo quisiera Maestra Celestina/ negrita linda como yo/ que algún día cuando camines por los adoquines/ cruzando las calles para el mercado/ para ir al centro y al malecón/ descubras que te estoy esperando/ que soy esta niña" (71) [I wish Ms. Celestina/ beautiful and Black like me/ that one day when you walk the cobblestones/ crossing the street toward the market/ to go to the city center or boardwalk/ you see that I am waiting/ that I am that girl] A brief section of the narrative afterward clarifies that specific knowledge about Cordero derives from now-digitized nineteenth-century newspapers that state the teacher of African descent was one of the first to have classes for Black students in San Juan, Puerto Rico in and around 1847. (71)

In Arroyo Pizarro's writings, Africa and the Diaspora also receive direct attention in the work "Soy de la Encendida Calle Antillana" [I Am from Lighted Antillean Street] as well as "Poema del turbante" [Poem of the Headscarf] in *Afrofeministamente* in which the latter states:

> dice que soy una mujer orgullosa/ de su tradición/ el turbante o guelé para los Yoruba/ tukwi para los de Botswana/ dhuku para los de Malawi/ Zimbabue y Ghana/ también llamado foulard en francés/ doek para los de Namibia/ turbante en afroboricua/ origen de la protección del universo/ guardians protectors del cabello/ hoy es belleza e hidalguía. (47)
>
> [they say that I am a woman who is proud/ of her traditions/ the headscarf or *guelé* for the Yoruba/ *tukwi* for the Botswana/ *dhuku* for the Malawi/ Zimbabwe and Ghana/ also called the *foulard* in French/ *doek* for those from Namibia/ headscarf in AfroBoricua/ source of protection from the universe/ protective guardians of the crown/ today it is beauty and nobility]

Reading *Afrofeministamente* with texts like "Poema del turbante" [Poem of the Headscarf] sheds light on one of Arroyo Pizarro's books published four years prior, *Las caras lindas* (2016) [The Pretty Faces].

This children's book of short stories, a short play and a heart-wrenching essayistic epilogue, presents some of the same themes as *Afrofeministamente* yet in a language, style, and clarity apropos for young readers. The stories emphasize Blackness, people of African descent, the beauty of Black hair, and *las caras lindas* [pretty faces] of Black folk. Here too we find references to African heritage in terms of religion, rebellion against slavery and oppression, and the quest for libertá [freedom]. Anti-bullying and antiracism also shape the interactions of the young protagonists in a book sprinkled with intermittent drawings, representations of African-ancestored individuals, male, female, young, and older. The covers, the pictures, the endnotes, and the editorial commentary all constitute critical parts of the book, and her *afroamor* [Afrolove] compels the reader to acknowledge her presence in addition to her voice. It closes with the author directly addressing the public as she describes her own experiences being bullied in school and her eventual *afroamor* [Afrolove] and liberation. She titles the epilogue, "Todas las mañanas volvía a ser negra: sin raza, una historia de bullying" [Every Morning I Awoke a Black Woman: Without Race, A Story of Bullying], and she concludes with the following:

> Treinta años más tarde, descubrí que he heredado el bello color negro de mis tatarabuelos provenientes de la gran madre patria África. Me he enterado por mi árbol genealógico que soy descendiente de reinados y gestas de valentía. He

sabido de gente valiente de mi color que luchó por su propia libertad y la libertad de muchos otros hombres y mujeres ... Ya no estoy triste, ni desubicada, ni sin raza. (70)

[Thirty years later, I discovered that I have inherited the beautiful black color of my great-grandparents who originated from the great mother-fatherland Africa. I realized from my genealogical tree that I am a descendent of valiant kingdoms and achievements. I have learned of valiant people my color who fought for their freedom and the freedom of many other women and men ... I am no longer sad, nor disoriented, nor without a race.]

The next page invites us to meet the author and provides a beautiful, brown-skinned, headscarf-bearing, African pendant-wearing, Yolanda Arroyo Pizarro along with her biographical information, including references to her daughter, "una preciosa hija de nombre Aurora, en quien se ha inspirado para escribir poemas, cuentos cortos y novellas." (25) [a precious daughter by the name Aurora, who has inspired her to write poems, short stories and novellas] She concludes with the following: "Es fanática de la Torre Eiffel, los juegos de domino y el chocolate oscuro." (75) [She is a fan of the Eiffel Tower, playing dominos and dark chocolate.]

The overall image is not too different from the one of Breonna Taylor that graced the cover of *O, The Oprah Magazine* at the height of her notoriety. Another woman of Caribbean descent, who was a titan in her own right, Cicely Tyson would also celebrate Black love and accomplishments in her formidable memoir *Just as I Am* penned in 2020 and published the following year. In it the nearly-centenarian would, on more than one occasion, reflect on Breonna Taylor as well as the challenges of being a Black woman. Among the many elucidating comments in the impressive tome, we find the following which also captures much of the spirit in *Afrofeministamente*:

We each have many faces, various ways of appearing and behaving. In one moment, we may show remarkable steadfastness, and in another an aching vulnerability. We can be at turns tranquil and belligerent, jubilant and despairing. We are inherently multifaceted and yet marvelously complete. (41)

Yolanda Arroyo Pizarro's poetry similarly and clamorously reaffirms her cultural awareness:

Soy lo afrofeministamente correcto/ visible y temible/ exijo igualdad racial para mí y mis hermanes (sic)/ exijo que se reconozcan mis experiencias/ y las de mi pueblo/ las de mi genealogía milenaria/ que sean colocadas/ en nuestros libros de historia/ nuestros libros de texto/ en nuestra ficción, narrativa y poética (89)

[I am Afrofeministly correct/ visible and fearsome/ I demand racial equality for me and my brethren/ I demand that others recognize my experiences/ and those of my people/ those of my millennial genealogy/ that they are inscribed/ in our history books/ our textbooks/ in our narrative and poetic fiction]

Let us also recognize, remember, and reaffirm Breonna Taylor and other Black women with *afroamor* enthusiastically, conscientiously, and *afrofeministamente.*

Notes

1 Lewis-Giggetts argues, "When joy is Black, it is the radical demonstration of our humanity – our laughter, our ancestral mandate to keep moving in a rhythm all our own – set in a cultural context and struggle specific to our experiences as members of the African Diaspora." (xxi)
2 *Afrocubanas* was first published in 2018 as *Afrocubanas: Historia, pensamiento y prácticas culturales.*
3 All translations in this chapter are mine, unless otherwise indicated. The Spanish word "historia" has two primary meanings: history and story. Both ideas would be applicable to the quotation above.

Bibliography

Arroyo Pizarro, Yolanda. *Afrofeministamente.* San Juan, Puerto Rico: Editorial EDP, 2020.

Arroyo Pizarro, Yolanda. *Las caras lindas.* San Juan, Puerto Rico: Editorial EDP, 2020.

Asante, Molefi Kete. *Afrocentricity: The Theory of Social Change.* Gilbert, AZ: African American Imagery, 2003.

hooks, bell. *Black Looks: Race and Representation.* Boston: South End, 1992.

hooks, bell. *Feminist Theory: From Margin to Center.* New York, Routledge, 2014.

hooks, bell. *Teaching to Transgress: Education as the Practice of Freedom.* New York: Routledge, 1994.

Lewis-Giggetts, Michae'l. "Dancing in the Rain and the Power of Black Joy as Resistance" *The Washington Post.* June 2020.

Lewis-Giggetts, Michae'l. *Black Joy: Stories of Resistance, Resilience, and Restoration.* New York: Gallery Books, 2022.

Martiatu, Inés María et al Editors. *Afrocubanas: History, Thought, and Cultural Practices.* New York: Rowman & Littlefield, 2020.

Tyson, Cicely. *Just as I Am: A Memoir.* New York: HarperCollins, 2021.

8 Centering Blackness: Reflections on the Summer of 2020

KIMBERLY EISON SIMMONS

In the summer of 2020, we witnessed powerful calls for social and racial justice. From Black Lives Matter demonstrations to the creation of DEI positions inside and outside the academy, the focus began to shift and center on race as a lived experience in the United States and beyond. What did it mean to be Black in the United States? How was Blackness experienced differently based on gender, color, social class, and sexuality? These questions surfaced in real-time, in the news, and on social media, and they forced us to revisit societal sensitivities around racialized groups. This reflective chapter explores class assignments and discussions I had with my students about Black Lives Matter during the summer of 2020 while contemplating the historical and contemporary racialized experiences of Black people in the United States, particularly Black women, following the deaths of Ahmaud Arbery, Breonna Taylor, and George Floyd.

Introduction

The summer of 2020 will be remembered for many things. From the COVID-19 pandemic to the Black Lives Matter demonstrations that swept the nation, it was a time of upheaval and change. For those in the academy, it was also a time of reflection and introspection.

As a cultural anthropologist who studies the African American and Afro-Latino/a experience regarding race and racism, gender, and identity, I was suddenly inundated with questions from my students about what was happening in the world around them. They wanted to know why George Floyd had been killed, why there were protests in the streets, and what it all meant for them and society. I realized my students were looking to me and their other professors for guidance and understanding. Since I was teaching *African American Cultures* that summer, I developed a class assignment using a variation of Photovoice to help students make sense of the racially charged summer of 2020. As a method, Photovoice was developed to shine a light on particular lived experiences using photography to generate discussions in communities (Carlson 2012). Caroline Wang and Mary Ann Burris developed this technique where participants were given cameras and asked to take pictures of people/items that were meaningful to them (Wang and Burris 1997).

In this chapter, I share and analyze this Photovoice assignment as a barometer for how students were processing the momentous events of the summer. This assignment asked students to center their own experiences with race and racism and the larger societal implications of what was happening around them that summer. It also asked students to consider how Blackness is experienced differently based on gender, color, social class, and sexuality. I hope that by sharing a discussion of this assignment, I can provide some insight into how students are thinking about structural racism, anti-Black police violence, their individual and collective responses, as well as the impact and broader societal issues that the summer of 2020 illuminated. In this way, this approach is situated in the context of culturally relevant pedagogy – a concept developed by anthropologist Gloria Ladson-Billings – where students' race and backgrounds are taken into account in the learning environment while also focusing on the relationship between educators and students (Ladson-Billings 1995). This concept has developed over time to incorporate the idea of sustainability (Paris & Alim 2017). I hope that after engaging in this assignment, students will continue to reflect on their lived experiences and use their voices to bring about change in their communities.

African American Images in the Media

During class, we discussed racialized images of African Americans in the media (in general) and social media (in particular). The media is a powerful tool that can shape public perception in various ways. When it comes to images of African Americans, the media has often been guilty of perpetuating stereotypes and negative portrayals. Black men, in particular, have been subjected to a wide range of damaging stereotypes, from the "thug" to the "brute" (Bogle 1994). Black women, meanwhile, have been portrayed as either hypersexualized or largely invisible (ibid). These distorted representations can profoundly affect how the wider world perceives African Americans. They can also lead to real-world consequences, such as discrimination and racial profiling.

These stereotypes are not only harmful to Black people, but they also serve to reinforce racist attitudes. As a result, many Black Americans have called for more positive and realistic depictions in the media. We witnessed this racial awareness during the summer of 2020 as there were calls for social justice, representation, and real change. Multinational corporations and others reconsidered marketing and branding materials. A prime example is when Quaker Oats announced that it was removing the image of Aunt Jemima, an image based on a racial stereotype, off their brand of pancakes and syrup. Still, with all the calls for change and resultant institutional/departmental statements on racism and police violence, much work must be done to combat these harmful stereotypes. These images and stereotypes were part of the societal backdrop as we discussed race and lived experience and how everything came to a head during the summer of 2020 in the United States.

Black Students and Activism

Race and racism continue to be among society's most important topics. For Black students, developing a Black consciousness is essential for understanding and combating the race-based inequalities that continue to exist in our world. Black consciousness is about more than just awareness of race; it is also about understanding the historical and social context of race in America, recognizing the unique experiences and perspectives that come with being Black in America, and using this knowledge to fight for justice and equality. In recent years, we have seen an increase in Black student activism on college campuses across the country. This activism is a critical development, showing that Black students use their education to empower themselves and their communities. Black students who develop a Black consciousness will be better equipped to challenge the status quo and create lasting change.

Developing Black consciousness among Black students is a critical step in the fight against race and racism. By critically examining how race and racism operate, Black students can develop the knowledge and skills necessary to challenge these systems. Additionally, by talking openly about race and racism with their peers, Black students can create a space for honest dialogue and support. Finally, Black students can use their experiences to engage in activism that pushes for societal change.

How do we connect the dots between racialized media images and student activism? How do we interact with images meaningfully to bring about social awareness and change? Social media allows us to interact with others, promote ideas, and discuss and even challenge different ways of thinking. During class discussions, with the Black Lives Matter demonstrations and the COVID-19 pandemic as both a backdrop and a reality, we discussed social media posts and the ways in which students felt compelled to raise their voices as a show of solidarity and resistance. The Photovoice assignment allowed them to reflect on an event that resonated with them, changed their lives, or impacted them. By sharing their images, they contributed individually to a collective project, telling a story about how race and racism continue to be lived.

Photovoice

> Photovoice is a process by which people can identify, represent, and enhance their community through a specific photographic technique. It entrusts cameras to the hands of people to enable them to act as recorders, and potential catalysts for change, in their own communities. It uses the immediacy of the visual image to furnish evidence and to promote an effective, participatory means of sharing expertise and knowledge. (Wang and Burris 1997: 369)

How do we shed light on different lived experiences? How do we begin to talk about race, gender, and social class as lived and differently experienced based on our own positionality?

Photovoice is a methodology that allows us to do that – it is a unique approach to storytelling that uses photographs to explore the interconnectedness of personal experiences and social issues. Wang and Burris developed this approach in the 1990s as a way to give voiceless people a platform to share their stories. It has since been used by groups ranging from indigenous peoples to survivors of domestic violence. By using photographs as a starting point, Photovoice allows people to share their stories in their own words, on their own terms. This honest, first-person storytelling can help challenge dominant narratives and reveal hidden racial truths. It can also empower marginalized groups by giving them a space to tell their stories and shape their narratives. In this way, Photovoice is important for promoting social justice and gender equality.

In class, we used a variation of Photovoice to provide a space for honest and open dialogue about race, gender, and other social justice issues. The photographs taken by the students were used as a starting point for discussion and reflection and to think about the hidden truths about the experiences of marginalized communities revealed in the photographs. Students were also given the option to select an image that resonated with them from social media. In this way, Photovoice provided a unique and powerful way to engage with social issues and create meaningful change for students individually and collectively.[1]

Photovoice Class Assignment
The Photovoice assignment read as follows:

"We are currently in the middle of the COVID-19 pandemic and at a critical point in our history in this country with police brutality, racial injustice, and conversations surrounding the ongoing Black Lives Matter movement. Coronavirus cases are on the rise, and there are conversations around the country taking place about individual/collective action and responsibility with regard to slowing the spread of the virus vs. individual rights and liberties. Several statements have been made by organizations and companies in solidarity with the Black community and communities of color. There is talk of change, inclusion, and transformation. When you think about this current moment, what are your thoughts and feelings? How have the pictures you have taken over the past 3 ½ months reflected your thoughts and feelings? Looking back at your pictures, select 4–6 pictures that capture/represent the following and add your pictures along with your name and a couple of sentences about the picture."

1. Early thoughts and feelings regarding the coronavirus pandemic (reaction to the extended spring break, classes going online, social distancing, masks, news coverage, fear/anxiety, etc.).
2. Thoughts and feelings as the reality of coronavirus set in (classes, end of the semester, social distancing, reality of quarantine, masks, news coverage, fear/anxiety, navigating the "new normal").
3. Thoughts and feelings with the reality of coronavirus and/or emerging images, news coverage of police brutality, racial inequality, and Black Lives Matter.
4. How you're navigating and finding and creating joy/happy moments during this time.

Here is a sample of some of the submissions below (all names have been changed):

Rosalind
Rosalind submitted a photo of a young, Black male in a police uniform. She wrote, "I thought this was relevant to the times because to me, this is my fiancé, James, and he is a good man and a good cop. In uniform others may see him as a threat, sell out, or as a protector, while in regular clothes he is treated as just a Black man."

Becca

Becca included an image of text messages between her and her boyfriend:
Becca: how is it
Boyfriend: got teargassed and they shooting rubber bullets
Becca: time to come get you? [large-eyed emoji]
Boyfriend: No there's more work to be done
Becca explained in her submission, "This was a text message between my boyfriend and I, while he was at the protest. I was 8 months pregnant so sadly I was not able to attend with him, but I was worried sick the entire time."

Ryan

Ryan included a photo of seven police officers in full riot gear. Their race and gender are undistinguishable. He wrote, "This photo really struck me as something powerful. This picture is from my city in front of a famous mural that was painted in response to NC House Bill 2. It's ironic that the riot police were there to control people protesting for equality while they stood underneath the 'All are Welcome' slogan."

David

David cited the poem "Ode to Black Skin" by Ashanti Anderson which appeared in the April 2019 issue of *Poetry* magazine.

Ode to Black Skin[2]
By Ashanti Anderson

> You are dark as religion. Remember God
> could not have named a modicum of light without you.
> You are plum, black currant, passion
> fruit in another woman's garden. You are Black
> as and as if by magic. Black not as sin, but a cave's jaw
> clamped shut by forgiveness. Color of closed wombs and bellies
> of ships, you, dark as not the tree trunk but its every cleft.
> I chart each crescent moon rising above fingernail
> and rub together my thighs for want of you. I try
> to find you where the pages of books meet. You hang
> where men or piano keys segregate. When I miss you,
> I remember the hickey the sun left on the back of my neck.
> If I forget, I smoke blunts down to my fingertips
> and beg you to come on my lips. This is how I pray for you
> when I'm not pessimistic. I bow to your darkness like I kneel
> beside a child's bed, confessing as gospel, *there's no monster here.*

David wrote, "Rioting had begun. The #BlackLivesMatter protests were underway in most state capitals and cities. I myself began to feel marginalized by a society where success had been my only goal. The poem *Ode to Black Skin* made me feel comfortable in the many situations that plague my young life. Then reminds me I am forever a Black mind, body, and soul and I relish in that fact."

James
James included a black and white photo shot from the back of a huge crowd at a demonstration in Charlotte, North Carolina. He wrote, "This was a photo I took at a Black Matters rally in downtown Charlotte. This picture is significant because of the climate we currently live in, and it was eye opening experience for me as well."

He also had a screenshot of the rapper Lil Baby from his music video, which James captioned, "Lil baby is a rapper that I'm a fan of. He released a song called "Bigger Picture" that was about the world that Blacks live in and the difficulties we face every day."[3]

Tina
Tina attached a collage of five photos of her at different protests: a black and white picture of her with a COVID mask and a handwritten sign that says BLACK LIVES MATTER; a color photo of Tina partially wearing a Kente cloth face mask and holding a George Floyd sign; a color photo of her and another Black woman in front of white police officers whose backs are to the camera; a black and white photo of Tina marching with her hands up alongside another Black male; and a color headshot of her with a Kente cloth facemask around her neck exposing her anguished expression.

Caption: Tina wrote, "I put this collage here because I consider myself a very Pro-Black very Black Militant, social activist. I am passionate about Black people, our mental health, progression, and betterment in society. I've always been pretty vocal about being Black throughout my life, but this was the first time I protested on the front line. The protest I was in prior to this was back in 2013 for Trayvon Martin where I was just becoming more socially & politically aware of what it meant to be Black in America. This year, in my new educated + experienced life I protested, and it was the most connected I felt not only to my community but to the Black leaders and activists that walked before me. It was a very emotional experience for me, especially given I'm at age where I understand it goes beyond just being Black and as a sister of 4, daughter, niece, granddaughter, and cousin, being able to fight for something that represented not only myself, but the personal Black lives I cared for was very touching. I also got the chance to voice myself in front of / to (sic) the police and felt like I needed to hold a Black Panther meeting after lol. (Btw I kept pulling my mask up during the protest lol)"

These submissions, individually and collectively, speak about racial awareness among students – an awareness with an eye on the past and another on present-day situations with race at its center. This awareness brought about a call to action for these students as many referenced the demonstrations and being directly or indirectly involved. Without a doubt, the summer events directly impacted their lives as what they had read about and what they saw on social media was playing out in real-time, in their actual experiences, creating a lasting impact. One of the pedagogical aims of having students reflect on their experiences in this way is with the hope that they will continue to use their voices to be an important force in the fight against racial injustice.

While the images and descriptions for the Photovoice assignment were uploaded to a Google document, and students were asked to review other submissions, we reviewed and discussed the submissions in class and focused on some of the personal and societal effects of the summer of 2020. Some students wanted to continue this reflection and opted to write their final papers on themes related to #BlackLivesMatter and #SayHerName and having the chance to write directly about Ahmaud Arbery, George Floyd, Breonna Taylor, and others we lost that summer due to racially motivated police violence.

The excerpts below were written by African American women students and speak to the issues of Black women in the context of Black Lives Matter and the role of social media. Tina's paper was entitled, "They Love to Hate Us: The Intersectionality of Gender and Race on Black Women."

> Black women are also still seen fighting for protection in society in movements such as Black Lives Matter. Granted Black women have a history of being at the forefront of social justice with historic figures such as Sojourner Truth, Assata Shakur, Angela Davis, Harriet Tubman and many more, they are still last in the fight of racial equality and justice. Most recently shown in the advocacy and fight for justice in the cases of George Floyd and Breonna Taylor, two Black individuals both killed unjustly by the police. While George Floyd case sparked national outrage, protesting, and resulting in the arrest of his murderers, Breonna Taylor's killers still remain free. It isn't that there hasn't been attention to her case, but it is simply the lack of care for the life of a Black woman in society.

Tina discusses how Black women have long been at the forefront of the fight for justice and equality in America. From early leaders like Sojourner Truth and Harriet Tubman to modern-day organizers like Alicia Garza and Patrisse Cullors, Black women have always been willing to put their lives on the line to make America a better place for all. This moment reveals that there is still more work to be done as Black women continue to face disproportionate levels of violence, poverty, and discrimination. Tina also focuses on Breonna Taylor and the lack of attention her case received in the media compared to George Floyd. She suggests that this lack of attention was because Breonna Taylor was a Black woman and that her life seemed to matter less as a Black woman. This sentiment is echoed in the #SayHerName Movement (Grant 2022, Martin 2021, Tynes 2021).

Becca's paper, "Evolution on Media," focused on the role of social media and how we witnessed police violence, and varied responses, on different platforms:

> Due to social media platforms, situations of injustice are spread quicker and more efficiently. This has helped in situations such as George Floyd, a Black man who had police called on him at a store after being accused of giving the clerk a counterfeit twenty-dollar bill. George Floyd then got into an altercation with four police officers who then killed him at the scene. Protests were held in his honor all around the world for weeks, petitions were sent around on all social media platforms to have his murderers arrested, which later happened. Around this same time Breonna Taylor, a 26-year-old Black woman was shot to death by police officers in her own home. The officers were acting on a search warrant for two men they believed were selling drugs, but these men lived nowhere near Breonna.
>
> Breonna Taylor's story has been plastered all over social media in hopes to get the officers who murdered her arrested. Some posts have been helpful with numbers of attorneys to call to help push for her murderer's arrest, petitions to sign, fundraisers for her family, and many other helpful tools to find justice. There have also been posts making jokes of the situation. They are still with the idea to arrest her murderers, but once again not in ways to be taken seriously. Posts such as putting "Arrest the Cops Who Killed Breonna Taylor" on different things such as Woody's feet from Toy Story, in appropriate pictures, because they think they will get people's attention, and many other jokes. Our generation makes it hard to be taken seriously in times when we need it the most. We are being watched by the younger generation and if they see us taking these situations lightly, they will do the same, and nothing will ever get resolved. We must be the change we want to see in the world.
>
> Overtime social media has made a big influence of the social injustices that Black people face. Racism has never gone away it is just filmed now. Black people are still getting lynched, treated poorly while fighting for our lives in hospitals, or even just giving birth. Black people are still getting beaten, raped, and killed by white people for no other reason than the color of their skin. We can see who these people are now and get justice. During these past few months when injustice has been at an all-time high many white people have lost their jobs and have been prosecuted for their wrongdoings against Black people. We have a long way to go, but we have also come a long way from where we started, and we will not give up until Black people are treated fairly in every aspect.

Here, Becca raises several issues. Social media has played an increasingly prominent role in social and political movements. The rise of platforms like Twitter and Facebook has allowed previously marginalized groups to share their stories and build momentum for change. The Black Lives Matter movement is a prime example of the power of social media. In the wake of police killings of unarmed Black men, women, and children, the #BlackLivesMatter hashtag became a rallying cry for social justice (Chambers and Harlan 2021; Hinderliter and Peraza 2021). The hashtag gave voice to the pain and anger of Black people across the country and helped to galvanize a new generation of activists.

Social media has played a significant role in raising awareness of police violence and fostering the growth of the Black Lives Matter movement. In the past, incidents of police brutality were often overshadowed by official narratives that sought to downplay or deny the severity of the abuse. However, social media has given survivors and witnesses a platform to share their stories, which has helped shine a spotlight on the issue of police violence. The Black Lives Matter movement has been particularly effective in using social media to spread its message and build support for its cause. By using hashtags, organizing online campaigns, and live-streaming protests, BLM has reached a global audience and galvanized support for its fight against police brutality.

Conclusion – #SayHerName

> Black women and girls as young as 7 and as old as 93 have been killed by the police, though we rarely hear their names. Knowing their names is a necessary but not a sufficient condition for lifting up their stories which in turn provides a much clearer view of the wide-ranging circumstances that make Black women's bodies disproportionately subject to police violence. To lift up their stories, and illuminate police violence against Black women, we need to know who they are, how they lived, and why they suffered at the hands of police. #SayHerName – https://www.aapf.org/sayhername

In recent years, Black students have been using social media to write about their lived experiences with race and racism. In this way, they use the platform to speak out against the injustices they see and demand change. Their writing gives voice to the voiceless and brings attention to the many ways in which race and racism continue to impact our society. In a world where we continue to make the case that Black lives matter, these students use their words to remind us that every life is valuable and deserves respect.

The Photovoice assignment reinforced the idea that students' experiences, situated in historical, political, social, and cultural contexts, have value – their lived experience is a source of knowledge. Black students use their personal stories to challenge dominant narratives and create a new understanding of race and racism. By centering Blackness, we tell a different story as the people become subjects of their own stories, transforming the way we think about race and racism by bringing the lived experience of Black people to the fore.

Photovoice and other reflexive assignments allow students to share their experiences in their own words. It also gives them a chance to be the experts on their own lives, rather than having their experiences dictated by others. It helps to build a sense of community and solidarity among Black students. By telling their own stories, Black students can assert their individuality and contribute to the collective narrative of the Black experience. In doing so, they are shaping the future of race relations in America and redefining what it means to be Black in America today. This shift is significant, as it allows for a more accurate representation of race and experience within society. It also helps to counter the long-standing narrative that has placed white people at the center of history. By amplifying Black students' voices, we can gain a deeper understanding of the lived experiences of people of color. In turn, this amplification can help to create a more just and equitable world.

Notes

1 The University of South Carolina had a Black Lives Matter project to collect stories (Voices of SC: Black Lives Matter), and I was part of the team. I gave a presentation based on the Photovoice class assignment. https://digital.library.sc.edu/exhibits/sc-blm/. Students knew the class project would be part of the Voices of SC: Black Lives Matter Project (and related discussions). I encouraged them to submit their reflections as well. I made minor edits to some of the submissions for this chapter.
2 The poem "Ode to Black Skin" appears here in its entirety, thanks to the expressed, written consent of the author, Ashanti Anderson.
3 The image was from a Lil Baby fan page (Lil baby 4PF Fan Page [lilbaby_1] Real Rap Tonight!! #blacklivesmatter, Instagram). At the time of this publication, the photo is no longer on the fan page, but it was posted during the summer of 2020. It was a screenshot from Lil Baby's *The Bigger Picture* music video focusing on Black Lives Matter demonstrations and the issues raised during the summer of 2020 (https://youtu.be/_VDGysJGNoI).

Bibliography

Anderson, Ashanti. "Ode to Black Skin" *Poetry.* Poetry Foundation. April 2019.
Bogle, Donald. *Toms, Coons, Mulattoes, Mammies, and Bucks: An Interpretive History of Blacks in American Films.* New 3rd ed., Continuum, 1994.

Carlson, Elizabeth D., et al. "Photovoice as a Social Process of Critical Consciousness." *Qualitative Health Research*, vol. 16, no. 6, 2012, pp. v4–131–852, https://doi.org/10.1177/1049732306287525.

Chambers, Veronica, and Jennifer Harlan. *Call and Response: The Story of Black Lives Matter*. Versify/Houghton Mifflin Harcourt, 2021.

Django, Paris, and H. Samy Alim eds., *Culturally Sustaining Pedagogies: Teaching and Learning for Justice in a Changing World*, Chapter 8, Teachers College Press (2017).

Grant, Rachel, et al. "Selling Breonna: Twitter Responses to Breonna Taylor on the Covers of O, The Oprah Magazine and Vanity Fair." *Journalism & Mass Communication Quarterly*, 2022, https://doi.org/10.1177/10776990221108646.

Hinderliter, Beth, and Steve Peraza. *More Than Our Pain: Affect and Emotion in the Era of Black Lives Matter*. Edited by Beth Hinderliter and Steve Peraza, State University of New York Press, 2021.

Ladson-Billings, Gloria. "Toward a Theory of Culturally Relevant Pedagogy." *American Educational Research Journal*, vol. 32, no. 3, 1995, pp. 465–91.

Ladson-Billings, Gloria. Culturally Relevant Pedagogy 2.0: a.k.a. the Remix. *Harvard Educational Review*, vol. 84, no. 1, 1 April 2014, pp. 74–84. doi: https://doi.org/10.17763/haer.84.1.p2rj131485484751

Martin, Jordan. "Breonna Taylor: Transforming a Hashtag into Defunding the Police." *The Journal of Criminal Law & Criminology*, vol. 111, no. 4, 2021, pp. 995–1030.

Tynes, Brendane. "What the Reimagination of Breonna Taylor's (After)life Reveals." *Feminist Media Studies*, vol. 21, no. 5, 2021, pp. 864–67, https://doi.org/10.1080/14680777.2021.1944892.

Voices of SC: Black Lives Matter. U of South Carolina. https://digital.library.sc.edu/exhibits/sc-blm/

Wang, Caroline, and Mary Ann Burris. "Photovoice: Concept, Methodology, and Use for Participatory Needs Assessment." *Health Education & Behavior*, vol. 24, no. 3, June 1997, pp. 369–387, doi:10.1177/109019819702400309.

9 The Groundwater Approach to Breonna Taylor and Others: Systematic Racism and African Americans

KERYN G. VICKERS

Memory Lane

As I pondered how to begin this chapter, I recalled my first real encounter with a police officer. I have seen them before while growing up in the streets of the Bronx, New York, or as we called it, uptown boogie down Bronx. However, one day I was playing with my middle school peers in the neighborhood behind our apartment and was walking through the park. A Black police officer happened to be walking through at the same time and engaged our group of Black kids. His utility belt intrigued us, and we specifically asked about his weapon and handcuffs. He said that he could not unholster and show his weapon but could show us his handcuffs. Secretly, we all feared the weapon and preferred the cuffs. So, one by one, he let us examine the equipment, feel its weight, and experience what it was like to have handcuffs put on us. He emphasized that he would not put them on tight because he did not want to hurt us. Ironically, when my turn came, my wrists were still so small he could not even place them on tight even if he wanted to, and that is when the officer said, "He never wanted to see any of us have handcuffs placed on us for real, and that we ought to do the right thing." The encounter set the foundation for my relationship with law enforcement; they were leaders in the community despite their weapons and cuffs; they were indeed one of us, who cared, and to keep it that way, I had to stay on the right side of the law. From that point on, I have made it my mantra or mission that when I see an officer of the law, I speak and engage them, so they never have to worry or consider me any threat; since they were and are leaders with power in the community.

Although I am unaware of Breonna Taylor's upbringing with law enforcement and could only make assumptions about it, Breonna Taylor did not lose her life because she strayed away from the law during the fatal incident at her apartment. What if she received the chance to speak and engage the officers non-threateningly? Would the outcome have been different, or would officers still exert power and influence over the situation? Unfortunately, we will never know if or how the outcome would have changed because Breonna Taylor cannot speak from the grave. The hypothetical questions surrounding the circumstances of Breonna Taylor's death remain a mystery. Still, we can address the idea of law enforcement as leaders with power in the community and how African American women meet their demise due to inhumane actions. I also write because I am sick and tired of having to think twice before going on a walk or run, for fear of being accused, shot at, or accosted because I am considered a threat simply because of my gender and the color of my skin. Again, I write to share truths, promote change, and offer hope!

My conversations with law enforcement intend to illuminate how an African American/Black, educated cisgender heterosexual male, father, and man of the cloth views this travesty of justice, summer of reckoning, and series of immoral acts that brought about the demise of so many like Breonna Taylor, listed with forty-nine other women of color since 2014 on #SayTheirNames website, and other victims such as George Floyd and Amadou Diallo. The #SayTheirNames website is a work-in-progress list of Black women killed in the United States by law enforcement and civilians. The website explains the mantra "Never Forget," which stems from the horrific loss of thousands of lives due to the September 11 terrorist attacks. Therefore, in the same spirit of "Never Forget," the #SayTheirNames website focuses on the fact that we must also "Never Forget" the Black lives taken unjustly and demand a change. Historically, there have been thousands upon thousands of Black people who lost their lives at the hands of law enforcement. Still, the website lists the forty-nine names submitted by individuals personally impacted by the tragedies, and some are included as part of the Black Lives Matter movement. So, in the same spirit of "Never Forgetting," I also pay homage to Breonna Taylor and the forty-nine women listed on the website. In addition to writing about Breonna Taylor and listing the names of other women, I share some of my conversations over the last few decades with officers who have provided insight into how and why these unfortunate events occur. These conversations and encounters transcend space, place, and time because they happened across the United States in various settings and ultimately landed in the laps of the next generation, our children. Hopefully, these narratives can help us understand how and why we need law enforcement to engage with African Americans justly because all our lives depend on it. Historically, African Americans in the United States consistently face micro and macroaggressions and life-threatening moments at the hands of the law. Over time these individual moments lead or accumulate into transgenerational oppression. Unfortunately, those individuals and circumstances receive the most press. They should receive significant press when lives are at stake or lost, like with Breonna Taylor, the forty-nine other women, George Floyd, and Amadou Diallo cases. Fortunately, not all law enforcement officers have ill will and evil intentions.

To illuminate my conversations with law enforcement, I invite readers to journey with me down memory lane as I share personal experiences in hopes of comprehending Breonna Taylor's case for all of us. Part of grasping tragedies such as Breonna Taylor's includes understanding the power dynamics between white law enforcement officers and the African American and, in some cases, low socioeconomic communities. We can only understand the power dynamics once we first understand and define an officer's position or place within society. My research determined that officers are executive leaders within our communities. I coupled my research with Andreescu and Vito (2010), who discussed how officers should conduct themselves in society using an exploratory study on ideal leadership behavior. I used Haberfield's research to explain the officers' responsibilities. After delving into Haberfield's research, I revisited my research on The Groundwater Approach to help us put the dynamics between systemic racism, African Americans, and white law enforcement in context within the United States. I discovered that the issues that African Americans face with white law enforcement officers are not germane only to the law enforcement agency but all agencies within the United States; the entire system is contaminated and needs cleaning. Even though law enforcement officers are executive leaders, and the system works in their favor, through my encounters with officers, I learned that officers still express fear and an attempt to escape consequences if their actions are unbecoming, as an officer when serving the community. After an unfortunate incident occurs and a life is lost, officers must only verbalize that they were fearful and seldom face ramifications. However, there is still hope because not all law enforcement officers abuse their power, act unbecomingly, or try to escape repercussions. Some officers choose another way. Therefore, I have hope and unapologetically offer hope by writing about my conversations with law enforcement officers. I write to pay homage to the many women like Breonna Taylor, the forty-nine others, and those unmentioned that law enforcement officers took away from us too soon. I pay tribute by writing about individuals hoping we do not forget them and that officers do not repeat these inhumane acts.

Conversations and encounters with the law illuminate the possibility of a unique law enforcement process for whites as opposed to Blacks, minorities, underprivileged, and lower socioeconomic classes especially. Law enforcement officers police white communities differently from Black ones. We know nothing is absolute, meaning that not all whites are affluent nor are all Blacks poor or from lower socioeconomic statuses. We also know that wealthy Blacks suffer at law enforcement's hands. However, law enforcers use unique protocols in white communities because they know there would be pushback if they did not. Too often, they do not care about Black pushback.

Furthermore, officers traditionally have held power, not just because they holster a weapon or taser. Officers assume control because there is one phrase they can utter, which almost always releases them from fault or negligence in cases like Breonna's and others such as Amadou Diallo in 1999. Many African Americans met their demise at the hands of officers who thought they could hide behind or seek refuge from consequences by uttering a phrase or string of seven words verbalizing their fear. If uttering a phrase can provide officers haven from punishment after taking a life, then the value of that life is mere words! The truth is that there is no price tag or amount of money equivalent to the value of someone's life. However, the law incorrectly devalued the lives of Breonna Taylor, forty-nine other women, and George Floyd. In Breonna's case, the law focused on the willful and wanton negligence of the officers destroying her neighbor's property when they unloaded their weapons. Breonna and her ex-boyfriend's lives, and even the property in their residence, were almost irrelevant. The law demonstrated what it valued and devalued. George Floyd's murder happened over the alleged purchase of goods with counterfeit currency. The law may not have appreciated Breonna and forty-nine other women of color, but they receive tribute here through my writing about conversations.

Although law enforcement officers may follow unique protocols for the white and affluent and devalue African American or minority life, especially those of lower socioeconomic status, some elders suggest a change is on the horizon. The elders I spoke with, who are members and, in some cases, leaders of the African American communities I connected to, in impromptu conversations, offered that things are improving. They are hopeful when we revisit the history of law enforcement, the origin of its creation in this country, and where it is today. Hope exists because elders see changes in the legal system. African Americans now have their day in court. Having a day in court without a conviction is not enough! A deceased African American's "day in court" will never equate to the erasure of days, weeks, months, years, and generations because of senseless acts by law enforcement. Although the officers committed unfortunate acts, the deceased are irreplaceable, my faith rises. Hope remains, and change may occur because we, African Americans, can respond to or approach these travesties through a Christian perspective (for those who believe) and find a better WAY to live with law enforcers and, more importantly, law enforcers with us. The better way does not always mean we must forgive and forget, but rather forgive and remember. Again, we pay tribute by writing their names, Breonna Taylor and the other forty-nine women listed on #SayTheirNames: Tanisha Anderson, Fanta Bility, Sandra Bland, Rekia Boyd, Ma'Khia Bryant, Eleanor Bumpurs, Celestine Chaney, Ta'Neasha Chappell, Dominique Clayton, Sharonda Coleman-Singleton, Michelle Cusseaux, Deborah Danner, Roberta Drury, Monica Goods, Titi "Tete" Gulley, Darnesha Harris, Meagan Hockaday, Cynthia Hurd, Susie Jackson, Latoya Denise James, Atatiana Jefferson, Aleah Jenkins, Kathryn Johnston, Bettie Jones, Alberta Odell Jones, Ethel Lance, Charleena Lyles, Katherine Massey, Jassmine McBride, Renisha McBride, Della McDuffie, Natasha McKenna, DePayne Middleton-Doctor, Mary Mitchell, Kayla Moore, Akira Ross, Priscilla Slater, Yvette Smith, Alberta Spruill, Aiyana Stanley-Jones, Brayla Stone, Geraldine Talley, Myra Thompson, Pamela Turner, Sharon Walker, Ruth Whitfield, Alteria Woods, Pearl Young, and many others unmentioned. Again, many of these women were killed by law enforcement and, in some cases, civilians are noted on the #SayTheirNames website, but all are worth noting.

So, in the spirit of remembrance, I share the conversations I have had with law enforcement officers over the years, which I characterize as narratives. The dialogues or narratives of law enforcement officers and others come from direct encounters with African American/Black police officers just as much, if not more, than white/Caucasian officers. I stress the officer's race because it speaks to the idea of race being the central focal point of police brutality against African Americans. Throughout my narratives, you will see that both Black and white officers are aware of the treatment officers render to white and affluent people, as opposed to those who are Black or from a lower socioeconomic status. Recalling the conversations allows for a perspective on an officer's call of duty, life, its value, and why some situations like Breonna's occur and lives are taken too soon. These officers and elders know fully well the history of law enforcement agencies in the United States and how African Americans did not start on the right side of the law in this country. Therefore, I also write to illuminate the struggles and attempts to mitigate transgenerational oppression that African Americans face with law enforcers. I use my narratives, experiences, and research to communicate clearly. Essentially, I attempt to help paint a new picture, orchestrate a new testimony, and touch the hearts of kinesthetic individuals; that change must and can occur because too many African American women have been taken from us ahead of their time. White officers have hidden behind power, privilege, and presumed fear for far too long. African American women's lives, such as our grandmothers, mothers, sisters, daughters, aunts, coworkers, friends, and acquaintances, are at stake, and their lives matter. So, I write as a tribute to the Breonna Taylors of our world who are taken from us and gone way too soon, and I write to change the narrative that, hopefully, no more lives are lost!

Officers as Executive Leaders

How do we conclude that officers are executive leaders with power within the community? How might the officers' actions and decisions impact the treatment of Black people? One potential answer to how law enforcement actions affected Black people appears in my research about higher education executive leadership and The Groundwater Approach, which focuses on an allegory of the fish, lake, and groundwater but can parallel the law enforcement industry. Although my research focuses on higher education, there is a direct correlation between educational leadership, law enforcement systems, and The Groundwater Approach. They are all interconnected by systemic racism, but there is hope.

In my doctoral research, *Lifting As We Climb: Investigating Nontraditional Pathways and Strategies to Executive Leadership for Black*s, I attempted to help Black or African American staff and administrators (BoAAs) who aspire to executive leadership roles within a higher education environment. Unfortunately, I noted insufficient BoAAs in executive-level positions; there were few efforts to increase the number of BoAA executives and a dearth of research to inform efforts. Throughout my research, I sought to answer a pivotal question and sub-questions: How did BoAA executives attain an executive leadership role at a predominantly white institution (PWI)? What challenges and obstacles did they encounter, and what specific roles, strategies, or responsibilities helped them overcome obstacles and facilitated upward mobility? However, the answers to these questions can help us understand how we define officers as leaders and how systemic changes must occur to protect Black lives genuinely.

Before I could answer my research questions, I first had to define an executive leader in the context of higher education. I described a Black or African American (BoAA) Higher Education Administrator as someone with budget authority and supervision over personnel. Additionally, a Higher Education Executive-Level Leader is a member of the Chief

Executive Officer's (e.g., Chancellor or President's) cabinet and typically has budget authority and oversight of personnel. Executive Leaders are in different parts of the higher education community, including academic affairs, student affairs, and business affairs. Under the umbrella of Business Affairs are the Vice President of Finance, Alumni Relations, Director of Security, and Information Systems (Moore and Sagaria, 1982; Sagaria, 1988; and Smith, 2013). If the Director of Security or Chief of Police is an executive leader within the higher education community who has oversight over personnel, and higher education is a microcosm of or mirrors society, it stands to reason that police officers and law enforcement would also be executive leaders in communities outside of higher education. Officers have power, authority over person(nel) or every person in the community and have the law on their side. Although an officer has power or perceived power, that power does not equal right, justice, fairness, or equitableness. In Breonna Taylor's case and some of the other forty-nine women who lost their lives at the hands of police officers, officers had power or perceived power, and did not act reasonably. Unfortunately, the display or use of force is subject to the one who can exercise it for evil or good. Therefore, law enforcement must manage their decisions and behaviors toward all people, especially Black women.

Andreescu and Vito, in their exploratory study on ideal leadership behavior: the opinions of American police managers noted that leaders are expected to generate a sense of purpose that motivates and directs followers so that they voluntarily make meaningful contributions to the organization. Essentially the leader is a source of guidance and inspiration (Andreescu and Vito, 2010). Andreescu and Vito also noted that police leadership directly impacts practitioners in the field and that police leaders recognize that leadership can be exercised at any department level. In other words, the Director of Security, Chief of Police or Sheriff, and regular patrol officers are all leaders responsible for properly exercising that leadership. Another author, Haberfield, in her book, *Police Leadership*, defined police leadership as the ability to make a split-second decision and take control of a potentially high-voltage situation that evolves on the street (Haberfield, 2006, 3).

Additionally, Haberfield made the case that "line (patrol) officers are the true leaders on the streets, using their leadership skills in daily encounters with the community" (Andreescu and Vito, 2010; Haberfield, 2006, 3). Andreescu, Vito, and Habberfield strongly argue that officers are executive leaders in the community and, as such, have influence over situations that arise and evolve in the street. Therefore, when community members like Breonna Taylor and the forty-nine other women encountered police and civilians, why do we have these unfortunate results? Is it the fish, lake, or groundwater that is the problem?

The Groundwater Approach

In my research, I explain how The Groundwater Approach helps build a practical understanding of structural racism and explains the pervasive nature of racism as it currently exists in the United States. The crux of The Groundwater Approach is that all our systems, institutions, and outcomes stem from a racial hierarchy on which the United States is built (Hayes-Greene and Love, 2018; Vickers, 2021). In 2013, Haynes-Greene and Love credited Camara Phyllis Jones with using an allegory of fish, lake, and groundwater to help make complex concepts easily understandable and provide a metaphor for structural racism. Before explaining the allegory, a discussion about structural racism is necessary. Haynes-Greene and Love noted that Jones' goal was to illuminate the fact that we live in a racially structured society; it causes racial inequality, and as a result, systems and system representatives treat people differently based on race regardless of their culture and behavior.

Furthermore, Haynes-Greene and Love noted that The Groundwater Approach illuminates the idea that racial inequalities look the same across all systems, that socioeconomic difference does not explain racial inequity, and that inequities are caused by systems regardless of people's culture or behavior. Ironically, these researchers examined national data from federal agencies such as health care, education, *law enforcement* (emphasis mine), child welfare, and finance, and found that African Americans were disproportionately negatively affected more than their white counterparts and thereby concluded that racial inequity is similar across all systems (Vickers, 2021). Haynes-Greene and Love determined that the system causes inequity, not the African American or minority's behavior. If we as practitioners embrace the truth about our systems and institutions (e.g., *law enforcement*) and that outcomes stem from a racial hierarchy on which the United States was built, we will recognize that we have a "groundwater" problem and need "groundwater" solutions (Hayes-Greene and Love, 2018; Vickers 2021).

The Groundwater Approach argues that there are three major components: the fish, the lake, and the groundwater. The three components are interconnected and work congruently. Love and Haynes-Greene posed a question using an allegory to explain a fish's demise. For the sake of this chapter, I will sum up the story. If a person has a lake in front of their house and one fish is floating belly-up dead, they will analyze the situation by asking what happened to the fish or what the fish did wrong to bring about its end. However, if the person saw that a school of fish were belly-up dead in their lake instead of one fish, they would ask what is wrong with the lake, not the fish. In other words, the lake or environment is contaminated, causing the fish unfavorable outcomes.

Additionally, from my research, it became abundantly clear that groundwater analysis is essential if many homes with lakes in the area and schools of fish are floating belly-up dead. Moreover, homeowners would want to know how all the lakes were contaminated and initiate an investigation of the groundwater (Hayes-Greene and Love, 2018). Upon examination of the groundwater, we discover that lakes do not appear to be connected on the surface but somewhat below it, and 95% of the freshwater on the planet is not above the ground where we can see it but below the surface in the groundwater (Hayes-Greene and Love, 2018). In the initial examination of the groundwater, researchers used an example of a fish (student) within the education system who was failing. Researchers determined that they would question the fish or student to determine what the fish or student could have done better to succeed. Alternatively, if a group of students or a school of fish is failing, an examination of the lake or educational system is necessary and not merely just a single fish (Hayes-Greene and Love, 2018). Therefore, if researchers are correct that The Groundwater Approach illuminates racial inequalities across all systems, we can apply The Groundwater Approach to law enforcement.

In our case, the fish or school of fish are African Americans in society, and the lake is the law enforcement system that disproportionately impacts African Americans. If researchers are correct, and indeed they are, the system negatively impacts African Americans regardless of their behavior. So, let us revisit the modern-day issues surrounding race and law enforcement that surfaced in recent years. There is a groundwater problem, and the law enforcement system is broken. Unfortunately, African Americans such as Breonna Taylor and other women faced their demise, not because of their actions! How might this be possible? Were these African Americans responsible for their demise, and not the system or the officers within it? If Andreescu and Vito are correct that law enforcement officers are community leaders who are aware of their perceived or actual power, then regardless of how African Americans (and women such as Breonna Taylor) behave, they should not and cannot be at fault. Officers should know their power and responsibilities and understand how The Groundwater Approach systematically advantages them. Consequently, if the officers were aware of their power and responsibilities, and exercised them appropriately, perhaps Breonna Taylor and the other forty-nine women would still be here today. Maybe another story will drive home the point that the groundwater is contaminated or flawed and needs cleansing, and officers who verbalize their fear through seven words to avoid consequences do not help.

Officers Express Fear

In 1999, my late father, Al Vickers, myself, and the late Deacon, Harold L. Jackman, were walking from a church in Parkchester, New York. We were on the corner of Benedict and Pugsley Avenue in the Bronx, and Deacon Jackman, a retired African American police officer, shared an intriguing viewpoint on the Amadou Diallo case. He recalled a story of being in a shootout and exclaimed that something jumped up and bit him. The culprits had shot him, and the bullet entered through his hip and body and then exited. He recalled unholstering his gun, firing at the suspects, and leaving the situation alive. After recounting that tale, Deacon Jackman, a retired police officer, looked at my father and me in the eyes and said seven words I will never forget. Deacon Jackman noted, in his case, and those like it, all the officer has to say is, "I was in fear for my life!" When an officer stands in court or is questioned about their actions, no matter how adverse and how much they disproportionately affect African Americans, Deacon Jackman said, "They utter those seven words and typically do not face dire consequences whether within their precinct or in court." He explained that officers did not face dire consequences in court and alluded to the fact that they frequently do not face the consequences within their precinct from their immediate supervisor.

Tim Bowen, an author who wrote an article on the *Phrase of the Week: To Get Off Scot Free*, noted that if someone avoided punishment for doing something that deserved punishment, that person got away scot-free. Whether or not the officer's fear is real or perceived, whether or not the officer was caught red-handed was irrelevant; all they had to say was seven words, "I was in fear for my life," and their actions are automatically justified – they can get off scot-free or essentially get away with murder. William V. Dunlap, a law professor at Quinnipiac University in Connecticut, who also wrote about the origin of the phrase "Scot-free," noted that the idea of scot-free originated from an early Icelandic term, "Skot," meaning a customary payment or tax paid to a lord, bailiff, or sheriff. Skot has since morphed from Icelandic to French as "escot" and ultimately into modern English as "scot." Dunlap notes that "scot' literally means "exempt from tax," and it has broadened to indicate "exempt from punishment" – as in "the prisoner got off scot-free." Therefore, suppose the law enforcement acts in unbecoming manners (e.g., unjustly shoots and kills an African American woman such as Breonna Taylor); all the officer has to say when faced with dire consequences, such as losing their job or worse, jail time, is "I was in fear of my life." They could be exempt from punishment or consequences, getting off scot-free. If we look at the Icelandic term "Skot" and apply it to our law enforcement situations, the customary payment or tax due to the Lord, bailiff, or sheriff would come from the law enforcement officer, which makes no sense. No law enforcement officer would willingly want to charge themselves or pay restitution for their actions; therefore, they get away with murder.

The scot-free concept may be unsettling when discussing unjustified police brutality against African Americans and may require unpacking comparisons or juxtaposition against previous research. According to Andreescu & Vito, the police officer, or patrol officer especially, is, in fact, a leader within the community and has influence or control over situations that occur and evolve in the street. Unfortunately, in the late Deacon Jackman's case, Deacon Jackman was justified in unholstering his gun and firing at the suspect. However, that is not necessarily true with Breonna Taylor, the other forty-nine women, and Diallo. How can an officer of the law, who has a weapon, and the law on their side, fear for their lives and act irrationally on the streets when encountering community members (e.g., Black fish) and not face the consequences? If officers are true leaders on the streets and use their leadership skills in daily encounters with the community (Andreescu and Vito, 2010; Haberfield, 2006, 3.) in better ways, perhaps the African American death toll at the hands of police would be minimal. Perhaps Taylor and the forty-nine other women exhibited behaviors that directly responded to fear for their lives. When can Black fish like Breonna Taylor and the other forty-nine African Americans and women of color receive their due process and justice? When is enough going to be enough? How long will officers be allowed to conduct illegal search and seizure of property and use obsessive police force against African American women, including the discharging of firearms that lead to the death of more African American women like Breonna Taylor at the hands of the system? If the system generally favors the white, affluent, and empowered populace, then the Breonna Taylors of this world will be waiting a long time for due process and erasure of the travesties of justice. We will still be asking the question – when will enough be enough – how many more have to die before officers can no longer conduct illegal searches and use obsessive force like discharging firearms against African American women and women of color?

If the system favors white and affluent communities, the system will continue to favor those communities unless a necessary and long overdue change intentionally occurs. Another way to look at this groundwater problem with law enforcement is to ask, "Why would an officer want to relinquish their power and privilege if it were not required?" They do not wish to relinquish that power; therefore, African Americans and women continue to suffer. Even if African American women like Breonna Taylor lost their lives as an unintended consequence (or unfortunate accident), officers still have the upper hand because of the seven words and fear factor. What superior officer, judge, or jury would not understand is how fear necessitates or debilitates actions on the part of the officers. We must tackle the groundwater problem of law enforcement officers in this country by addressing the notion that they are fearful and use that fear as a valid excuse, regardless of the unintended consequences.

To address the notion of law enforcement officers, fear, and privilege, I recall more narratives. One other time, right after I graduated from my alma mater, DePauw University, in Greencastle, Indiana, I worked as an assistant women's basketball coach. I also worked for the police department, enforcing parking (e.g., on a golf cart writing parking tickets). One evening, I had to ride with one of the white patrol officers in the squad car during their shift change. I was sitting in the front passenger seat, and he stopped a white male in a vehicle on a dark, dirty, and dusty dirt road due to a traffic violation. The university officer was a fully sworn-in officer of the law with all rights, privileges, and responsibilities therein. He even had a holstered weapon if necessary. However, as I sat in the front seat, my heart started beating profusely in my chest because I realized I was still vulnerable. As the officer went to approach the car, I sat in the car thinking to myself, what if this white person decided to shoot the officer and then turn on me because I was in the car and could be a witness? However, thankfully the situation was resolved amicably, and the officer returned to the patrol car unscathed, gave the person a warning, and we drove off. While leaving the scene, I divulged how I felt to the officer, and he quickly exclaimed that he was fearful because you never know what you will get, even at a traffic stop. If the Greencastle, DePauw University Police Officer was in fear of his life during a routine traffic stop and he was a veteran officer who was close to retirement, in retrospect, I cannot help but wonder if that situation would have ended differently had he stopped an African American suspect.

In the early 2000s, I talked with a New Hanover County law enforcement officer. The officer was an African American who would go nameless for fear of retaliation. Still, they shared a powerful perspective about their jurisdiction and lack of access to affluent white communities instead of African American and low socioeconomic neighborhoods. The officer shared that they are allowed on an island just off the Carolina coast, home to the wealthy, after first notifying residents that they plan to come onto the island. The

African American officer exclaimed that some white affluent government dignitaries on the island needed protection. I quickly retorted that the system protects the affluent white community in this case because they have time to "clean up" or hide any evidence or illegal paraphernalia before the officers arrive. The residents on the island know when the officer(s) plan to come. The New Hanover County officer exclaimed that my assessment was correct. Suppose the New Hanover County officer is right, the officers protect the affluent white upper-class residents on the island. In that case, the groundwater must be examined because African Americans such as Breonna Taylor and the other forty-nine women certainly did not get prior notice of the officer's arrival or time to "clean up" their act before officers arrived. In this case, Jones's theory holds some weight or water – we live in a racially structured society, and it causes racial inequality. As a result, systems and system representatives treat people differently based on race, regardless of their culture and behavior (Hayes-Greene and Love, 2018). However, this needs to change, and I still hope it will!

Still Hope

The idea of change and hope being on the horizon is possible. While in Wilmington, North Carolina, on 17th street, at a local gas station, across the street from the Music & Arts store, I had another encounter with an African American New Hanover County Sheriff. As I was standing in line, waiting to purchase my snacks, the officer stood behind me. I immediately turned to him and said, "Thank you for your service," – and I knew he had a hard job due to the climate in our country. The officer retorted that he appreciated my recognition of his service and said, "It is rough since the senseless killing of African Americans at the hands of police." My response was, "There are bad apples in every industry but social media, and the 'system' highlights all these cases now." The officer said, "You're absolutely right; not all of us are bad, and we try to do the right thing, and most of us got into law enforcement for all the right reasons." I nodded and said, "That's correct," as I recalled my initial encounter as a youth in my neighborhood with the officer who encouraged us to stay on the right side of the law. Then I said, "The irony is that we may all be up in arms about the systemic mistreatment of African Americans by law enforcement, but if something happens, we must call you all anyway to help rectify the problem. So, we're in a Catch-22," and the officer agreed.

Upon reexamining my conversation with the officer at the gas station, keeping the definition and examples of a Catch-22 in mind, some things become more apparent. African Americans and those from lower socioeconomic status find themselves in Catch-22 situations with law enforcement because they are subject to rules, regulations, or procedures over which they have no control, and to fight it often means to accept it. Acceptance may mean that African Americans find themselves at the mercy of law enforcement and suffer when some officers create arbitrary rules to justify and conceal their abuse of power. In some cases, covering the abuse of power could mean officers utter seven words like "I was in fear of my life" to justify their reckless behavior, which can result in more African American lives lost.

African Americans and those from lower socioeconomic status may face Catch-22 situations while dealing with law enforcement officers, but not all officers abuse their power. As I reflected on the rest of my experience with the officer at the gas station, the revelation that not all officers are bad apples or abuse their power became clearer. I recall paying for my snacks and leaving the gas station. However, I do not remember this officer's name, badge number, or personal story, but there is hope because he is trying not to be a bad apple in the bunch. More to the point, if we apply The Groundwater Approach to the officer at the gas station, he was trying to be part of the solution of saving the fish (African Americans, minorities) rather than using the flawed system to bring about their demise. Yes, the officer knew his responsibility was to serve and protect all. Still, in this instance, we focused on African American/Black people and perhaps those from low socioeconomic status.

There is even more hope still for all. While teaching a first-year seminar course at the University of North Carolina Wilmington, another encounter with a white law enforcement officer changed my narrative that the system *always* (emphasis mine) disproportionately affects African Americans. While watching my students give their presentations, in the front of the room, one of the students leaned up against the intercom system, and it accidentally called the university police. I told the police dispatcher that all was well and that a student had accidentally hit the police call-button on the intercom. A minute later, Chief David Donaldson, who is white, knocked on the classroom door. He was downstairs outside the building when the call came and decided to do a courtesy check. When he saw me, he told the class, "I don't know what you're doing up here; I can tell you Vickers is one of the best advisors and instructors on campus; you have got a good one." He walked out of the room, and I ran after him and asked if he would spend some time in the classroom discussing law enforcement and what the university does to support students, faculty, staff, administrators, community affiliates, and visitors, and he immediately agreed. Chief Donaldson spent the next unplanned hour with my diverse students sharing stories of how he and other officers have gone above and beyond the call of duty to save, support, and encourage patrons from all walks of life. From that day, I made it a point to invite Chief Donaldson to my class every semester, and the students appreciated the alternative narrative about officers in our community.

The New Hanover County Sheriff officer and University Chief of Police provide an alternative narrative, and there is still hope. However, I must ask the question: are their actions like an examination of the lakes and their attempts at change futile? In other words, do their singular actions, conversations, and perspectives profoundly change the groundwater issue of the flawed law enforcement system? How would our thoughts and attitudes change if I divulged that Chief Donaldson was also awestruck by the tragedy of George Floyd and volunteered to be one of the pallbearers who carried George Floyd's casket when he arrived in our Southern State? Would that change our narrative about white officers? Alternatively, is there an element of truth to the statement that if more officers were like Chief Donaldson, who operated within the system, perhaps there would not be a need to carry Breonna's casket at all because the officers would have lifted her, and many of the other forty-nine women up while they were yet alive. Contaminated groundwaters are hard to filter and clean, but it is not impossible. Chief Donaldson did not have to step up when he did – so there is hope for us yet! In addition to getting more officers like Chief Donaldson in the mix to change the course, flow, and current of the groundwater, we cannot change the groundwater issue of the flawed law enforcement system without impacting or dealing with other connected systems, such as our judicial branch.

Not too long ago, I sat with two other African American men at a graduation ceremony at the University of North Carolina Wilmington in Trask Coliseum. One man was in his early 80s, the other in his 50s, and I was in my 40s. Three different generations were sitting and discussing the systemic police brutality and injustices relative to African Americans. The elder in our group said that while we may think the police brutality and issues were harsh, he had hope. He said, back in my day, "Someone would just go missing, never to be seen or heard from again, and everyone knew what happened. . .but now at least officers are being charged and going to trial." Changes to the police and judicial system are afoot due to the examination of the groundwater issue that law enforcers target African Americans unjustly. Now, there is a level of accountability that exists, and could it be that an officer's expression of "I was in fear of my life" will not hold water soon because they are the ones in authority and power and have had the law and system on their side for a long time! Again, there is hope from an elder, but is that enough to change the law enforcement and judicial system's contaminated groundwater flow? It may not be enough, but it is more than what we had before, and it is undoubtedly a start and a massive step in the right direction. It is a start for those Black fish like our children who still have a fighting chance to one day see, enjoy, and live in clean lakes, because the fresh water from the ground is pure and uncontaminated.

Bibliography

Bowen, Tim. "Phrase of the Week: To Get off Scot Free." *One Stop English – Macmillan Education*, 3 July 2006, https://www.onestopenglish.com/your-english/phrase-of-theweek-to-get-off-scot-free/145661.article#commentsJump. Accessed 16 June 2023.

Dunlap, W. V. "What Is the Origin of the Phrase 'Scot-Free'?." *Guardian.co.uk*, 3 January 2011, https://www.theguardian.com/notesandqueries/query/0,5753,2732,00.html#:~:text=IN%20MACBETH%20you%20may%20recall,Free%20because20of%20colloquial%20speech. Accessed 16 June 2023.

Haberfield, M. R. *Police Leadership.* Prentice Hall, 2006.

Hayes-Greene, Deena, and Bayard P. Love. *The Groundwater Approach: Building a Practical Understanding of Structural Racism.* p. 6, 2018, https://www.isbe.net/Documents/Groundwater-Approach.pdf.

Vickers, Keryn. *Lifting as We Climb: Investigating Non-traditional Pathways and Strategies to Executive Leadership for Blacks.* 2021. University of North Carolina Wilmington, EdDdissertation. UNCW Library, http://dl.uncw.edu/Etd/2021-1/vickersk/kerynvickers.pdf

Viviana, Andreescu, and Gennaro F. Vito. "An Exploratory Study on Ideal Leadership Behaviour: The Opinions of American Police Managers." *International Journal of Police Science & Management*, vol. 12, no. 4, July 2010, p. 17, https://journals.sagepub.com/doi/pdf/10.1350/ijps.2010.12.4.207?casa_token=Wo0EtBvejsAAAAA:G7cwois1kXsu5k9EHFydZsltvRxogE8l8paeH07Ee5JASkRUi0Vf40dclMjVhBX0EcuwDwyvRlwC0Q.

Wikipedia. "Joseph Heller's Catch-22 (logic)." 14 March 2023,https://en.wikipedia.org/wiki/Catch-22_(logic). Accessed 16 June 2023.

#SayTheirNames. Mar. 2014, https://sayevery.name/take-action. Accessed 17 June 2023.

Part III The Legacies of Black Women: Respect, Empowerment and Hope

10 A Legacy of Hope: Changing the Narrative for Black Girls (Who Become Black Women)

Sheka Houston and Tammy Taylor

There is a long history of violence against Black girls and women without fanfare or consequence in this country. During enslavement and throughout the Jim Crow period in America, Black women were beaten, raped, and subjugated. In the Antebellum and Jim Crow South, white men abused and raped Black women, as if they were entitled to do so, without consequence or remorse. The French term "droit du seigneur" is translated as "the right of the Lord," establishing a position of societal inferiority for Black females. Too often, Black girls were victims of these horrific crimes and unable to be vindicated because of their place in society. Although such flagrant disregard for Black girls and women no longer exists, both groups continue to face subjugation and marginalization based on their race, class, and gender in blatant and less obvious ways and through subtle microaggressions and adultification.

Microaggressions are negative, gender-based actions that many Black women experience at work, making them feel undermined and subjected to discrimination. Microaggressions can be comments or actions expressing prejudice toward a marginalized group member (Barrett). The remarks, questions, and actions are painful because they are related to a person's membership in a group that has been oppressed and subject to stereotypes. Microaggressions can take a psychological toll on the mental health of those victimized. That toll could lead to experiencing anger, depression, and lower work productivity (Desmond-Harris, 2015). Microaggressions have been cited as the reason why Black teachers are walking away from the profession at staggering rates of 17%, twice the rate cited for other reasons such as low wages (Tarada, 2021).

Like the harmfulness of microaggressions to Black women, the adultification of young Black girls is just as damaging. Adultification is dehumanization that robs Black girls of their childhood innocence. Adultification happens not only with Black girls but with Black children in general. It causes them to be perceived as more adult-like and biologically older than they are. There are two forms of adultification. The first form is the process in which children function at more mature developmental states because of situational context and necessity, often in communities with few resources. The second form of adultification is a social or cultural stereotype based on how adults perceive children without knowledge of children's behavior and verbalizations. Adultification was noted in a Georgetown study revealing that Black girls are considered to be "grown" and in less need of the care and nurturing of adults. Black girls are referred to as "fast" or promiscuous at early ages and disciplined at higher rates in school. These perceptions are based on the dominant culture's views of Black females and the unwillingness to see the buffoonery of thinking Black girls need less care and nurturing than white girls of the same age (Anspach, 2015). In this chapter, we hope to interrupt this narrative around the adultification of Black girls and focus on how embracing our deep Africana heritage can change the trajectory of these young ladies on their journey to becoming productive and successful women.

We will interrogate the misrepresentation of Black girls through the lens of educators. We will also provide a guide to help these young ladies to rise above assigned roles that will no longer be accepted. We will explore the Africana Womanism paradigm as defined by Dr. Clenora Hudson-Weems, progenitor of the concept. Hudson-Weems identified the elevation and empowerment of the Africana race and community as the center of consciousness for the Africana womanist. She postulates that Africana men, women, and children share a unique connection, allowing the triad to form a bond that will impact the Africana community. As an academician, she has spent her life challenging the status quo; her legendary work, identifying Emmett Till as the catalyst of the modern Civil Rights Movement, positioned her as an authority on the Black Community. However, her careful examination and presentation of Africana Womanism as a theoretical construct have confirmed her as an expert and authority in the Black Community and Higher Education (the Academy) (Hudson-Weems, 2020). We will carefully examine each of Hudson-Weems' eighteen characteristics of Africana Womanism to lead Black girls away from nasty stereotypes assigned to them by a corrupt and racist society to become Black women embracing who they are and learning to live up to and fulfill their proper roles in society.

In May 2020, a 9 minutes and 29 seconds video changed the world as we once knew it, forever. This 9 minutes and 29 seconds video captured the blatant disregard for Black life as George Floyd lay dying in the streets at the intersection of Chicago Avenue and 38th Street in Minneapolis, Minnesota, with the entire world watching. Mr. Floyd's death did not occur as a result of Black-on-Black crime. His death was experienced at the hands of Minneapolis, Minnesota, law enforcement. His death created a long-due response to the cruel and brutal treatment of Blacks in America by police. Enraged, the Black community demanded answers after this disturbing tragedy. Black Lives Matter protests were seen across the world to express the hurt, anger, sadness, and discontentment of the world in response to this very public murder. Most of the world did not know that on March 13, 2020, a much less public murder had occurred. A police-involved murder that was equally cruel took place with possibly even more reckless abandonment; the heart-rending and senseless death of Breonna Taylor in Louisville, Kentucky. Shortly after midnight on that sad and tragic morning of March 13, as the world was preparing to shut down because of the deadly and mysterious coronavirus (COVID-19) that was claiming the deaths of thousands of people each day around the globe, Breonna Taylor's home was raided by Louisville, Kentucky police officers. Ms. Taylor was a 26-year-old Black emergency medical technician with no criminal records. No one in Ms. Taylor's home had a police record, yet three white police officers dressed in plain clothes entered her home, shooting at least thirty-two times, striking Breonna Taylor five times, and killing her senselessly. This heartbreaking and sad episode did not receive public outcry until much later when many Americans joined the #SayHerName campaign that began over a decade ago when it became painfully apparent that Black women and girls as young as 7 and as old as 93 have been killed by the police, though we rarely hear their names (Anspach, 2015).

Knowing their names is a necessary but not sufficient condition for lifting their stories, providing a much clearer view of the wide-ranging circumstances that make Black women's bodies disproportionately subject to police violence. To lift their stories and illuminate police violence against Black women, we need to know who they are, how they lived, and why they suffered at the hands of the police (Anspach, 2015). #SayHerName took a front-and-center role following the attention brought to Breonna Taylor's death after George Floyd was murdered. Unfortunately, many more Black women have lost their lives at the hands of police, and their names have been left off of the long lists of victims across the country who have died as a result of police brutality. The #SayHerName campaign has revealed how gender, race, and sexuality have made Black women targets for police brutality. During the period of enslavement for Africans in America, Black women were lynched alongside Black men. However, they were also more likely to suffer from the additional trauma of sexual violence and are still suffering from it in many instances today. Civil rights leader, Malcolm X, brought attention to the ill-treatment of Black women in one of his famous speeches when he stated: "The most disrespected person in America is the Black woman. The most unprotected person in America is the Black woman. The most neglected person in America is the Black woman" (Desmand-Harris, 2015). Although Malcolm X made the speech in 1962, some would argue that his argument still holds today in some instances. The #SayHerName campaign categorized, in some instances, the unpublicized stories of Black women who have died at the hands of police into the categories of driving while Black, policing poverty, casualties of the war on drugs, violence instead of treatment, death in custody, guilt by association, violence, unseen and unsupported women, the use of excessive force against Black mothers and their children, and no sympathy (Anspach, 2015).

These and so many other experiences have caused Black communities to be traumatized for centuries. Members of these communities have begun to think that dysfunction and despair are a natural part of the lives of the individuals in their communities. Educators, politicians, social justice advocates, and others must take a stand to save these communities from daily pain and misfortunes. Rescuing communities, in essence, means rescuing the children who are the legacy of hope of those communities that many hold on to during these tumultuous and unsettling times.

The challenges of rescue efforts for the children lie in the fact that without systemic changes where their daily environments can be impacted, it is difficult to effect and sustain lasting change. Children suffering from trauma caused by seeing the life choked out of their mother by someone who has sworn to protect and serve their community are the same children who show up to school each day too angry to engage in their learning. This repeated disregard for school can result in an exit from high school before graduation, resulting in another statistic related to trauma, that of a high school dropout. Becoming a high school dropout leads to possibly engaging in illegal or reckless activities that can lead to incarceration. This vicious cycle is a very popular one for students living their lives in traumatic environments each day.

A recent study from Georgetown Law confirms that Black girls feel the sting of adultification bias creating a rare form of discrimination that only Black girls experience. The new report, "Listening to Black Women and

Girls: Lived Experiences of Adultification Bias," reveals findings from groups that assessed whether the original study aligns with the real lives of Black girls and women, as well as what should be done to address adultification bias (Blake, 2019). These traumatic experiences of young Black girls seriously impact their lives as Black women. Unfortunately, the established societal position of inferiority for Black women has created a laissez-faire governmental response toward the disenfranchisement of Black girls. Using a theoretical construct like Africana Womanism can give Black women a platform to use their voices to actively engage and promote discourse surrounding race, class, gender, cultural awareness, and other important topics, especially in schools. Khalifa et al. (2013) posit race, ethnicity, and color as important to every educator's context. Every educator faces unique challenges and obstacles that must be overcome. However, some things are consistent across classrooms, grade spans, schools, regions, and the world. Educators must be willing to engage in crucial conversations surrounding race, gender, class, and cultural awareness to shed light upon hidden agendas and taboo topics to improve our girls' lives.

Young Black girls are conditioned at early ages to believe that their God-given beauty and temperament are not enough or inappropriate. These girls often become insecure about their physical attributes, including the length and texture of their hair. Black girls are frequently asked to tone down their behavior when exhibiting exuberance and excitement because they need to be more ladylike. We find Black girls sometimes looking to mainstream society to determine their standards. The uncertainty of who they are and how they fit into a society that has created a standard for them, including a standard of beauty that may not match any of the attributes they possess, has caused little Black girls not to be able to appreciate their authenticity – and see and love themselves for who they are.

For some, this begins with the cycle of trying to assimilate to become what they believe beauty to be. Consequently, social media, music videos, and blockbuster films add to the image many of these young ladies aspire to emulate. Many of them also become victims of the aspect of adultification that matures them and grows them up far too quickly based on society's opinion that Black women and girls are hypersexual. These unfortunate situations can lead to teen motherhood, gang affiliations, and drug and alcohol abuse. Black women have been forced to find their voice and speak up for themselves for centuries. This way of being has been passed down through generations. Therefore, by design, Black girls are strongly opinionated and extremely vocal. These characteristics sometimes get Black girls labeled as hostile, angry, and adversarial in school. These stereotypes lead to Black girls being punished more harshly in school because they are so misunderstood. Black girls are twice as likely than white girls to be disciplined for dress code, cell phone violations, and loitering. Black girls are 2.5 times more likely to be disciplined for disobedience. Black girls are three times more likely to be disciplined for fighting, disruptive behavior, and bullying or harassment. Black girls in K-12 schools are 8% of the enrollment but 13% of student suspensions. Disparities also exist at the Juvenile Justice level. Black girls are 20% more likely than white girls to be formally petitioned, 2.7 times more likely to be referred to Juvenile Justice, and 1.2 times more likely to be detained than white females.

When Black girls vocalize differences in opinions or argue a position, they are often viewed as disrespectful and uncooperative. A Georgetown study proved that adults have less empathy for Black girls than their white peers. This lack of empathy toward Black girls results in white girls being viewed as more innocent and needing protection and comfort. They are viewed as being more vulnerable and in need of adult interventions. It is critically important that educators have situational awareness when it comes to Black girls and the adultification they face. Black girls have to be empowered to be authentic and secure in themselves. Educators must also treat Black girls in age-appropriate manners no matter how strong or tough they are perceived. Additionally, Black girls must be encouraged to embrace who they are in a way that allows them to learn and grow as they develop into the beautiful, intelligent, and astounding Black women they will someday become (Blake, 2019).

Reverend Deborah Jackson (2022) poses a question. She asks, "Is there any way out of the morass that has left us fractured, distressed and despairing?" Reverend Jackson also answers the poignant question, as we and many academicians would answer. She claims that the answer to this question is found in the theory and praxis of Africana Womanism in a healing and restorative way (Hudson-Weems, 2022). In her seminal Foreword in the recently released book, *Africana-Melanated Womanism: In It Together* (2022) Reverend Jackson hails Africana Womanism as the antidote to society's ills. She explains that Africana Womanism represents a model through which we can operate in the world while being comforted by a grounded sense of self, an esteeming and nurturing sense of others, and an uplifting focus on the world that is restorative (Hudson-Weems, 2022).

Reverend Jackson carefully categorizes the eighteen characteristics of Africana Womanism as conceptualized and articulated more than three decades ago by Dr. Clenora Hudson-Weems to make it very clear who a Black woman is. She has explicated Africana Womanism into the following categorical design:

The Africana Womanist
Who She Is: Self-Naming, Self-Defining, Spiritual, Whole
How She Functions: Mothering, Family-Centered, Nurturing, Male Compatible, Respectful of Elders, Genuine in the Sisterhood
How She is Viewed: Respected, Recognized, Strong, Authentic
How She Works in the World: Flexible Role Player, Adaptable, Ambitious, In Concert with Males in the, Struggle

(Debra Jackson, Foreword)

The term "Africana" represents Africa and the African diaspora which includes Afro-Latin, Afro-European, and Afro-American countries and people, as well as their experiences and cultural ideologies with an Afrocentric perspective (Hudson-Weems, 2004). The characteristics of Africana Womanism include the following: Self-Namer, Self-Definer, Family-Centered, Male-Compatible, Strong, Whole and Authentic, Spiritual, Respectful of Elders, Adaptable, Ambitious, Mothering, Nurturing, Family-Centered, Genuine in Sisterhood, In Concert with Males in the Liberation Struggle, Flexible Role Players, and Respected and Recognized. The Africana Womanism paradigm is complete and holistic in its ability to educate, unite, and inspire the Africana community. Therefore, this transformational standard of excellence can be used as a model to help young Black girls find their place in their communities and society as a part of the hope for Africana communities near and far. This feat can be accomplished by embarking upon the necessary journey of helping Black girls understand their values and worth as they develop into strong, amazing, and successful Black women. We can begin this journey by applying Reverend Jackson's categorical analysis of Dr. Clenora Hudson-Weems's Africana Womanism construct.

Who She Is

The first step in this process is to help these young ladies to determine who they are. This self-awareness will manifest as a result of helping them discover the power of self-naming and self-defining who they are. Helping these young ladies connect to their spirituality and assuring them that they are whole beings can lead them on the path to an incredible journey of self-discovery. Molefi Asante claims that in African cosmology, the concept of Nommo says that it is through the proper naming of a thing that its essence comes into existence (Hudson-Weems, 2020). Therefore, Black girls must learn to define what they want to be called and what they are willing to answer. Black women, since antiquity, have been self-namers. Even during slavery, when white enslavers tried to label Black women as breeders, those strong Black women named themselves "mother" (Hudson-Weems, 2022).

In Toni Morrison's well-known novel, *Beloved,* she says, "Definitions belonged to the definer, not the defined." As such, Black girls can define themselves in a way that demands respect. In this regard, these young ladies will define their reality without having to assimilate into the norms and conditions that society has imposed upon them. Permitting young ladies to connect with their spirituality is imperative in helping them connect with themselves. Dr. Clenora Hudson-Weems says that the Black woman's sense of wholeness is compatible with her cultural consciousness and authentic existence (Hudson-Weems, 2022). After discovering who she is, a young Black girl must also connect with how she functions.

How She Functions

According to Hudson-Weems, a major cornerstone of Africana Womanism is the centrality of the family (Hudson-Weems, 2022). Elechi Amadi posits, "Men and women need each other emotionally and, of course, for survival." (71) Although, over time, society has tried to wedge a gap between Black men and Black women, it is imperative that the Africana community commits to not falling for these deliberate divisive antics. In *Africana Womanism Reclaiming Ourselves*, Hudson-Weems makes it clear that in the Black community, neither women nor men can afford to conclude that the other gender is irredeemable or refuses to work together (43). Young Black girls must be taught to be at peace with who they are and embrace their natural instinctive nurturing and mothering qualities. In the Africana community, women are committed to caring for the entire family. The beauty of having mothering and nurturing qualities for the Black woman is that one does not have to be an actual mother to possess and embody these amazing qualities. As such, Black women can be found to be genuinely caring and protective of their environments and those who are a part of them.

Additionally, Africana women hold elders in their lives in high esteem. Hudson-Weems claims that as spiritual and religious people, African women have been taught to practice the greatest regard for elders in their community because they are looked to for wisdom and guidance (47). Another important aspect of Africana Womanism that must be handed down to young Black girls is that as Africana people, we realize we have to save ourselves and each other from the vestiges of a corrupt and colonized society. Teaching them to care for and support each other will tremendously help them learn how to support one another genuinely. When Black women realize they can support one another and not engage in declared or undeclared competition, the sisterhood can be strengthened and used to create bonds that cannot be broken because they are genuine in the sisterhood.

How She Is Viewed

Remaining strong and recognizing that strength is necessary for the survival of any community is imperative to the people who make up that community. Since antiquity, Black women have been a source of natural strength and resiliency. Hudson-Weems explains: If the Africana woman (girl) lacks self-love, which can result from accepting white Beauty, she will inevitably exude a negative sense of herself, thereby assuming a "zero image." This negative self-image could result in her allowing herself to be disrespected, abused, and trampled on by her male counterpart. Because this sometimes happens, no one can realistically deny that gender issues do not constitute a critical concern in the Africana community. The Africana womanist demands respect for and recognition of herself in order to acquire true self-esteem and self-worth, which in turn enables her, among other things, to have complete and positive relationships with all people (45). Hudson-Weems believes that the true Africana womanist seeks both wholeness (completeness) and authenticity (cultural connection) in her life. Collectively, wholeness and authenticity are powerful tenets of the Africana womanist; her heritage also strongly stresses the importance of an entire family unit (46).

How She Works in the World

The natural ambition and responsibility must be cultivated in Black girls. It can be viewed as quite a daunting task for some because Black girls are often made to feel inferior or subpar. However, it is the norm in the Africana community to teach young ladies the importance of self-reliance and resourcefulness early on (48). Another natural aspect of the Africana community for women is the Africana womanist's ability to be adaptable. Black women can be adaptable and do not require separate spaces to operate and show who they are. This adaptability leads to the Black woman's ability to be flexible role players. Hudson-Weems states, "While Africana women do believe in and respect traditional roles, it must be remembered that those roles have never been as clear-cut in the Black community as they are in the White community." (43) Finally, the intertwined destiny of all Africana people speaks volumes to the dependence upon the participation of the male sector in the Africana womanist's struggle (40). As explained by Hudson-Weems, throughout history, the white man has often been viewed as the enemy of the white woman in her struggle; however, the Africana man does not necessarily hold that position with the Black woman (42). She also clarifies that Africana men and women share a similar space as oppressed people, and as such, they cannot afford division based solely on gender (42).

Conclusion

In conclusion, Dr. Clenora Hudson-Weems postulates that Africana men, women, and children share a unique connection, allowing the triad to form a bond that will have lasting impacts on the Africana community.

> The key descriptors of the Africana womanist are very important, as they ulti-mately bring forth an overall holistic environment and existence for both the Africana womanist and her entire family. Clearly refining a paradigm relative to who the Africana womanist is and has always been, and could conceivably enable us to better resolve the existing conflict between Africana women and particularly the gap characterizing modern day male/female relationships. An end to the gender divide must now come forth! Envisioning this could possibly be the answer to a conceivable resolution for all humankind via the belief in the ultimate salvation of all: "For faith is the substance of things hoped for, the evidence of things not seen." (Hebrews 11:1) (49)

As educators, we recognize the crucial need for mindfulness to be always present. The tragic circumstances surrounding Breonna Taylor's death make educators, who possess a fiery passion for what they do, pause and ponder how to move forward. Breonna's death provoked us to act and advocate for the Black women and girls who continue to be disrespected and mistreated. Therefore, we must be ever mindful that we are responsible for changing this narrative by creating a new one. Providing a paradigm to which young Black girls can connect in a manner that changes their lives forever is the beginning of the needed restoration of the Africana community. The tenets (character-istics) of Africana Womanism are timeless and enduring in our journey to excellence toward perpetuity and collectivity in the Africana community.

Bibliography

Anspach, Rachel, Anspach, Rachel, Kimberle, Crenshaw, Rachel, Gilmer, Luke, Harris and Andrea Ritchie. *Say Her Name: Resisting Police Brutality Against Black*

Women. African-American Policy Reform, July, 2015, https://www.aapf.org/_files/ugd/1187fd_7db4f9a2e9e94cce9ac6c03b290916d4.pdf. Accessed 18 July 2022.

Blake, J., Eptein, R., and Gonzalalez, T. Girlhood Interrupted: The Erasure of Black Girls' Childhood. Center on Poverty and Inequality, Georgetown Law 2019. www.law.georgetown.edu. Accessed 3 April 2022.

Blake, Jamilia and Rebecca Epstein. Listening to Black Women and Girls: Lived Experiences of Adultifcation Bias. Center on Poverty and Inequality, Georgetown Law 2019. www.law.georgetown.edu. Accessed 14 April 2022.

Desmond-Harris, J. What Exactly Is a Microaggression? Vox, 16, Feb 2015, www.vox.com/2015/2/16/8031073/what-are-microaggressions. Accessed 3 April 2022.

Hudson-Weems, C. (2022). *Africana Womanism: Reclaiming Ourselves Africana-Melanated Womanism*. Cambridge Scholars Publishing.

Hudson-Weems, C. (2020). *Africana Womanism: Reclaiming Ourselves Africana-Melanated Womanism*. Routledge.

Hudson-Weems, C. (2004). *Africana Womanist Literary Theory*. Africa World Press.

Hudson-Weems, C, Editor. (2023). *Africana-Melinated Womanism: In It Together*. Cambridge Scholars.

Jackson, Deborah (2023). *Africana-Melinated Womanism: In It Together*. Hudson-Weems, Editor. Cambridge Scholars.

Jones, F. *Malcolm X Stood Up for Black Women When Few Others Would*. Zora, 7 August 2020, https://zora.medium.comncludim-x-stood-up-for-black-women-when-few-others-would-68e8b2ea2747. Accessed 18 July 2022.

Khalifa, M. A., Dunbar, C. and Davis, J. E. (2013). Derrick Bell, CRT, and Educational Leadership 1995-Present. *Race, Ethnicity, and Education, 16*(4), 489–513.

Terada, Y. *Why Black Teachers Walk Away*. The Research Is In, 26, March 2021, www.edutopia.org/article/why-black-teachers-walk-away. Accessed 3 April 2022.

11 Disrespected and Devalued: A Common American Experience for Black Women

ANGELA Y. DOUGLAS

The year 2020 began with the World Health Organization (WHO) looking at a mysterious virus quickly spreading across the globe, infecting and killing an enormous amount of people. On March 11, 2020, WHO declared a worldwide pandemic – COVID-19, the novel coronavirus. News outlets were obsessed with COVID-19 (Courtney). Starting in January 2020, the 24-hour news cycle repeated and gave all updates about the coronavirus, no matter how incremental. The network news reported almost nothing else. Important information slipped by, including murders and police-involved shootings. In February 2020, a trio of local vigilantes followed, harassed, and killed Ahmaud Arbery, a young Black man, because he was jogging while Black in the neighborhood (Dakin). In March 2020, a botched police raid left Breonna Taylor, a young Black woman, dead in her hallway after the police sprayed her apartment with bullets (Waldrop). These deadly tragedies went underreported for months.

Coverage of police-involved deaths of civilians and unjust murders of Black Americans have not been fair or balanced. In recent years, due to cellphone and other camera footage (i.e., dashcams, body cameras, and surveillance cameras), more and more police-involved tragedies are being reported. Over the last five years, United States law enforcement, on average, shot and killed civilians three times more than other wealthy countries (Jones and Sawyer). According to the Washington Post's Fatal Force database, police in the United States shot and killed over 1,000 people in 2020. Over 400 of those police-involved shootings happened between January and May 2020. Black Americans are killed by police more than two times the rate of white non-Hispanic Americans. Additionally, arrests have not been consistent in cases where Black victims are murdered. Nearly three-quarters of the unsolved murders in large American cities had Black victims (Lowery et al.).

Some have argued that the nation has become desensitized to Black people being murdered, even unjustly, by the hands of vigilantes or due to deadly force by police officers.

Murdering Black people, with or without cause or justice, is not new. However, it should still be in the news. By June 2020, it quickly became the year of "No Justice, No Peace." This chapter examines the shared experience of being disrespected and devalued as a Black person in America, especially as a Black woman. It uses Breonna Taylor's death and a few notable cases and settlements to highlight the common issues around the devaluing of Black women – visibility, activism, and accountability.

On March 12, 2020, in Louisville, Kentucky, Breonna Taylor and her boyfriend, Kenneth Walker III, had an enjoyable day. They ate dinner out, then went back to her apartment to settle in for the night by playing cards and watching the movie *Freedom Writers*. They went to sleep in peace, with plans for a future – together. Breonna and Kenneth had known each other for many years. They dated on and off, as young couples sometimes do. At ages 26 and 28, respectively, they were finally in a place to take their relationship more seriously. Breonna Taylor loved to help others. Family members and friends described her as soft-spoken, loving, respectful, and kind. Perhaps, that is why she chose to be an emergency room technician. She drew to calmness, even in scary moments. Going to bed that night, she had no idea her life would be endangered and lost in just a few hours. An unanswered knock on the door in the wee hours of March 13 ended this young lady's life and further frayed the relationship between police and the Black community. According to numerous reports, eyewitnesses, and Mr. Walker's statements, the police knocked but did not identify themselves after the residents' repeated requests. The police rammed the door, and Mr. Walker said he felt endangered by who he thought was an intruder. He did not know it was the police. Within his rights, Mr. Walker grabbed his legally owned firearm to defend himself, his girlfriend, and their home. When the police forced open the door without identifying themselves, they were met with a single shot from Mr. Walker's gun. That shot hit one of the officers in the thigh. From outside, the officers responded with a "hail of gunfire," 32 shots, into the apartment and the neighboring apartment. Mr. Walker was not injured. Ms. Taylor was struck five times. Mr. Walker frantically called 911, and their mothers pleaded for assistance. Afterward, he was met with and arrested by the police, who had shot at them and killed Breonna.

He stated, "I thought they were there to help me, but really, they were the ones who just hurt me." Breonna Taylor died in the hallway of her apartment (Duvall and Costello). The police had a no-knock warrant to search for illegal drugs and money owned by Jamarcus Glover. Yes, someone who was neither Taylor nor Walker. Glover was Taylor's ex-boyfriend. They had ended their relationship in 2018, two years before that fateful night. In his post-tragedy interviews, Glover confirmed she was not involved with any of his legal or illegal dealings (Bailey et al.).

Despite having arrested Glover at a different address, police executed this warrant, resulting in Breonna's demise. The warrant, police intrusion, and death were due to the lies police told themselves, each other, and the judges. So, one would think justice would be swift and mighty. Nevertheless, is Breonna's death her fault? Maybe she would have been still alive if she had not dated anyone with past drug convictions, opened the door at nearly one o'clock in the morning to a strange knock, or did not allow her boyfriend to stand his ground against whom they thought were intruders. Maybe she would have been still alive if she was a Black man, a white woman, or in a better neighborhood.

Not until the highly publicized 8-minute, 46-second video of George Floyd's murder at the knee of Minneapolis police officer Derek Chauvin did we learn more about the Arbery and Taylor tragedies. Social unrest and disruption have played a vital role in how victims are seen and remembered. Visibility indicates the ability to see and be seen and how well one sees or is seen.

The Invisibility of Black Victimhood

Black people have had to lean into great public outrage, response, and activism because of the denial or delay in accountability surrounding violence against them. Historically, Black people have been frequently denied fundamental human rights, exploited physically and sexually, and otherwise oppressed. Before the Civil War Amendments, 13th–15th, Black people were not considered citizens of the United States or covered by the protections provided in the United States Constitution (Douglas 86–87). During that time, they were seen as commodities, not people with rights and freedoms. Their humanity was invisible to society. Therefore, they experienced tremendous terrors and degradation.

Black people were treated horribly during their enslavement, including long work hours, horrendous work and living conditions, brutal whippings and beatings, and frequent sexual assaults. They were used as test specimens for surgical and medical experiments (Domonoske, 2019). Although often stripped of their children, Black women were forced to become breeders to keep the slave trade going. Also, they had to care for the white enslavers' children. Jim Crow laws of the American South did so much to perpetuate biases against and block the rights of Black people, especially Black women. In 1965, Daniel Moynihan, policy advisor to President Lyndon Johnson, authored a report titled "The Negro Family: The Case for National Action," more commonly known as the Moynihan Report. It highlighted what he saw as the breakdown of the traditional Black family structure. He argued that the high rates of single-parent households contributed to a cycle of poverty and social problems. Moynihan used the term "Welfare Queens" to describe Black women perceived as intentionally exploiting the public assistance programs. He suggested they intentionally remained unmarried and had more children to receive increased benefits (Turner). This oversimplification of complex social and economic issues haphazardly placed endless blame on whether Black women received public assistance. It has become commonplace to assume that Black women are lazy and abusively reliant on public assistance to care for their families. This poor characterization has further advanced and perpetuated the stigma and shame associated with women, especially Black women, needing and seeking help.

Furthermore, violence against Black people, even in cases of known police brutality, was and continues to be a conversation challenging the victimhood of Black people. Black people's pain, physical and mental, has been wholly disregarded. This subjugation laid the foundation for today's biases and stereotypes against Black people. In many ways, we were made invisible to society and the laws of the land. Like many before, Breonna's death was not immediately highlighted in the news or other media. CNN first released the story on May 13, 2020, when her family issued a lawsuit against the officers and the City of Louisville, Kentucky. However, the details of Breonna's death did not spread until about two weeks later. Breonna's story became attached to George Floyd's murder and finally gained traction. On May 25, 2020, Officer Chauvin rested his knee, with his total body weight, on George Floyd's neck as he lay belly-down on the ground and was held by four other officers until Floyd died. Eight minutes and forty-six seconds of cellphone-captured video allowed viewers a front-row seat to Mr. Floyd's pleas, cries for help, and gasping until his body became lifeless. Using the suffocating restraint, the officers took less than 10 minutes (9 minutes, 29 seconds) to kill Mr. Floyd. This public lynching took the airwaves by storm, and uprisings occurred across the nation and the world, illuminating the absurdity of America's commitment to democracy and racism. However distorted or corrupt, officials were forced to share more transparency and details about Breonna Taylor's and Ahmaud Arbery's deaths. Nonetheless, this begs the question: Are Black people worthy of being victims?

When covering crimes against Black people, the media lead with stories about the victims' criminal pasts and questioned their behaviors. It is common to question the actions of Black victims of violence and wrongdoing as if they deserve it. Doing so preserves the notion that Black people are not worthy of protection or defense and that violence against them is justified. The circumstances surrounding these deaths are reminiscent of earlier tragedies. Black victims are presumed guilty of disgraceful or illegal behavior – in court, in the court of opinion, and the news. Whatever happened to the adage "Do not speak ill of the dead?" Does that not apply to Black people? Before anyone can conceptualize the brutal murders, Black victims' characters are assassinated. The press and others heavily criminalize them. Their pleas are ignored, and they are coldly murdered.

Why do the news media characterize white perpetrators as sick or mentally ill? Why do white mass murderers get more sympathy and warrant more dignity than unarmed Black victims? Young white men have fired in schools, clubs, and malls, killing masses, including innocent schoolchildren. Most news outlets have attempted to characterize these murderers as sufferers of mental illness or bullying. For other white male perpetrators, notably, Kyle Rittenhouse or George Zimmerman (a white Hispanic man), self-defense and stand-your-ground were touted as justification for their commission of murder. However, Black victims' actions are questioned, from Trayvon Martin and Tamir Rice to Sandra Bland and Atatiana Jefferson.

They should not have resisted, defended themselves, or been a 12-year-old child playing outside with a toy gun in the case of Tamir Rice. Despite knowing he was out for a jog through the neighborhood, Arbery was often called a trespasser, potential vandal, and thief. Before his autopsy and toxicology reports came back, Floyd was characterized as a frequent drug abuser (Xiong). He was also called a criminal, thief, and someone with a problem with authority. Breonna Taylor, described as sweet and kind by friends, family, and coworkers, the Emergency Room Technician, was often referred to as someone who regularly dated drug dealers (Bailey et al.). Despite her excellence, Breonna was characterized as a ghetto or hood chick. These descriptions suggest that Black people cause their murders. Somehow, they should know their actions would cause their deaths. In many cases, Black people have been victims of character and physical assassinations.

Intersectionality and the Plight of Black Women

Black women have continued to experience pervasive discrimination and bias in the United States. Using an intersectional lens to the structural and socio-cultural barriers that prevent Black women from achieving equity, inclusion, and justice, the legacy of American slavery and Jim Crow laws and more con-temporary forms of racism and sexism readily contribute to the biases against Black women. Intersectionality is a crucial framework that acknowledges the interconnected nature of various social identities and systems of oppression (Best). The term, coined by Kimberlé Crenshaw in 1989, recognizes that individuals can simultaneously experience multiple forms of discrimination and disadvantages due to race, gender, class, sexuality, and more (Crenshaw). Racial and social constructs have narrowly defined Black people throughout history. Black women's unique experiences and challenges can be acknowl-edged and addressed through intersectionality. This approach underscores the understanding that the struggles of Black women cannot be fully compre-hended or effectively combated without considering the intersecting impacts of racism, sexism, and other forms of oppression (Crenshaw 1991). Therefore, Black women's experiences and challenges may feel extremely common – but only in part – to others, particularly Black men and white women. The weight of multiplied bigotry compounds the experience of oppression for and biases against Black women (Martin).

There is a long history of Black women being portrayed as one-dimensional characters. The *Jezebel* stereotype portrays Black women (and girls) as promiscuous and hypersexualized. The concept aims to justify sex-ual and physical exploitation against Black women and the adultification of Black girls. It reduces Black females to mere sex objects for the enjoyment and pleasure of others. This damaging trope prevents Black women from being seen as people deserving of dignity and respect. In this country, demands on Black women to care for others, put others' needs before theirs, and deny self-care and interests have rendered Black women insignificant in their own lives. The historical *Mammy* stereotype portrays Black women as nurturing, self-sacrificing caretakers who exist solely to serve and support white families. It emerged during slavery when Black women were forced into such domesti-cated roles. It perpetuates that Black women are subservient, unthreatening, and devoid of aspirations. The unrealistic monikers of *Sapphire, Angry Black Woman, and Strong Black Woman* diminish Black women's emotions, needs, and voices. Black women are not allowed to be vulnerable or require assis-tance. These stereotypes suggest that Black women should not be prioritized or valued in their lives or anyone else's. Our culture becomes so *tilted* with these frames that it stigmatizes Black women into shame (Harris-Perry 108). The weight of this shame is incredibly restrictive, often preventing Black women from defining themselves beyond these stereotypes. As a result, they find themselves confined, unseen, marginalized, and subjected to oppression. Framing Black women so narrowly perpetuates the trauma of enslavement. This trauma prevents Black women from taking center stage in their lives and in social justice movements. The activism of Black women becomes entangled at the intersection of race, class, and gender, yet their advocacy is poised to bring benefits to others. Many of us learn to persist and persevere, *Lift As We Climb.*[1], and somehow make *BlackGirlMagic*[2] happen. At some point, it should be our turn to be vulnerable and prioritized, to be included and equal. After all, self-care is not selfish. Melissa Harris-Perry writes in her 2011 book entitled *Sister Citizens*:

> The silence in Black political agendas and national partisan organizing are in areas where Black women have the most critical needs. African American women struggle at the intersection of multiple forms of marginalization and find that their political labor often leaves them. . .less well. (299)

Historically, Black women have consistently led social justice movements, tirelessly advocating for equality, empowerment, and systemic transformation. Activists like Angela Davis, Audre Lorde, Kimberlé Crenshaw, and Tarana Burke have significantly contributed to feminist and civil rights movements. They all emphasize the importance of centering the experiences and voices of Black women, making the narratives more inclusive. Are Black women real victims? Do they create their problems? Are Black women seen as Black or women? Does it matter when they are portrayed poorly? Black women challenge and disrupt prevailing narratives perpetuating inequality and discrimination (Bliss; Cho et al.; P Collins; Gillespie and Brown; Weasel). These individuals often develop a critical consciousness through their lived experiences and can see through the veneer of mainstream norms and ideologies. This outsider-within-perspective allows individuals to challenge and resist dominant discourses, providing alternative ways of understanding and knowing the world. It enables them to critique and confront the systems of oppression that affect their lives and advocate for social change. By bringing their marginalized perspectives to the forefront, Black women can challenge the status quo and offer new ways of thinking and being that center the experiences of marginalized communities (P. Collins).

Despite the fight for freedoms and protections under racial and gender banners, often Black women have been highly marginalized and have not been the biggest beneficiaries of their protests. On the front lines, from the

Underground Railroad and Suffrage to Black Lives Matter and #MeToo, Black women have played significant roles in the battles for freedom, inclusion, and justice. Leading the war against sexual harassment and exploitation, and police brutality against Black bodies, Black women founded the #MeToo and Black Lives Matter movements. In incredibly ironic fashion, these movements have garnered great exposure and, in some cases, resolved issues on behalf of Black men and white women (Nishaun). "Because of the prioritization of Black men in the Black Lives Matter movement, Black women are again rendered invisible in the very reform movement originated to empower Black people" (Martin).

Activism is rooted in the understanding that addressing Black women's unique needs and concerns is essential for achieving true social justice and dismantling the intersecting systems of oppression. With intersectionality, Black women have long learned that they can set the agenda, but often they must rely on the intersection of their platitudes to receive the changes they seek.

In 2014, Crenshaw also launched the #SayHerName campaign through the African American Policy Forum (AAPF) to give voice to the many Black women who lost their lives to police violence. It acknowledges that Black women face unique and compounded forms of discrimination and violence. The campaign emphasizes that Black women's experiences of police violence and systemic racism are not simply an extension of the experiences of Black men or white women. Black women face a distinct set of challenges and biases shaped by their race and gender. They may be subjected to racial profiling, gendered violence, sexual harassment, or the erasure of their stories and experiences. According to the AAPF website (AAPF.org), many women were experiencing a mental health crisis, and police were called to conduct welfare checks. AAPF chronologically identifies Black women who have suffered and died due to police brutality and sexual assault. Its "Defund the Police" campaign became controversial, primarily because it was misunderstood. Police departments have been heavily militarized over the years. The "Defund the Police" campaign requested a more equitable distribution of resources to support strategies to increase community safety and wellness (Martin). Unfortunately, most of that got lost in translation. Critics often misinterpret it as a call to abolish police departments altogether. However, proponents generally advocate for reimagining public safety, wherein specific responsibilities traditionally assigned to police can be better handled by specialized professionals (i.e., social workers, psychologists, and more). Thus, there would be a reduction in the likelihood of unnecessary use of force and police violence. The inconsistency in messaging and the criticisms against some of the messengers have challenged the success of the "Defund the Police" campaign.

Despite these challenges, it has sparked discussions and public discourse on police reform and reallocation of resources.

Lawsuits as Social Activism

Lawsuits have had significant implications for the Black community regarding equality and justice. Historically, the Black community has faced systemic discrimination and injustices, including racial profiling, police brutality, housing discrimination, employment discrimination, and voting rights suppression, among other issues. Lawsuits have been a means for individuals or organizations to seek redress and fight against these injustices. Attorney Ben Crump is known for advocating for victims of police brutality and racial injustice, specifically within the Black community. He has been involved in several high-profile cases that have resulted in settlements, policy changes, and increased awareness of the issues. Over the last few years, he has significantly increased lawsuit payout amounts.

Additionally, he is comprehensively attaching riders on lawsuits involving Black women who seek more than a check. These riders demand change. Crump has advocated for broader adoption of body camera technology and mandatory use policies, comprehensive police reforms at all levels of government, de-escalation training, use-of-force policy changes, and more.

When Black individuals or advocacy groups file lawsuits, they often aim to challenge discriminatory practices, policies, or systems that perpetuate inequality. They are not simply compensation lawsuits. Lawsuits can be instrumental in bringing attention to specific cases of injustice, raising public awareness, and holding those responsible for discriminatory actions accountable. Furthermore, successful lawsuits can lead to legal precedents and landmark decisions that establish new legal standards or interpretations, which can benefit the Black community and other marginalized groups.

Well-known cases in US Black history demonstrate how lawsuit outcomes may result in changes to policies, practices, or laws that promote equality and justice. *Brown v. Board of Education* (1954) challenged racial segregation in public schools, ruling that the separate but equal doctrine was unconstitutional. The Supreme Court ruled in the case of *Griggs v. Duke Power Co* (1971) that employment practices that disproportionately affected African Americans could be deemed illegal under the Civil Rights Act. This decision expanded the scope of protection against employment discrimination. Regents of the *University of California v. Bakke* (1978) challenged affirmative action policies in college admissions.[3] It limited racial quotas, emphasizing that race could affect admissions decisions to promote diversity.

Additionally, lawsuits can provide a platform for marginalized voices to be heard and amplify their demands for justice. They can catalyze broader social and political movements by galvanizing public support, mobilizing communities, and putting pressure on lawmakers and institutions to address systemic inequalities. It is important to note that while lawsuits can be powerful tools in the pursuit of justice, they are not a comprehensive solution to the deeply rooted issues the Black community faces. Other forms of activism, community organizing, education, and policy changes are essential in creating lasting change and achieving true equality and justice.

Studies have shown that Black women are less likely to receive settlements for police violence or discrimination. According to the National Women's Law Center's website, Black women received settlements less frequently than Black men who experienced similar violence. They make 64–67 cents for every dollar paid to white non-Hispanic males (Letterman). More than white women and men of any race, Black women are more likely to be incarcerated and face harsher sentences. Black women face discrimination on both, leading to unique experiences of inequality and injustice, but are often left out of the public debates (Crenshaw; Crenshaw). There is growing concern around these occurrences across sections: police brutality and legal injustice, insurance, medical malpractice, and employment. There is a significant disparity in most settlements, of all types, awarded to Black women compared to white women and others in the United States. Even in cases where they have suffered similar or worse than others, Black women are more likely to receive lower to no settlement recompense.

In 2017, Justine Damond, a white Australian American woman, was killed by police when an officer fired into her home after being spooked by a noise. Despite testifying that there was an earnestly perceived threat, the court convicted the officer-shooter for killing the unarmed woman in her home (Romero). Initially, the officer was sentenced to 12.5 years. Recently, his charges and sentence were overturned in court. With a change in conviction from third-degree murder to manslaughter, Moor received a sentence of less than five years. Ms. Damond's family received a settlement judgment for $20 million from the City of Minneapolis. At the time, it was the largest of its kind. Well, it was the largest settlement for police-involved death until George Floyd. His family received $27 million from the City of Minneapolis (Associated Press). Floyd's killer was convicted and sentenced to 22.5 years.

Discrimination against Black women, through these payout discrepancies, becomes more transparent and arguably better positioned for real policy change. Breonna Taylor's family received $12 million in a civil settlement by the City of Louisville (J Griffith). Along with the $12 million settlement, the City of Louisville passed Breonna's Law. It bans no-knock warrants and requires body cameras to be worn (and on) during the execution of search warrants. In April 2021, the state of Kentucky also placed more restrictions on no-knock warrants due to Taylor's death and demands from activism surrounding her death (Waldrop et al.). Breonna's killers were found justified in her case. Eventually, they were hesitantly fired, which led to the firing of the police chief. US Attorney Garland brought forth charges against Brett Hankison for rights violations of Taylor and her next-door neighbors. Hankison is the *former* officer who aimlessly fired into the side of Taylor's apartment. These federal charges came shortly after his acquittal for wanton endangerment of Taylor's neighbors. Additional investigations led to federal charges of other officers who falsified information to secure the fatal warrant and lied to investigators. One has pleaded guilty and has been presumably working with federal agents to build their cases against her coworkers (Bowman; Waldrop). In the 2023 federal trial against Brett Hankison, the predominantly white jury could not reach a unanimous verdict, resulting in a mistrial. Although a mistrial is not an acquittal, a new trial can be an incredibly difficult feat. As the family's attorney said, ". . .we live another day to fight for justice for Breonna." (Lovan)

Black women have experienced invisibility and lack of accountability across multiple sectors of society. Workplace discrimination is an ongoing area of research and concern. Black women are less likely to be hired, paid competitively, or promoted (Browne). These disparities occur even when controlling their education and experience. Neither is the great equalizer for Black women (Banks). Underrepresentation in data, news reporting, and public discourse often lead to underreporting by Black women who may fear they will be further deprioritized and subjected to cumbersome state-sanctioned oppression and retaliation. Numerous studies have highlighted the persistent racial biases that permeate hiring practices, limiting employment opportunities for Black women. Bertrand and Mullainathan found that resumes with Black-sounding names were less likely to receive callbacks and interviews than identical resumes with white-sounding names. Discriminatory practices that encourage racial inequalities further hinder Black women's access to employment. Black women earn fractional amounts compared to whites and Black men (Letterman et al. 145–163; Roux; Browne). Black women are significantly underrepresented in senior management roles, limiting their opportunities for advancement and influence (Dorrian; Del Ray).

According to a study of discrimination cases filed with the Equal Employment Opportunity Commission (EEOC), Black women, in particular, are less likely to receive a monetary award than white women (Ponce de

Leon and Rosette). Intersectional class-action lawsuits have shed light on pay and promotion discrimination against Black women and exposed the hostile and toxic cultures in which they must work (Letterman; Browne). The landmark case, *Dukes v. Wal-Mart Stores Inc.*, revealed significant pay disparities and systemic discrimination against female employees, particularly Black women. These lawsuits underscore the importance of legal remedies and organizational accountability in combating discrimination. Despite the decision reversal[4] in *Dukes v. Wal-Mart Stores, Inc.*, there were great successes in battling against race and sex discrimination in corporate America, namely Bank of America and Merrill Lynch. In August and September of 2013, Bank of America, specifically its Merrill Lynch division, settled at $160 million for Black American brokers (Becker) and another $39 million for female brokers (McGeehan).

Tech giant, Google, has been sued by Black, white, Asian, and nearly all other groups of employees, citing racial or gender discrimination resulting in pay, hiring, and promotion disparities. Google has had to compensate many employees and applicants over the last few years. In 2018, Google agreed to pay $118 million to settle a class-action lawsuit brought by women who alleged gender discrimination at the company (Bunn). In 2021, Google reached a settlement with the U.S. Department of Labor amounting to over $3.8 million. The settlement addressed allegations of systemic compensation and hiring discrimination in Google's facilities in Washington and California. The settlement covered over 5,500 current employees and job applicants to resolve these claims. Also, in 2021, three former Google employees, including two Black women, filed a lawsuit against the company. The class-action lawsuit filed by attorney Ben Crump claimed the company paid Black women less than their male counterparts and fostered a hostile work environment for them. It has gained the attention of the California Department of Fair Employment and Housing, which has also launched an investigation. While not all lawsuits are specific to Black women, they exemplify the intersectionality of race and gender.

The social media company, Pinterest, faced turnover due to an alleged hostile work environment, including claims of sexual and racial harassment. Black employees left employment with little to no financial package; however, some white employees received substantial severance packages (Levenson). In 2020, two Black women from Pinterest's public policy team, Ifeoma Ozoma and Aerica Shimizu Banks, quit their jobs because of the underpayment in wages compared to others, racial and sexual discrimination, and the hostile work environment. Despite their earlier attempts to resolve these issues, Ozoma and Banks found Pinterest unresponsive to their concerns and needs.

Their public fight led to a settlement of less than one year's income for each. By contrast, just a few months later, Pinterest settled a monumental gender discrimination lawsuit with its former COO, Francoise Brougher (E. Griffith; Min; Paul). Brougher, a French American woman, settled for $22.5 million (Min; E. Griffith). Pinterest has not so much as offered Ozoma or Banks an apology. Due to the lawsuits and public discourse, Pinterest pledged $50 million to study and improve its diversity and inclusion. Ozoma and Banks, after getting this "slap in the face," are pushing large tech firms, like Pinterest, to go beyond diversity and inclusion – toward equity and transparency. After the numerous employment issues raised by the 2020 settlements and prior complaints, Pinterest executives and board members found themselves in a subsequent lawsuit alleging they were

> personally engaged in, facilitated, or knowingly ignored the discrimination and retaliation against those who spoke up and challenged the company's white, male leadership clique. As a result of the defendants' illegal misconduct, the company's financial position and goodwill and reputation among its largely female user base (which Pinterest's success depends upon) were harmed and continue to be harmed. (The D&O Diary)

In 2021, The Employees Retirement System of Rhone Island settled the lawsuit for a $50 million earmark to go toward diversity, equality, and inclusion to improve Pinterest's toxic culture (Levenson).

Similarly, Uber investigated its practices and implemented several changes to address the issue of diversity and inclusion as a response to lawsuits filed by Black female engineers and a former employee's, a white woman, blog post on the company's culture of sexism, racial discrimination, harassment, and retaliation (Guynn). After the revelations of sexual harassment and workplace misconduct, Uber underwent significant organizational changes, including ousting critical executives, implementing new policies, and improving workplace culture (Siddiqui).

The global e-commerce behemoth, Amazon, has faced several lawsuits related to employment discrimination, including allegations by Black women, women in general, and other diverse groups (Jeans). These lawsuits highlight concerns regarding discrimination, harassment, and lack of diversity within the company. In recent years, Black women have filed lawsuits against Amazon, accusing the company of fostering a hostile work environment where racist and sexist comments were prevalent, and they experienced unequal treatment in promotions and compensation. It was described as having a glass ceiling for Black women (T. Collins). Reports have highlighted allegations of racial and gender bias, inadequate representation of women and minorities in leadership positions, and a toxic work environment. Amazon has publicly acknowledged these concerns and stated its commitment to addressing them (Del Ray; Long). It will be interesting to compare the results of implemented initiatives to improve diversity and inclusion before and after the pending lawsuits.

The #MeToo movement shed light on the experiences of Black women who faced sexual harassment and misconduct. However, the movement initially gained prominence through the stories of predominantly white women, shaking the entertainment world immensely. The movement has led to the exposure, arrest, conviction, or punishment of numerous individuals across different industries for their improper behavior toward women. From Harvey Weinstein, Bill Cosby, various Fox News anchors, Larry Nassar, Charlie Rose, and Matt Lauer, many high-profile men have been held accountable for their sexual improprieties with women. In most cases, lawsuit settlement amounts and terms have not been disclosed (Carlsen). Many women were mostly satisfied when their stories were heard, and the accused men had career-ending results. Companies terminated contracts with all of them.

Weinstein and Cosby faced time in prison. Hollywood producer, Weinstein, was a significant catalyst for the *#MeToo* movement. In 2020, he was convicted of rape and sexual assault against multiple women, primarily white actresses. He was sentenced to 23 years in prison. Renowned comedian and actor Bill Cosby was convicted in 2018 for drugging and sexually assaulting Andrea Constand in 2004. He was sentenced to three to ten years in prison. Over 60 women, primarily white models, and actresses, have presented similar allegations. After serving three years, he was released, and the Pennsylvania Supreme Court threw out his 2018 convictions due to a negotiated $3.38 million settlement with the complainant and prosecutor. Cosby continues to have legal issues concerning the additional allegations of past sexual misconduct against women.

The #MeToo movement created an unprecedented milestone when it gained attention in connection with the highest position in the United States, the Presidency. During the 2020 Democratic Primary's presidential debates, Elizabeth Warren publicly confronted fellow candidate and former Mayor of New York, Michael Bloomberg, on his use of nondisclosure agreements (NDAs) for women who alleged sexual harassment against him. Former President Donald Trump battled civil allegations regarding sexual misconduct in court. The consequences of his pattern of utilizing provocative language to fuel racial and sexual discrimination eventually caught up to him. Trump's brazen and vulgar comments targeting women and individuals of different ethnicities disgraced the seat of office. Subsequently, in May 2023, a jury granted E. Jean Carroll $5 million in compensation, holding Trump accountable for sexual abuse and defamation (Nawaz et al.).

The incidents mentioned above predominantly affected white women. However, there has been a growing recognition of the necessity of intersectional analysis, acknowledging Black women's distinct challenges. Due to their historical marginalization and lack of voice, particularly in matters of sexual harassment, Black women have remained invisible and unheard for extended periods. In this context, the #MeToo movement emerged as a crucial catalyst for resolving and addressing long-standing issues. Perhaps one of the most well-known cases was the one against Robert Kelly, "R Kelly", the world-renowned musical genius. In 2021, after decades of allegations of crimes against underage girls and sexual exploitation of young women (Savage), Kelly was found guilty on federal charges, including racketeering and sex trafficking. Another prominent music executive, Russell Simmons, faced accusations of sexual assault and harassment. He stepped down from his businesses and faced public scrutiny. Tavis Smiley, a TV host and author, faced allegations of sexual harassment from several women who worked on his show. PBS suspended him, and his contract was subsequently terminated. These examples highlight the need to recognize the experiences of Black women within the broader context of the #MeToo movement. Black women can face intersecting forms of discrimination and may encounter specific barriers when presenting their truths. Efforts to ensure inclusivity, listen to diverse voices, and address the particular experiences of Black women are essential for creating a more comprehensive and equitable movement against sexual harassment and misconduct.

From insurance premiums and payouts to medical care, there is plenty of documentation of discrimination and bias against Black women in everyday situations. Black women are often charged higher insurance premiums than white women for the same coverage, despite similar circumstances and risk profiles. They are also more likely to be denied insurance coverage and claims. Increasing data collection for comparison and transparency in pricing can significantly reduce disparities and promote fairness. The Center on Race, Inequality, and the Law at the NYU School of Law has studied homeowners' insurance disparities. The data from this study has encouraged a class-action lawsuit against State Farm in an Illinois federal court (Adriano).

Discrimination and disparity lawsuits within the U.S. healthcare system have shed light on the alarming discrepancies experienced by white and Black women in cases of medical malpractice. Numerous cases have highlighted a disturbing pattern where Black women often face significant challenges and inequalities when seeking medical attention. White women received more attentive care than Black women, who experienced delayed diagnoses, inadequate treatment, and preventable harm due to the systemic issue. Black women have a maternal death rate of 2.9 times that of white women (Mossburg and Romine). Such disparities have resulted in lawsuits against healthcare providers, exposing the deep-rooted bias and negligence that disproportionately affects Black women. These lawsuits serve as a crucial step toward addressing the injustices within the healthcare system, demanding equitable treatment and accountability for all patients, regardless of race or ethnicity.

Famed tennis star Serena Williams used her personal story of medical discrimination during the birth of her daughter. Sharing her story publicly, she has shed light on the tendency of medical professionals to overlook or downplay the concerns of Black women, leading to inadequate care and delayed diagnoses. Kira Johnson died shortly after giving birth via C-section. Her medical team dismissed and downplayed her complaints of severe pain, ultimately leading to her death. Her husband was told that his wife was not a "priority." In depositions and testimonies from medical staff, there was an admission of blatant racism against Black women. A surgical technologist stated that she says an extra prayer when Black patients enter the hospital because of institutionalized racism. This implicit bias refers to the unconscious attitudes and stereotypes that influence decision-making and can gravely impact patient outcomes (Mossburg and Romine). These stories and lawsuits catalyze discussions and efforts to address and rectify bias and cultural incompetence, aiming to ensure equitable and quality patient care.

The culture of accountability and transparency is imperative in addressing these issues and ensuring Black women are no longer disproportionately affected by discriminatory practices. Despite potentially encountering substantial legal hurdles, lawsuits serve a vital purpose in increasing awareness and revealing entrenched systemic biases. They highlight the urgent need for reform and the importance of addressing intersectional discrimination. Black women are fighting for equal treatment, fairness, and transparency through these battles. Ultimately, Black women demand a more inclusive and equitable landscape where individuals are assessed on their merits and not subject to discriminatory practices.

From freedom to suffrage and sexual harassment to affirmative action, Black women remained at the forefront of social movements while undervalued and marginalized. The idea that things cannot change for marginalized groups until their interests align with those of men or white women is rooted in power dynamics and privilege. This perspective suggests that progress or societal change is contingent upon gaining the support or approval of a dominant group. It implies that the concerns and needs of Black women are less important or valid unless they are seen through the lens of Black men's or white women's interests.

Through the intersectional lens, it is essential to center Black women in movements for social justice and activism. They use the movements' incremental successes along racial and gender lines to promote progress and equality for themselves. Centering Black women in these social movements is crucial when lifting veils of secrecy and providing equality, inclusion, and justice for Black women. A genuinely equitable society recognizes and values all individuals' diverse experiences, perspectives, and interests. It acknowledges and addresses the systemic barriers and biases that have historically marginalized certain groups and works toward creating an inclusive and just society for everyone (P. Collins). It is vital to challenge and question progress if it is only possible through the lens of one group to bring about transformative social change.

Notes

1 *Lifting As We Climb* is the motto of the National Association of Colored Women's Clubs, founded in 1896 as the National Association of Colored Women. Great activists like Mary Church Terrell (co-founder), Ida B. Wells, and Harriett Tubman were members. The organization has focused on equality and promotion of Black Americans since its founding. The motto refers to our ability to "climb above the stereotypes" about Blacks. This organization has had a profound impact on my life. As a child, I was the first junior *Barbarette*, a local NACWC's Federated Youth Club chapter. My older sisters were members, so I had to tag along. I graduated and was a presented debutante of the organization. Beyond championing oratorical competitions and holding state office, I received great experience and training in advocacy, leading meetings, and community service. The organization is a big part of who I am today.

2 *Black Girl Magic* is a term used to celebrate and uplift Black women. Controversially, several people claim its origin. However, Beverly Bond, founder of Black Girls Rock, trademarked it.

3 Affirmative action has remained a contentious issue with ongoing debates. Despite its role in accelerating progress for white women, arguments for its reversal have primarily hinged on race, not gender. On June 29, 2023, the Supreme Court reversed its previous decision regarding using race as a determinant for college admissions. In two cases, *Students for Fair Admissions v. Harvard University* and *Students for Fair Admissions v. University of North Carolina*, the Supreme Court ruled that affirmative action based on race for college admissions violated Title VI of the Civil Rights Act of 1964 and the equal protection clause of the 14th Amendment. "U.S. Supreme Court Issues Landmark SFFA College Affirmative Action Decision." JD Supra, 29 June 2023, web.archive.org/web/20230702104641/https://www.jdsupra.com/legalnews/u-s-supreme-court-issues-landmark-sffa-3730254/.

4 Ironically, the decision reversal had more to do with legal technicality than an assessment of wrongdoing. In 2004, in Federal District Court, the judge certified the pursuit as a 23(b)2 class action. It was an attempt on behalf of the attorneys to avoid multiple lawsuits for similar remedies – back pay claims. However, Wal-Mart Stores Inc. appealed the decision pushing it to the Supreme Court under the case heading, *Wal-Mart v. Dukes*. In 2011, the Supreme Court found that the assembled plaintiffs did not have enough in common to pursue a class-action suit.
Fisher, Daniel. "Supreme Court Dumps Wal-Mart Sex-Discrimination Class Action." Forbes, 11 August 2011, www.forbes.com/sites/danielfisher/2011/06/20/supreme-court-dumps-wal-mart-sex-discrimination-class-action/?sh=5a7930806206.

Bibliography

Adriano, Lyle. https://Www.Insurancebusinessmag.Com/Us/News/Breaking-News/State-Farm-Hit-by-Class-Action-Lawsuit-Claiming-Racial-Discrimination-430895.Aspx.

"Ahmaud Arbery Shooting: A Timeline of the Case." *The New York Times*, 8 Aug. 2022, www.nytimes.com/articlencludd-arbery-timeline.html?searchResultPosition=5.

Associated Press. "Police Officer Who Fatally Shot Justine Damond Gets Nearly Five Years in Prison." *The Guardian*, 21 Oct. 2021, www.theguardian.com/us-news/2021/oct/21ncludie-damond-police-officer-mohamed-noor-sentenced.

Bailey, Phillip M., Darcy Costello, and Tessa Duvall. "Exclusive: Breonna Taylor Had Nothing to Do with Illegal Drug Trade, Ex-Boyfriend Says." *The Courier-Journal*, 27 Aug. 2020, www.courier-journal.com/story/news/local/breonna-taylor/2020/08/27/breonna-taylor-had-no-ties-drugs-ex-boyfriend-says/5641151002/.

Banks, Nina. "Black Women's Labor Market History Reveals Deep-Seated Race and Gender Discrimination." *Economic Policy Institute*, 19 Feb. 2019, www.epi.org/blog/black-womens-labor-market-history-reveals-deep-seated-race-and-gender-discrimination/.

Becker, Amanda. "BofA's Merrill to Settle Racial Bias Suit for $160 Million." *Reuters*, 28 Aug. 2013, www.reuters.com/article/us-merrilllynch/bofas-merrill-to-settle-racial-bias-suit-for-160-million-idUSBRE97R13X20130828.

Best, Rachel Kahn, et al. "Multiple Disadvantages: An Empirical Test of Intersectionality Theory in EEO Litigation." *Law & Society Review*, vol. 45, no. 4, 2011, pp. 991–1025.

Bertrand, M., & Mullainathan, S. "Are Emily and Greg More Employable Than Lakisha and Jamal? A Field Experiment on Labor Market Discrimination." *American Economic Review*, vol. 94, no. 4, 2004, pp. 991–1013.

Bliss, James. "Black Feminism Out of Place." *Signs*, vol. 41, no. 4, 2016, pp. 727–49.

Bowman, Emma. "4 Current and Former Officers Federally Charged in Raid That Killed Breonna Taylor." *NPR*, 4 Aug. 2022, www.npr.org/2022/08/04/1115659537/breonna-taylor-police-charges-ky.

Brice, Makini. "Behind $12 Million Breonna Taylor Settlement, "Black America's Attorney General Benjamin Crump." *Reuters*, 16 Sept. 2020, www.reuters.com/article/us-global-race-usa-taylor-crump/behind-12-million-breonna-taylor-settlement-black-americas-attorney-general-benjamin-crump-idUSKBN2671NJ.

Browne, Irene. "Explaining the Black-White Gap in Labor Force Participation among Women Heading Households." *American Sociological Review*, vol. 62, no. 2, 1997, pp. 236–52.

Bunn, Curtis. "Black Women Allege Google Fosters 'Racist Culture' in Lawsuit against the Company." *NBC News*, 22 Mar. 2022, www.nbcnews.com/news/nbcblk/black-women-allege-googles-racist-culture-lawsuit-company-rcna21008.

Carlsen, Audrey, et al. "#MeToo Brought down 201 Powerful Men. Nearly Half of Their Replacements Are Women." *The New York Times*, 23 Oct. 2018, www.nytimes.com/interactive/2018/10/23/us/metoo-replacements.html.

Chavez, Nicole, and Christina Carrega. "Breonna Taylor Settlement Is among Largest Payouts Linked to a Police Shooting." *CNN*, 16 Sept. 2020, www.cnn.com/2020/09/16/us/police-shooting-lawsuits-breonna-taylor-settlement/index.html.

Cho, Sumi, Kimberlé Williams Crenshaw, and Leslie McCall. "Toward a Field of Intersectionality Studies: Theory, Applications, and Praxis." *Signs*, vol. 38, no. 4, 2013, pp. 785–810.

Collins, Patricia Hill. *Black Feminist Thought: Knowledge, Consciousness, and the Politics of Empowerment*. Routledge, 2009.

Collins, Terry. "Black Amazon Manager Sues the Tech Giant, Execs Alleging Discrimination and Harassment." *USA TODAY*, 1 Mar. 2021, www.usatoday.com/story/money/business/2021/03/01/charlotte-newman-sues-amazon-claiming-discrimination-harassment/6877253002/.

Courtney, Joe. "Text–- H.R.748–- 116th Congress (2019-2020): CARES Act." *www.congress.gov*, 27 Mar. 2020, www.congress.gov/bill/116th-congress/house-bill/748/text.

Crenshaw, Kimberlé. "Demarginalizing the Intersection of Race and Sex: A Black Feminist Critique of Antidiscrimination Doctrine, Feminist Theory and Antiracist Politics." *University of Chicago Legal Forum*, vol. 1989, no. 1, 1989, pp. 139–167, chicagounbound.uchicago.edu/cgi/viewcontent.cgi?article=1052&context=uclf.

Crenshaw, Kimberlé. "Mapping the Margins: Intersectionality, Identity Politics, and Violence against Women of Color." *Stanford Law Review*, vol. 43, no. 6, 1991, pp. 1241–1299.

The D&O Diary | A Periodic Journal Containing Items of Interest From the World of Directors & Officers Liability, With Occasional Commentary, www.dandodiary.com/wp-content/uploads/sites/893/2020/12/Pinterst-derivative-complaint.pdf.

DakinIe. "A Timeline of the Killing of Ahmaud Arbery and the Case against 3 Men Accused of His Murder." *CNN*, 12 Nov. 2021, www.cnn.com/2021/10nclud/ahmaud-arbery-case-timeline/index.html.

"Death of George Floyd, Trial of Derek Chauvin: Timeline of Key Events." *Los Angeles Times*, 19 Apr. 2021, www.latimes.com/world-nation/story/2021-04-19/timel ine-key-events-george-floyd-death-derek-chauvin-trial.

Del Rey, Jason. "Amazon Hit by 5 More Lawsuits from Employees Who Allege Race and Gender Discrimination." *Vox*, 19 May 2021, www.vox.com/rec ode/2021/5/19/22444177/amazon-five-more-lawsuits-employees-all ege-race-and-gender-discrimination-charlotte-newman.

Del Ray, Jason. "Bias, Disrespect, and Demotions: Black Employees Say Amazon Has a Race Problem." *Vox*, 26 Feb. 2021, www.vox.com/recode/2021/2/26/22297554/ amazon-race-black-diversity-inclusion.

Domonoske, Camila. "NPR Choice Page." *Npr.org*, 2019, www.npr.org/seI/the two-way/2018/04/17/603163394/-father-of-gynecology-who-experimented-on-slaves-no-longer-on-pedestal-in-nyc.

Dorrian, Patrick. "Black Female Amazon HR Employee Settles Job Discrimination Suit." *News.bloomberglaw.com*, 11 July 2022, news.bloomberglaw.com/litigation/ black-female-amazon-hr-employee-settles-job-discrimination-suit.

Douglas, Angela Y. "Questions Arise: The Political, Legal, and Social Implications of the Trayvon Martin Tragedy." *The Trayvon Martin in the US: An American Tragedy*, edited by Emmanuel Harris II and Antonio D. Tillis, Peter Lang, 2015, pp. 83–94.

Dukes v. Wal-Mart Stores, Inc., 603 F.3d 571 (9th Cir. 2010).

Duvall, Tessa, and Darcy Costello. " 'Say Her Name. Don't Say Mine': Breonna Taylor's Boyfriend Remains Haunted by Her Death." *USA TODAY*, 28 Oct. 2020, www. usatoday.com/story/news/nation/2020/10/28/breonna-taylor-case-boyfriend-kenneth-walker/6052969002/.

Early Resolution Conciliation Agreement between the U.S. Department Of Labor Office Of Federal Contract Compliance Programs and Google LLC 1600 Amphitheatre Parkway Mountain View, California Part I. Preliminary Statement. 15 Jan. 2021.

"Federal Judge Sentences Three Men Convicted of Racially Motivated Hate Crimes in Connection with the Killing of Ahmaud Arbery in Georgia." *www.justice.gov*, 8 Aug. 2022, www.justice.gov/opa/pr/federal-judge-sentences-three-men-convic ted-racially-motivated-hate-crimes-connection-killing.

Gillespie, Andra, and Nadia E. Brown. "#BlackGirlMagic Demystified: Black Women as Voters, Partisans and Political Actors." *Phylon (1960-)*, vol. 56, no. 2, 2019, pp. 37–58.

Griffith, Erin. "Pinterest Settles Gender Discrimination Suit for $22.5 Million." *The New York Times*, 14 Dec. 2020, www.nytimes.com/2020/12/14/technology/ pinterest-gender-discrimination-lawsuit.html.

Griffith, Janelle, et al. "City of Louisville Reaches Settlement with Breonna Taylor's Family." *NBC News*, 15 Sept. 2020, www.nbcnews.com/news/us-news/city-louisvi lle-reaches-settlement-breonna-taylor-s-family-n1240115.

Guynn, Jessica. "Uber Agrees to Pay $4.4 Million to Settle EEOC Sexual Harassment and Retaliation Probe." *USA Today*, 18 Dec. 2019, www.usatoday.com/story/ tech/2019/12/18/uber-sexual-harassment-investigation-me-too/2694091001/.

Harris-Perry, Melissa. *Sister Citizen: Shame, Stereotypes and Black Women in America: For Colored Girls Who've Considered Politics When Strong Isn't Enough.* 2014. New Haven: Yale.

Hayes-Greene, D., & Love, B. P. (2018). *The Groundwater Approach: Building a Practical Understanding of Structural Racism.* The Racial Equity Institute.

Hurt, Emma. "15 Months after Ahmaud Arbery's Death, Georgia Repeals Citizen's Arrest Law: NPR." *Web.archive.org*, 27 Nov. 2021, web.archive.org/web/20211127022901/www.npr.org/2021/05/11/995835333/in-ahmaud-arbe rys-name-georgia-repeals-citizens-arrest-law.

Institute of Medicine (US) Committee on Understanding and Eliminating Racial and Ethnic Disparities in Health Care. *Unequal Treatment: Confronting Racial and Ethnic Disparities in Health Care.* Edited by Brian D. Smedley et al., National Academies Press (US), 2003. doi:10.17226/12875.

Jeans, David. "Amazon Targeted with Five Lawsuits from Employees Claiming Discrimination and Retaliation." *Forbes*, 19 May 2021, www.forbes.com/sites/davidjeans/2021/05/19/amazon-five-racial-discrimination-lawsuits/?sh=2a71c e597293.

Jones, Alexi, and Wendy Sawyer. "Not Just 'a Few Bad Apples': U.S. Police Kill Civilians at Much Higher Rates than Other Countries." *Prison Policy Initiative*, www.priso npolicy.org/blog/2020/06/05/policekillings/.

Letterman, Margaret R., et al. "Major Choice and the Wage Differential between Black and White Women." *Journal of Applied Social Science*, vol. 12, no. 2, 2018, pp. 145–63.

Levenson, Michael. "Pinterest Agrees to Spend $50 Million on Reforms to Resolve Discrimination Allegations." *The New York Times*, 25 Nov. 2021, www.nytimes. com/2021/11/24/technology/pinterest-discrimination-settlement.html.

Long, Katherine Ann, and Manuel Villa. "Amazon Data Showed Big Jump in Diversity among Senior Leaders — after Definition of 'Executive' Was Loosened." *The Seattle Times*, 22 May 2021, www.seattletimes.com/business/amazon/amazon-data-sho wed-big-jump-in-diversity-among-senior-leaders-after-definition-of-executive-was-loosened/.

Lovan, Dylan. "Mistrial declared after federal jury deadlocks in trial of ex-officer in deadly Breonna Taylor raid." AP News, 16 November 2023, www.apnews.com/arti cle/breonna-taylor-federal-civil-rights-trial-police-6346bbfdc0d6a522e3088dfa8 0d61cc5.

Lowery, Wesley, et al. "Killings of Black People Lead to Arrests Less Often Than When Victims Are White." *The Washington Post*, www.washingtonpost.com/graph ics/2018/investigations/black-homicides-arrests/.

Martin, Jordan. "Breonna Taylor: Transforming a Hashtag into Defunding the Police." *The Journal of Criminal Law and Criminology (1973-)*, vol. 111, no. 4, 2021, pp. 995–1030.

McGeehan, Patrick. "Bank of America to Pay $39 Million in Gender Bias Case." *DealBook*, 7 Sept. 2013, archive.nytimes.com/dealbook.nytimes.com/2013/09/06/bank-of-america-to-pay-39-million-in-gender-bias-case/.

Min, Janice. "Pinterest and the Subtle Poison of Sexism and Racism in Silicon Valley." *Time*, 22 Mar. 2021, time.com/5947561/pinterest-gender-discrimination-racism/.

Moore, K. M., & Sagaria, M. A. D. (1982). "Differential Job Change and Stability among Academic Administrators." *The Journal of Higher Education, 53*(5), 501–513.

Mossburg, Cheri, and Taylor Romine. "Widower of Black Woman Who Died Hours after Childbirth Files Civil Rights Lawsuit against Cedars-Sinai." CNN, 7 May 2022, www.cnn.com/2ncludingus/california-civil-rights-lawsuit-cedars-sinai/index.html.

National Women's Law Center. (2019). *Unlocking Opportunity for African American Girls: Acall to Action for Educational Equity.* Retrieved from https://www.naacpldf.org/wp-content/uploads/Unlocking-Opportunity-for-African-American_Girls_0_Education.pdf

Nawaz, Amna, and Matt Loffman. "Breaking Down the Verdict as Jury Finds Trump Liable for Sexual Assault and Defamation." *PBS NewsHour*, 9 May 2023, www.pbs.org/newshour/show/breaking-down-the-verdict-as-jury-finds-trump-liable-for-sexual-assault-and-defamation.

Nishaun T. Battle. "From Slavery to Jane Crow to Say Her Name: An Intersectional Examination of Black Women and Punishment." *Meridians*, vol. 15, no. 1, 2016, pp. 109–36.

Paul, Kari. "Pinterest's $22m Settlement with Executive Is a 'Slap in the Face,' Black Former Workers Say." *The Guardian*, 18 Dec. 2020, www.theguardian.com/technology/2020/dec/18/pinterest-gender-discrimination-lawsuit-black-workers.

Ponce de Leon, Rebecca, and Ashleigh Shelby Rosette. "'Invisible' Discrimination: Divergent Outcomes for the Non-Prototypicality of Black Women." *Academy of Management Journal*, vol. 65, no. 3, 8 Feb. 2022, https://doi.org/10.5465/amj.2020.1623.

Roberts v. Texaco Inc., 36 F. Supp. 2d 1238 (S.D.N.Y. 1999).

Romero, Dennis. "Texas Police Officer Shoots Woman to Death inside Her Home." *NBC News*, NBC News, 13 Oct. 2019, www.nbcnews.com/ncluus-news/texas-police-officer-shoots-woman-death-inside-her-home-n1065451.

Roux, Mathilde. "5 Facts about Black Women in the Labor Force | U.S. Department of Labor Blog." *Blog.dol.gov*, 3 Aug. 2021, blog.dol.gov/2021/08/03/5-facts-about-black-women-in-the-labor-force.

Sagaria, M. A., D. (1988). "Administrative Mobility and Gender: Patterns and Processes in Higher Education." *The Journal of Higher Education, 59*(3), 305–326.

Savage, Mark. "R Kelly: The History of Allegations against Him." *BBC News*, 28 Sept. 2021, www.bbc.com/news/entertainment-arts-40635526.

Siddiqui, Faiz. "Uber to Pay up to $4.4 Million to Alleged Gender Discrimination Victims after EEOC Investigation." *Washington Post*, 18 Dec. 2019, www.washingtonpost.com/technology/2019/12/18/uber-pay-million-victims-alleged-gender-discrimination-following-eeoc-investigation/.

Smith, S.L. "African American Females in Senior-Level Executive Roles Navigating Predominantly White Institutions: Experiences, Challenges and Strategies for Success" PhD dissertation, The University of Texas at Austin, 2013.

Turner, Jennifer L. "Beyond 'Welfare Queens' and 'Baby Mamas': Low-Income Black Single Mothers' Resistance to Controlling Images." *Black Matrilineage, Photography, and Representation: Another Way of Knowing*, edited by Lesly Deschler Canossi and Zoraida Lopez-Diago, Leuven University Press, 2022, pp. 53–72.

Waldrop, Theresa Waldrop, Eliott C. McLaughlin, Sonia Moghe, and Hannah Rabinowitz. "Breonna Taylor Killing: A Timeline of the Police Raid and Its Aftermath." *CNN*, 4 Aug. 2022, www.cnn.com/2022/08/04/us/no-knock-raid-breonna-taylor-timeline/index.html.

Weasel, Lisa H. "Embodying Intersectionality: The Promise (and Peril) of Epigenetics for Feminist Science Studies." *Mattering: Feminism, Science, and Materialism*, edited by Victoria Pitts-Taylor, NYU Press, 2016, pp. 104–21.

Williams, Serena. "How Serena Williams Saved Her Own Life." ELLE, 5 Apr. 2022, www.elle.com/life-love/a39586444/how-serena-williams-saved-her-own-life/.

Wolfson, Andrew. "Breonna Taylor Settlement One of Largest Ever in U.S. For Black Victim of Police Shooting." *The Courier-Journal*, 15 Sept. 2020, www.courier-journal.com/story/news/local/breonna-taylor/2020/09/15/breonna-taylor-settlement-may-largest-ever-black-victim-police-shooting/5804320002/.

Xiong, Chao. "A Timeline of Events Leading to George Floyd's Death as Outlined in Charging Documents." *Star Tribune*, 4 June 2020, www.startribune.com/a-timeline-of-events-leading-to-george-floyd-s-death-as-outlined-in-charging-documents/570999132/?refresh=true.

12 For Black Girls Who Grow Up Too Quickly: An Open Letter to My Daughters

Louis L. Woods

My Dearest Maya and Zora,

It pains me to explain to you both that we live in a nation where a Black woman can be slaughtered inside her apartment in the middle of the night by government officials sworn to protect and serve all American citizens. While others will attempt to justify the actions of the Louisville police officers for botching a no-knock warrant, the fact remains that this would never happen to a white woman. Somehow police officers across the nation can de-escalate dangerous civilian encounters and bring white men into custody wearing body armor and brandishing weapons of war. Police officers have arrested white men after committing mass murder in churches, synagogues, mosques, grocery stores, elementary schools, movie theaters, and countless other social environments. Despite the police officer's ability to disarm murderous white men across the country, what Breonna Taylor's murder suggests is that Black people are not even safe within their own homes. The murder of Breonna Taylor also heartbreakingly reveals how this nation has consistently treated African American women. Throughout American history, thousands of African American men have been lynched, most often for being accused of mistreating white women. Yet, the molestation, abuse and murder of Black women remained commonplace.

In a 1962 speech, Malcolm X once said, "The most disrespected person in America is a Black woman. The most unprotected person in America is a Black woman. The most neglected person in America is the Black woman."[1] While over 60 years have passed since Malcolm X made these insightful comments, the reality is that Black women remain unprotected by law in America.

Too often, Black girls are treated more like adults than innocent children. Maya, while you were only eleven years old, a white woman at our neighborhood park, asked you if your five-year-old sister was your child. Maya, do you remember that problematic incident? This is a tangible example of how this "adultification" occurs daily for Black girls across this nation.[2]

As infuriating as the racial and gendered discrimination you endure today is, believe me, it was worse in generations past. For example, in 1850, a 14-year-old Black girl named Celia was purchased by a 56-year-old widower named Robert Newsome. Newsome had a special cabin made for Celia away from the slave quarters. Between 1851 and 1855, Celia was repeatedly raped by Newsome, delivering two children. In March 1855, Celia was pregnant again and in a relationship with a Black man named George. Frustrated with Newsome's frequent disruption of their relationship, George gave Celia an ultimatum to stop her sexual relationship with Newsome or risk losing his companionship. Pressured by George and infuriated with his consistent sexual assault, Celia told Newsome it was over and threatened to hurt him if he came to her cabin again. Indignant, Newsome asserted his ownership of Celia and promised to come to her cabin that night. In anticipation of an unwanted visit, Celia procured and hid a large tree branch near her fireplace. When Newsome attacked her, she fought him off, grabbed the tree branch, and clubbed Newsome to death. She spent the remainder of the morning hours burning Newsome's dead body inside her fireplace. Weeks later, she confessed to the murder asserting she had a legal right to defend herself against unwanted sexual advances. At trial, Celia's defense argued that she killed Newsome in self-defense resisting his improper behavior. Despite having a law stating, "every person who shall be convicted of rape" or "by forcibly ravishing any woman of the age of ten years or upwards shall be punished by imprisonment in the penitentiary not less than five years," the Missouri courts rejected Celia's defense plea. They argued that as property, Black women were incapable of being raped.[3] The Missouri courts ruled that Black women did not possess bodily autonomy and were legally incapable of fighting off the unwanted sexual advances of white men.[4] Celia's harrowing story reveals Malcolm X's insight and contextualizes the Breonna Taylor tragedy. Black women remain unprotected by societal structures.

Despite the many ways American society has attempted to belittle Black women, your mother and I were both thrilled to raise Black girls. Your mother and I believe in an African tradition that names have power. We named you both after powerful and prolific African American female writers. Maya, you are named after Maya Angelou, and Zora, you are named after Zora Neale

Hurston. We named you after these inspirational women for a reason. When we named you both after these literary giants, we wanted you to know that your name and family legacy were powerful and purposeful. There is power in both your name and your DNA. You come from a long line of powerful Black women. Your namesakes and ancestors forged a powerful resilience in the face of unimaginable repression.

Nevertheless, they persisted so you could prosper and thrive despite an unrelenting tsunami of racism. While this remains true, it is not intended to undermine or minimize the legitimacy of your current and future grievances with the nation of your birth (I say the nation of your birth because every generation of African Americans has been made to feel unwelcomed here). Rather an appreciation of relative racial progress is simply a recognition that our people have come a long way from the plantations that once commodified Black bodies.

However, while we are no longer enslaved, racism is far from stagnant. White supremacy is dynamic, fluid, and ever-evolving. Until now, we have seen three major systems of Black denigration (slavery, segregation, and mass incarceration). However, we cannot afford to be naïve and believe that our current brand of racism is the only way some white Americans seek to maintain racial dominance. If history can teach us anything, trust me with an assurance that there will be other systemic forms of Black belittlement. Now the quintessential challenge for you both, my lovely young daughters, is this: as long as you remain within the nation of your birth, you must find a way to live within this profoundly discriminatory society. And if you choose to remain inside the geographic boundaries of the nation of your birth, you must also find joy, happiness, and fulfillment in a profoundly anti-Black and anti-female country. You must never internalize the messages this nation has for Black women. John Henrick Clarke once said, "Powerful people cannot afford to educate the people they oppress, because once you are truly educated, you will not ask for power. You will take it."[5] This sentiment is especially true when contemplating the current political backlash against teaching Black history. African American history empowers Black students by highlighting the heroes who survived unimaginable mistreatment and provides a sense of purpose with their people's generationally endured struggle. Daughters, please remember this, people who begrudgingly acknowledge your humanity cannot possibly celebrate your many gifts. You both most find ways to use their judgement as fuel. Seek validation from your tribe, and never use the perceptions of some white people as a barometer to evaluate your greatness. Remember, if Black people had taken to heart what some white people said about them, we would have collectively slit our wrists in the year 1620. We must strive for greatness despite what the nation of our birth says about our potential to accomplish our dreams.

As you grow into young women, remember this fact: generations of remarkable Black people have already lifted the heaviest of burdens. As Nikole Hannah-Jones reminds us, "Black people were enslaved here longer than we have been free."[6] To be specific, from 1619 until 1865, the majority of African Americans were enslaved. That is 246 years of unfreedom for our ancestors within a self-proclaimed democratic nation. Adding 246 years to the year 1865 is the year 2111 (when African Americans have been as free as their ancestors were enslaved in the nation of their birth). Assuming you can live long enough to witness the breakeven period for fundamental African American freedom and bodily autonomy, Maya, you will be 101, and Zora will be 95 years old. Additionally, you cannot be free in a democracy without the right to vote. For Black people, their enfranchisement was codified in the year 1965 by the Voting Rights Act. We enjoyed 48 years of unmolested access to the franchise until 2013 when the Supreme Court ruled in *Shelby County v. Holder* that the preclearance section of the Voting Rights Act was no longer needed. This provision asserted that states with a history of disfranchising African Americans could not change statewide voting laws without federal oversight. While African Americans could vote after 2013, the nationwide voter ID laws have made it much more difficult to do so. This is the horrible legacy of nationwide Black disfranchisement: From 1619 to 1965 there was a 346-year era exclusion of Black democratic participation (except for a few years of United States military supervision during Reconstruction). Adding 346 years to the year 1965 is the year 2311. Assuming you both lived long enough to see the breakeven period for Black access to the ballot within this self-celebrating democracy, Maya, you would be 301 years of age, and Zora, 295 years old. That is how long it will take before Black people have been able to vote as long as this essential freedom has been denied to our people within a democratic republic. Racism mathematics reveals the generational enormity of our ancestors' degradation.

While Black access to American freedom and democracy is new, fighting for our dignity against all odds is not. We have always been embattled here. James Baldwin once said, "In America, I was free only in battle, never free to rest – and he (or she) who finds no way to rest cannot long survive the battle."[7] The reality in this insight exemplifies the exhaustion inherent in living among people whose identity, too often, is predicated upon our collective marginalization and their relative privilege over Black and brown folks. Toni Morrison once said, "If you can only be tall because somebody's on their knees than you have a serious problem." Morrison further argued, "And my feeling is that white people have a very, very serious problem. And they should start thinking about what they can do about it."[8] In 2016, Maya, the father of one of your swim teammates told me that President Donald Trump was elected "because the role of the white man had been diminished." Before the 2008 and 2012 elections of Barack Obama (the 44th president of the United States), white men had won 43 consecutive times. How fragile must your ego be if the election of a single Black man to the presidency could "diminish a white man's role" in America? In any sporting event or by any metric, we would call a 43 and 1 record a dynasty. For too many white folks, a singular loss to a Black or brown person represents an unsettling diminishment. Imagine the level of delusion necessary to perceive the election of the first Black man to the presidency in conspiratorial logic. For some white people, it was more plausible that the first Black president was a "Kenyan, Muslim, Spy" than the belief that white men were defeated in a fair election by a member of a historically marginalized group. Antiracist activist Tim Wise once asked white participants in antiracist workshops, "What's good about being white?" Most of them responded by highlighting their relative privilege, "I can receive a bank loan," "I can live wherever I want," and "The police don't harass me."[9] Essentially, these respondents said the best thing about being white was not being Black. Some of your white countrymen's ego strength is drawn from their relative privilege and resulting from our collective oppression; this means that Black excellence and your greatness will inherently be perceived threateningly. My beloved daughters, understand it is not your responsibility to make them feel comfortable.

As a father, my primary job is keeping you both safe. Your holistic safety is not just physical but also intellectual, spiritual, and emotional. Safeguarding your emotional health remains among the most daunting aspects of parenting because, in an anti-Black country, Black love remains a revolutionary act. Loving you despite how we are treated in this country is my priority. When discussing the formidable prospect of raising healthy Black children, James Baldwin astutely commented:

> ...having barely escaped suicide, or death, or madness, or yourself, you watch your children growing up and no matter what you do...you are powerless... against the force of the world that is out to tell your child(ren) that (they have) no right to be alive. And no amount of liberal jargon...does anything to soften or to point out any solution to this dilemma. In every generation, ever since Negroes have been here, every Negro mother and father has had to face that child and try to create in that child some way of surviving this particular (nation), some way to make that child who will be despised not despise [herself].[10]

This struggle that Baldwin articulated remains relevant. Your mother and I strive to provide you with the tools to navigate within a society determined to convince you that Black people deserve the treatment we have been made to endure. Please remember that slavery, segregation, and mass incarceration are not an indictment on us. Instead, these systems of oppression are a damnation of this nation. Our people have survived the unfathomable with dignity, grace, and faith that future generations will have to endure less.

Believe me, I know that living here as a Black person is not easy. Zora, at 7 years old, your journey through white supremacy is just beginning. At your tender age, I already recognize that when we vacation in the Caribbean, you are never ready to return to the country of your birth. As a second grader, you understand where your humanity is and is not affirmed. Maya, as you enter your teenage years, I see you struggling to grapple with the weight of what it means to be both Black and a woman here. American society has always been, currently is, and will likely always be a profoundly sexist and anti-Black nation. While the prospect of widespread racial and gendered enlightenment of our fellow citizens remains doubtful, never internalize the hatred of your countrymen. Although the oppression is traumatic, it is not personal. They have nothing against you as an individual because their hatred cannot see beyond your skin color or your gender. They are not attacking your characteristics because many cannot affirm your humanity, and individuals who deny your human dignity cannot appreciate your many personal gifts. While recognizing their dehumanizing treatment of you is not personal, does not make the sting of marginalization hurt any less. The reality is that anti-Blackness is culturally cultivated and normalized. Their racial socialization and fragile racial identities too often require our subjugation. When people's sense of self is dependent upon being better than Black folks, they have surrendered their power to us and predicated their flimsy ego strength on their ability to defeat us in societal competition. And, rather than accept a defeat, they often fain victimization or bemoan the "unfairness" of the competition rather than admit they were bested by their so-called "inferiors."

Because our greatness is as begrudgingly acknowledged as the affirmation of our humanity, my beloved girls, you will have to find your intrinsic value. What will be among your greatest challenges will be to forge an unbreakable sense of self-worth independent of what society says about your abilities? Remember not to rely on validation from people incapable or unwilling to acknowledge your humanity. Seek validation from your tribe (the family and friend network that uplift you) alone. Remember that you both were born smart enough. You possessed all the gifts you needed to actualize your dreams within your DNA. Struggle is your inheritance. Stubborn resistance to white supremacy will become a part of your legacy.

Despite the persistence of white supremacy in the country of your birth, I remain encouraged as I ponder the future opportunities for you both. Not out of some naïve sense that many of your white countrymen will one day become racially rehabilitated. Rather, I find hope in our family's generational legacies despite consistently predictable racial and gendered oppression. When I said that greatness was in your DNA, that was not a hyperbolic statement. When he died in 1920, William Smith, a formally enslaved ancestor (your great, great, great, great grandfather), owned a cotton gin, a sawmill, a convenience store, and 768 acres of property in Caddo Parish, Louisiana. John Milton Smith, your great, great, great grandfather, was the first in our family to attend college in the 1890s (he went to Bishop Normal College in Marshall, Texas). Milton farmed and taught Blacks to read and write in the family sanctuary: Republican Baptist Church. John Milton's daughter, Orenzia Smith, your great-great-aunt, was a registered nurse in 1945. Melvin James Grant, Milton's grandson, and your great grandfather, received a bachelor's degree from New York University (NYU) in 1950, when approximately 2 percent of African Americans obtained this education level.[11] Two years later, Melvin got a master's degree from NYU and, in 1962, received a second master's degree from City College in New York City. Melvin retired as an NYPD Lieutenant and taught in the police institute at the University of Illinois, Champaign-Urbana. Vera Baquet, your Grammy, received both a bachelor's and master's degree from the State University of New York (SUNY) at Stony Brook and was a daycare director. Victoria Rivera, your grandma, got a bachelor's degree from City College and her Medical Doctorate from Yeshiva Medical School. I received a bachelor's degree from SUNY Stony Brook and my master's and Ph.D. from Howard University. Your mother received her bachelor's degree from Fisk University and her master's degree from Indiana University. Assuming you all follow in the substantial educational tradition of your ancestors, you both will be the sixth-generation college and fourth-generation graduate students. Despite persistent racism, that familial, educational legacy personifies greatness. These familial, educational accomplishments took place amidst soul-crushing racial oppression. Milton went to college as segregation was nationally sanctioned by the landmark 1896 *Plessy v. Ferguson* Supreme Court ruling. Orenzia became a registered nurse shortly after the United States Red Cross racially segregated blood plasma (created by Charles Drew – a brilliant Black medical doctor). Melvin received his master's degree two years before the 1954 *Brown v. Education* Supreme Court ruling, which made public school segregation unconstitutional. Grandma Vicki received her MD during the ravages of the crack epidemic, and Grammy Vera obtained her master's degree following the racial fallout of the Los Angeles race riots just after the inflammatory Rodney King verdict. Your mother and I obtained our graduate degrees after the horrendous government response to Hurricane Katrina which showcased the federal ineptitude. It took your government three days to get water to displaced American citizens in the sweltering tropical summer heat of New Orleans. These educational accomplishments occurred despite unrelenting national racial animus. Despite white supremacy, our family has been able to prosper. I am confident it will continue to do so as you both find your way in the world.

Finally, in addition to our substantial familial and educational legacy, my confidence in both of your prospects remains optimistic because no one in our family has ever started life with as many unearned privileges. Maya, before you were born, your mother and I had already been married for nearly four years, had our advanced degrees, and had bought our first home. Zora, not long after you were born, we moved the family into our second and more expensive home in an exclusive part of town. While Maya remembers it well, Zora, you probably have no recollection of our first home. Both of you have had passports before your first birthday. For the past eight years, your grandmothers have been retired in the US Virgin Islands. Except for the Covid lockdown, you have been to the Caribbean twice a year for your entire life. You have seen a world where you are a racial majority, where your humanity is daily affirmed, and you represent the national standard of beauty.

This latter point is significant because in the country of your birth, Blackness is vilified, and white people walk around the nation with their chests stuck out, insisting on the necessity of continuing the enjoyment of their "majority" status. James Baldwin once stated that "the world is not white; it never was white, cannot be white. White is a metaphor for power," and people clinging to power and representation "have lost their own" identity. Essentially, a loss of identity is the loss of one's reality and moral authority.[12] Baldwin was referring to the foundational disconnection from reality when many white people assert an identity predicated upon being a racial "majority." To begin with, the United States' population consists of less than 5 percent of the world's population. According to the PEW research center, "more than half of all people live in" the following seven countries: "China, India, the United States, Indonesia, Pakistan, Nigeria and Brazil." Additionally, "China's population is greater than the entire population of Europe (744 million) or the Americas (1.04 billion) and roughly equivalent to that of all nations in Africa (1.427 billion)."[13] While the United States population is the third largest country on earth, according to the Brookings Institute, between

2000 and 2019, "the white population share declined nearly nine points, to 60.1 percent." Also, in 2019, "for the first time, more than half of the nation's population under age 16 identified as" nonwhite.[14] According to the United Nations (UN), "sixty-one percent of the global population lives in Asia (4.7 billion), 17 percent in Africa (1.3 billion), 10 percent in Europe (750 million)," and only "5 percent in Northern America (370 million)." In addition to these current trends, the UN estimates that between now and 2050, "more than half of global growth" is "expected to occur in Africa." By 2050, the "population of sub-Saharan Africa is projected to double."[15] Baldwin's assertion that the world has "never been white" remains undeniable. You girls are the first generation of our family to normalize living, for weeks at a time, as members of the nonwhite global racial majority. You both know that if the political climate in the nation of your birth ever reaches an untenable status, many places will be populated by Black and brown people. While being in the majority is nice, what is more important is that we are not the presumed suspects in these Black and brown spaces. You both know and have ready accessibility to a society where your humanity is daily affirmed, populated by Black people, and surrounded by blue water. While this situation does not exist for most Black people, and most of our people will never be able to enjoy repatriation status, for you and us, living in the country of birth remains a choice. As your adoring father, knowing that you can achieve greatness – like the many generations of ancestors before you, despite white racism, and that if white supremacy becomes too much to endure, you have a readily available escape valve into a humanity-affirming Black country – brings me both joy and solace. Know that I love you both with all my heart, that having you remains the greatest accomplishment of my life, and that I will always be here for you both. I love you more than you can fathom – Your dad.

Louis Lee Woods II, Ph.D. (Maya and Zora's dad).

Notes

1 https://zora.medium.com/malcolm-x-stood-up-for-black-women-when-few-others-would-68e8b2ea2747. (Accessed May 18, 2022).

2 https://www.law.georgetown.edu/news/research-confirms-that-black-girls-feel-the-sting-of-adultification-bias-identified-in-earlier-georgetown-law-study/ (Accessed August 1, 2022).

3 The Revised Statues of the State of Missouri, Revised and Digested by the Thirteenth General Assembly During the Session of 1844 and 1845, State Slavery Statues, Folder, 1844, Law Library of the Library of Congress, 30.

4 McLaurin, Melton A. *Celia: A Slave,* (Athens: University of Georgia Press, 1991).

5 https://www.goodreads.com/author/quotes/51016.John_Henrik_Clarke. (Accessed August 1, 2022).

6 *The 1619 Project: A New Origin Story,* Nikole Hannah-Jones et al. eds., (One World: New York, 2021): 35.

7 Baldwin, James. *I Am Not Your Negro,* (New York: Vintage Books, 2016): 47.

8 https://www.youtube.com/watch?v=6S7zGgL6Suw. (Accessed September, 28, 2019).

9 Wise, Tim. *White Like Me: Reflections on Race from a Privileged Son,* (New York: Soft Skull, 2011).

10 Baldwin, James. *The Cross of Redemption: Uncollected Writings,* Randall Kenan, et al. eds., (New York: Pantheon Books, 2010): 60.

11 https://nces.ed.gov/programs/digest/d13/tables/dt13_104.20.asp. (Accessed August 1, 2022).

12 Baldwin, James. *The Cross of Redemption: Uncollected Writings,* Randall Kenan, et al. eds., (New York: Pantheon Books, 2010): 129.

13 https://www.pewresearch.org/fact-tank/2022/07/21/global-population-projected-to-exceed-8-billion-in-2022-half-live-in-just-seven-countries/. (Accessed August 1, 2022).

14 https://www.brookings.edu/research/new-census-data-shows-the-nation-is-diversifying-even-faster-than-predicted/. (Accessed August 1, 2022).

15 https://www.un.org/en/global-issues/population. (Accessed August 1, 2022).

13 Sororidad, resiliencia y cimarronaje: Breonna Taylor en el contexto hispano de la mujer negra

CRISTINA CABRAL

El año 2020 es significativo en la historia de la humanidad, pues marca el inicio de la primera pandemia global, debido al covid-19, que nos obligó a cumplir con una larga cuarentena de más de un año de confinamiento con estrictas medidas de seguridad sanitaria en todo el planeta, muchas de las cuales aún se encuentran en vigencia. Mientras estábamos encerrados en nuestras casas, atemorizados ante el avance de un virus mortal y descono-cido, tuvimos la oportunidad de ver múltiples escenas de solidaridad y apoyo hacia las víctimas de la epidemia y hacia los arriesgados trabajadores quienes expusieron sus vidas en cumplimiento de distintas labores comunitarias. Fue el inicio de la generalización de la vida virtual y remota como forma de tra-bajo y relacionamiento social. Llamo a este periodo "etapa de romantización de la pandemia", pues estuvo caracterizado por la emergencia de artistas que actuaban al aire libre, en forma voluntaria y gratuita, o desde los balcones de sus casas para todo quien quisiera disfrutar; periodo donde la presencia de cisnes que navegaban con elegancia en las tranquilas y cristalinas aguas de los canales de Venecia parecían pura fantasía. Ante tantas imágenes televisivas de animales que deambulaban libremente por las ciudades, algunos casi creímos que se trataba de un metafórico regreso al paraíso terrenal. Así, una parte del mundo, un grupo social, mayormente intelectual, liberal y europeo, proyect-aba el inicio de la pandemia.

Sin embargo, en la otra orilla del Atlántico, ese mismo año, pero en otro grupo social, ocurría un hecho muy alejado de las idílicas imágenes europeas. En los Estados Unidos las imágenes televisivas daban alerta del abuso y bru-talidad policial ante el asesinato de un hombre negro a sangre fría, frente a las cámaras, que capturaron la mirada desafiante de su homicida blanco, como en los viejos tiempos. Este acontecimiento causó gran impacto a nivel nacional y potenció la reactivación e internacionalización del movimiento *Black Lives Matter*[1]. Las imágenes del asesinato de George Floyd, ocurrido el 25 de mayo del 2020, que mostraban al hombre asfixiado bajo la pierna de un policía en Minneapolis, darán la vuelta al mundo recordándonos, una vez más, sobre el racismo sistemático y la violencia institucionalizada hacia la población afrodescendiente presente en los Estados Unidos. El asesinato de Floyd detonó un estallido de protestas sociales que se originaron en los Estados Unidos y se expandieron hacia el resto del mundo; bajo el lema *Black Lives Matter* millones de personas salieron a las calles a denunciar y protestar contra las condiciones de marginalidad y abuso en las cuales, la mayor parte de los afrodescendientes vive en los Estados Unidos, Europa y el resto del mundo.

Aprendimos a vivir en una realidad donde la eficacia de los medios de comunicación masiva se determina con base en el impacto que provoca una noticia en la audiencia, y este impacto depende, en gran medida, de las imágenes y videos que acompañan a la noticia. Cuanto más impactantes sean las imágenes obtenidas mayor será la cobertura de los medios y el interés de la audiencia. Desafortunadamente, muchos casos de abusos y delitos cometidos no cuentan con un video que los respalde; por lo que, no son tan atractivos para los medios y esto conduce, finalmente, a que la noticia se desvanezca en pocos días o no trascienda al nivel que debería. Esto sucedió en el caso del asesinato de Breonna Taylor, ocurrido en marzo del 2020, dos meses antes al de Floyd. Breonna era una joven afroamericana de veintiséis años, que trabajaba como paramédica en el hospital de la ciudad y fue asesinada en su apartamento tras la súbita interrupción de la policía a medianoche sin anunciar su presencia. La ausencia de un video policial que reporte el trágico suceso determinó, en parte, la ausencia de una amplia cobertura e información por parte de los medios; así como, la tardanza en el enjuiciamiento y, finalmente, la acusación oficial de solo uno de los policías. El hecho de que el abogado de la familia de la víctima demostrase que se habían cometido varios errores de procedimiento y que Breonna no fuera la persona buscada, sirvió como base para la compensación económica con la cual normalmente se resuelven los casos de abuso policial en los Estados Unidos y que todos los contribuyentes del estado pagan. Pese a la ausencia de un video, el reporte no oficial de los hechos sucedidos fue muy elocuente y nos expuso a otra mujer afroamericana víctima indefensa de un sistema racista.

El caso de Breonna Taylor brinda una visión extrema del estado de vulnerabilidad, marginalidad, omisión e invisibilidad en el que se encuentra la mujer negra en el contexto político, social y étnico de los Estados Unidos en el siglo XXI. Debemos tener en cuenta que hechos similares ocurren a diario en distintos países, en muchos de los cuales, ni siquiera llegan a ser noticia, puesto que solo se reportan como otro número para una víctima perdida en un archivo, el cual, a muchos no les importará. Serán los familiares de esas víctimas, sus madres organizadas, quienes inicien el arduo camino de búsqueda de sus hijos e hijas y el esclarecimiento de su desaparición. El fundamento de este capítulo es asumir el caso de Breonna como otro ejemplo de la violencia que enfrenta la mujer negra, latina, indígena o mestiza en nuestras sociedades. Estas acciones están siendo tácitamente legitimadas por la sociedad y, dada su frecuencia, se tiende a la normalización de una conducta agresiva por parte de cierto grupo hacia determinados sujetos a los cuales, ya no se los percibe como víctimas sino como merecedores de la agresión.

La situación de vulnerabilidad y violencia enfrentada por la mujer negra es histórica, ha ocurrido desde su llegada al continente como mercancía y continúa en la actualidad en todo el continente y el resto del mundo. Histórica es también, su resistencia ante la adversidad y resiliencia, lo cual le permitió desarrollar estrategias creativas de sobrevivencia, protección y desarrollo de sí misma, su familia y su comunidad. Junto a los desafíos históricos abordados en varios estudios sobre la diáspora africana en las Américas, el siglo XXI presenta nuevos desafíos a la mujer que se agudizan durante el periodo de pandemia y pospandemia. Entre estos desafíos, se señala mayor incidencia en los casos de covid-19 y/o sus variantes, aumento del número de víctimas por brutalidad policial, desplazamientos[2], feminicidios[3] y abuso doméstico, aumento del número de individuos diagnosticados con trastornos de atención hiperactiva, bipolaridad y enfermedades mentales que van desde la depresión hasta situaciones extremas que pueden culminar en el suicidio. Muchos de estos casos no son de origen genético sino social, pues surgen y se desarrollan en determinados ambientes sociales. Las estadísticas de todos los países indican que las mal llamadas "minorías" sufren el mayor impacto en todos los problemas anteriormente mencionados, siendo las mujeres y los niños los más vulnerables del grupo. Este artículo destaca algunos de los desafíos que enfrenta la mujer afrodescendiente en la cultura occidental contemporánea de las Américas y presenta un reporte general de diversas formas de asociación y organización de dichas mujeres para enfrentar y superar los nuevos desafíos.

Sororidad y cimarronaje

Sororidad y cimarronaje son términos que sintetizan la ruta transitada por las mujeres afrodescendientes en todo el mundo; por razones de espacio, este capítulo selecciona ejemplos de algunos países en Latinoamérica.

El economista norteamericano Ragnar Nurkse acuño el término "círculo vicioso de la pobreza" para referirse a la constelación de fuerzas que actúan en cadena dificultando o impidiendo el desarrollo de los países más pobres. En la década de los 70 varios organismos internacionales, como la Organización de Estados Americanos[4], y no gubernamentales comenzaron a hablar del "círculo de la pobreza" donde quedan atrapados millones de sujetos víctimas del capitalismo y sus políticas. Todo esto llevó a considerar que otras opciones políticas, tales como el socialismo y demás tendencias izquierdistas, tendrían el potencial de liberar a los sujetos empobrecidos y brindarles una vida más digna e igualitaria con el resto de la sociedad. En forma simple y esquemática el "círculo de la pobreza" se inicia con un sujeto empobrecido, cuya situación lo conduce a tener una baja calidad de salud y educación, lo cual resulta en la obtención de un trabajo precario con un nivel de ingresos bajos que lo hace permanecer inevitablemente en su situación inicial de pobreza. Este diagrama socioeconómico no admite movilidad estructural ascendente para los sujetos, sino que los mantiene atrapados en una estructura social fija a pesar de todo esfuerzo laboral que se intente.

A pesar de los cambios políticos ocurridos en el continente americano durante los siglos XX-XXI y los distintos gobiernos surgidos de tipo liberal o conservador, pasando por dictaduras militares y populismos, en referencia a la mujer afrodescendiente se constata que su situación social permanece básicamente siendo marginal, aunque existan ciertos avances personales, pero no colectivos. Pongamos como ejemplo a Uruguay, considerado uno de los países más estables en términos económicos, políticos y sociales del continente con base en su índice de producto bruto per cápita y variables sociopolítico-culturales que lo definen como una democracia de tendencia liberal que garantiza los derechos humanos de sus habitantes. Un informe del 2011 del Fondo de Población de las Naciones Unidas respecto a la población afrouruguaya indica: "La pobreza entre la población afrodescendiente se eleva a casi el 40 % más del doble que en el resto de población"[5] (2). El informe aduce una acumulación histórica de la inequidad que se refleja en la ubicación desfavorable de la población afrodescendiente en la distribución del ingreso en los hogares como consecuencia de una discriminación múltiple. Nótese la situación de la mujer afrodescendiente:

> La combinación de la condición de ascendencia afro o negra junto con otros atributos hace que ciertos grupos de población presenten una situación más comprometida en términos de bienestar. Es el caso de personas afro o negras, que además son mujeres y jóvenes frente al desempleo: la tasa de desempleo para personas con esta triple combinación de atributos –afro, mujer y joven– es once veces superior a los varones no afro de 30 y más años de edad (25,4% versus 2,3%, año 2010). (3)

Los datos estadísticos mencionados sustentan algunas de las observaciones realizadas por Marvin Lewis en su estudio del año 2003 sobre la literatura afrouruguaya[6] donde el crítico señala que gran porcentaje de los afrouruguayos están internamente colonizados, que no se perciben como sujetos subalternos y están en busca de ser un componente integral del resto de la sociedad. Sin embargo, destaca Lewis, este proceso de integración social ha sido enlentecido a través de los años debido a la discriminación existente contra los afrodescendientes; y concluye que la marginalización de los afrouruguayos y el alcance de su condición marginal es resultado del prejuicio racial y la estratificación social del país (8).

Elegimos a Uruguay como punto de partida intentando situar a la mujer afrodescendiente en el mejor escenario posible; sin embargo, se constata que su situación permanece siendo la peor en la estructura social. Estas cifras del informe son más drásticas en otros países latinoamericanos. Con base en lo anterior, debemos abordar el tema de la mujer afrodescendiente ponderando otras variables que trascienden las diversas estructuras políticas existentes. Para la mujer afrodescendiente y su comunidad, el "círculo de la pobreza" no es el inicio de su rueda social atrapante sino el resultado de una estructura racista y discriminatoria sistemática vigente en las sociedades americanas que la sitúa en el escalafón más bajo de la estructura social; por ende, la mantiene en una situación marginal y de extrema vulnerabilidad respecto al resto de la sociedad. O sea, el racismo y la discriminación son las primeras barreras impuestas a la población afro en general con la cual inicia su círculo de pobreza. Pese a toda posible buena intención, los gobiernos americanos capitalistas o socialistas, no lograrán resolver la histórica situación marginal en la que permanece sumergida la mayor parte de la población afro hasta no eliminar el racismo sistemático y la discriminación presente en sus sociedades. Leyes y acciones afirmativas promovidas en algunos países no lograron desarticular una estructura mental establecida durante el colonialismo, y que aún continúa vigente, que discrimina en términos de género y etnia. Racismo y patriarcado es la herencia de toda mujer afrodescendiente; por ello, ya cansadas del abuso y comprometidas en la sobrevivencia de su familia, comunidad y en su propia autoestima, la mujer afro comenzó a crear su ruta de escape hacia una vida mejor en forma individual o en asociación con otras mujeres. Este capítulo brinda homenaje a todas las cimarronas dispersas en la historia y en el mundo por su valor, compromiso y enseñanzas; a ellas les debemos nuestra cuota de libertad y dignidad alcanzada; por ellas, seguimos resistiendo y construyendo. Entre muchas otras y desde los Estados Unidos, recordamos a Harriet Tubman, libertadora de esclavizados; a Rosa Parks, que tuvo la valentía de decir "basta" y provocar el mayor boicot de ómnibus en

Montgomery que antecedió al movimiento por los derechos humanos; a Alicia Garza, Patrisse Cullors y Opal Tometi, creadoras de Black Lives Matter, movimiento antirracista con mayor repercusión en el mundo. La lista de activistas es infinita, las hubo y las hay alrededor del mundo, no poseemos un listado completo de nuestras hermanas en lucha, sea individual o colectiva, porque muchas veces ellas necesitan proteger su identidad por motivos de seguridad y otras veces, su labor es invisibilizada por el poder político. Este capítulo es un reporte breve y general de algunas de las estrategias desarrolladas por la mujer afro en Latinoamérica destinadas a enfrentar y resolver situaciones cotidianas.

Resistencia y resiliencia

En el prefacio del libro sobre literatura afrouruguaya, Lewis señala que su estudio se centra en la representación literaria y la resistencia desarrollada en la cultura afrouruguaya. En cuanto a los aspectos de resistencia el crítico clarifica: "resistance to total domination by the majority Eurocentric culture through popular expression associated with the African heritage" (7) ["Resistencia a la dominación total de la cultura mayoritaria eurocéntrica a través de la expresión popular asociada con la herencia africana"]. Como ejemplo de resistencia cultural llevada a cabo por la mujer afro en Uruguay se menciona la labor desempeñada por el grupo Afrogama.

En el año 1995, en Montevideo (Uruguay) surge Afrogama, un grupo de mujeres que, mediante el arte, buscan la reapropiación y resignificación de la cultura afrouruguaya para generar cambios tendientes a la equidad etno-racial y de género. Afrogama procura ajustar las asimetrías sociales y desarrollar una educación popular. Son mujeres afrodescendientes transmisoras y difusoras de la cultura afrouruguaya que han sido/son activistas en diversas organizaciones sociales, políticas y/o feministas y que resolvieron reunirse en un grupo con características propias con una mirada integradora hacia el aporte masculino y la diversidad cultural de sus integrantes. A nivel artístico, el grupo se especializa en la performática coral, plástica corporal, percusión de instrumentos y el teatro. Su género musical fundamental es el *Candombe* sumando otros ritmos de raíz africana; su vestuario y danza están vinculados a las deidades africanas de los *Orixas*. Bajo la dirección de Chabela Ramírez, Afrogama pretende abarcar la dimensión humana de las expresiones artísticas proyectadas hacia la comprensión de la cosmovisión africana y plural. Regularmente el grupo participa en encuentros culturales, seminarios y espectáculos; así como también, en convocatorias de protestas sociales y políticas renovando su compromiso con el colectivo afro, el feminismo, la lucha antirracista, antisexista y anticlasista como admite su directora. Una de las carencias fundamentales que enfrenta la mujer afrouruguaya es la ausencia de vivienda propia, situación que se agrava ante la realidad de ser madre soltera de bajos recursos y jefa de hogar. Procurando una solución a este problema social crónico, la organización Mundo Afro, a través de su Grupo de Apoyo a la Mujer Afro (GAMA), crea, en el año 2005, el programa de viviendas cooperativas UFAMA (Unidad Familiar Mundo Afro) que será considerado como la primera acción afirmativa del Estado uruguayo hacia el colectivo afro. Varias de las mujeres de Afrogama tuvieron una participación directa en todo el programa y algunas de ellas se beneficiaron a cambio de horas de trabajo en la construcción del edificio cooperativo.[7]

Las nociones de lugar y desplazamiento son centrales en el discurso poscolonial[8] . En las sociedades poscoloniales el "lugar" no alude simplemente al territorio, sino a una compleja interacción de lenguaje, historia y medioambiente; alude a un espacio cultural donde se forja la identidad de un grupo. Este concepto de "lugar" destaca la importante labor desarrollada por las Tejedoras de Mampuján y justifica su inclusión en este estudio. Las Tejedoras de Mampuján son un ejemplo de resistencia, sanación y resiliencia de la mujer campesina afro tras el impacto devastador del conflicto armado en Colombia. En el año 2000, un grupo de paramilitares aterrorizó a la población de Mampuján, una zona rural de la costa caribeña colombiana, asesinando campesinos después de acusarlos de ser guerrilleros, y obligando al resto de la población a abandonar el territorio. Estos mismos paramilitares habían masacrado a más de un centenar de personas, por lo que se consideró la región como una "ruta de la muerte". Las sobrevivientes de la masacre de Mampuján huyeron dejando atrás sus pertenencias, y llevaron con ellas sus recuerdos y el luto por sus seres queridos asesinados. Tras el desplazamiento forzado y como forma de sobrevivencia física y emocional, estas mujeres transformaron su dolor en arte creando tapices con figuras de tela sobre personas, lugares, situaciones y eventos de su comunidad; en otras palabras, a través de los tapices recrearon el "lugar" de pertenencia del grupo. Esta idea de perpetuar la memoria de su comunidad en los tapices fue imitada por otras comunidades de mujeres desplazadas. Inicialmente los tapices sirvieron para comunicar la dolorosa experiencia, pero rápidamente se convirtieron en una herramienta para el manejo del duelo, la integración comunitaria, la producción cultural e incluso la recuperación económica del grupo a través de la creación de la Fundación ASVIDAS[9]. Con el apoyo de las Naciones Unidas, las tejedoras han visitado numerosas zonas donde hubo masacres en Colombia, ofreciendo talleres grupales para que las familias hablen de su dolor y elaboren su experiencia colectiva por medio de la manufactura de tapices. Las Tejedoras de Mampuján han recibido muchos reconocimientos, como el Premio Nacional de Paz en 2015. Varias organizaciones, internacionales y gubernamentales, han organizado exposiciones de los tapices las cuales tienen como objetivo la visibilización y divulgación del trabajo artesanal como elemento clave dentro de la memoria del conflicto.

Cultura y empoderamiento

Tras siglos de sometimiento físico y emocional y como resultado de ello, uno de los problemas fundamentales enfrentado por multitud de mujeres en el mundo es la baja "autoestima". Los factores que generan la autoestima de una persona son multidimensionales y su análisis excede el propósito de este capítulo. Cuando la baja autoestima se presenta en la mujer afro puede hablarse de una situación doblemente complicada, en cuanto que, dicha mujer posee la convicción de pertenencia a un grupo asumido como "inferior" y, al mismo tiempo, reconoce su ubicación marginal o subalterna dentro del grupo. O sea, esta mujer queda emocionalmente atrapada entre las barreras del racismo y el patriarcado asumiéndose, consciente o inconscientemente, culpable de una situación que no puede controlar; siendo, sin embargo, víctima de una doble discriminación étnica y de género actuando en conjunto. Por ello, numerosas organizaciones de mujeres afro e indígenas en todo el continente se han agrupado con el propósito de aumentar la autoestima y empoderar a las mujeres en sus comunidades. Al respecto y entre varias, mencionamos al Centro Afroboliviano para el Desarrollo Integral y Comunitario y al grupo afrocolombiano Proceso de Comunidades Negras (PCN).

La situación de las mujeres indígenas y afrodescendientes en Bolivia ha estado marcada por altos niveles de pobreza, exclusión y discriminación en los diferentes espacios de la vida cotidiana. En la actualidad, las comunidades afrobolivianas se localizan en distintas regiones del país; sin embargo, es en la región de Los Yungas, en el departamento de La Paz, donde se encuentra su mayor concentración. Los Yungas es considerada una de las zonas más hostiles del continente para habitar debido a su ubicación en una zona de difícil y peligroso acceso rodeada de la jungla y la montaña. En la vida cotidiana de los/as afrobolivianos/as se presentan elementos sincréticos de la cultura afro y la aymara reflejada en su vestimenta y en la mezcla de creencias ancestrales de origen africano y andino. Las mujeres afrobolivianas han sido marcadas con una serie de prejuicios discriminatorios: "Parecemos extranjeras en nuestra propia tierra" afirma una representante de la comunidad de Los Yungas. Estas mujeres estuvieron presentes en la lucha por incorporar los derechos del pueblo afrodescendiente en la Nueva Constitución Política del Estado; reflexionan y trabajan de manera organizada, sobre la situación de subordinación que viven y en la conquista de sus derechos como mujeres afrobolivianas. Desde el año 2012, el Centro Afroboliviano para el Desarrollo Integral y Comunitario y el Programa ComVoMujer de la cooperación alemana coordinan acciones a partir de un plan de trabajo con el objetivo de fortalecer y empoderar a las mujeres de la zona. De allí surge la creación de un curso de liderazgo sobre violencia política hacia las mujeres, como un proceso formativo dirigido a lideresas afrobolivianas para potenciar sus capacidades en la prevención y erradicación de todo tipo de violencia por razones de género y etnia.

En Colombia, el conflicto armado sostenido en el país durante décadas es uno de los capítulos más trágicos en la historia de los pueblos latinoamericanos y sus consecuencias sociales, políticas, psicológicas y económicas adquieren dimensiones infinitas. Una doble consecuencia del conflicto es, por un lado, el desplazamiento de campesinos obligados a abandonar sus tierras y pertenencias; por otro lado, su reubicación en zonas urbanas marginales donde viven en estado de pauperización total o relativa. Ante esta situación, un número de lideresas afro han surgido en las zonas de conflicto con la tarea de enfrentar la violencia y reubicar a su comunidad en zonas seguras. Estas mujeres han sufrido amenazas de muerte por parte de los grupos criminales que defienden los intereses de las corporaciones beneficiarias de las tierras despobladas, los grupos paramilitares, el ejército nacional y el narcotráfico. Danelly Estupiñán es una lideresa activista en la zona del Pacífico colombiano; ella ha sido sometida a un seguimiento o vigilancia constante, la han fotografiado y han asaltado su casa, en una aparente represalia por su trabajo sobre los derechos humanos, en el que defiende a las comunidades negras de Buenaventura, el puerto más grande del Pacífico colombiano. Debido al incesante acoso de sus oponentes, Estupiñán decidió huir del país al enterarse de la existencia de un plan para matarla. Las mujeres afrodescendientes como Estupiñán, luego de haber perdido a padres, esposos e hijos durante años de derramamiento de sangre, están asumiendo valientemente roles activos en la defensa de sus comunidades ancestrales. No obstante, el enfrentar a empresas y organizaciones criminales que buscan imponer proyectos de desarrollo, extracciones mineras y operaciones de narcotráfico en sus territorios las ha puesto en peligro constante.[10] "La emergencia sanitaria causada por el covid-19 acentuó las existentes condiciones de discriminación y violencia que por generaciones han vivido las comunidades negras, afrocolombianas, raizales y palenqueras del país". Esta fue una de las principales conclusiones del seminario organizado en el año 2020, por la Jurisdicción Especial para la Paz y la Comisión de la Verdad[11] donde se insistió en la urgencia de tomar medidas que promovieran la paz territorial en medio de la pandemia. Mariposas de Alas Nuevas Construyendo Futuro es una red colectiva de mujeres, en Buenaventura, que ponen en riesgo sus propias vidas para ayudar a las víctimas de la violencia de género. "Construir la paz en medio del conflicto requiere que las mujeres asuman prácticas de autoprotección como parte de combatir la violencia y desarraigar las causas de la violencia", señala Bibiana Penaranda y David Sulewski en el año 2018.[12]

Defensa y cimarronaje

Desde su arribo al continente americano la mujer africana y su descendencia han tenido un largo y activo protagonismo en las luchas por la libertad. Durante el colonialismo, la mujer esclavizada se hizo cimarrona (esclava fugitiva) huyendo a zonas remotas y creando los llamados "palenques", poblados de esclavos que huían de las plantaciones y se autoproclamaban libres. En el palenque la cimarrona se convertiría en una campesina, que aseguraba las provisiones para la comunidad; en sanadora, encargada de la salud física y espiritual del grupo; o en soldado que tomaba las armas para asegurar la defensa del palenque. Mientras unas mujeres huían hacia la libertad, otras mayores o imposibilitadas se quedaban en la plantación facilitando la huida de otros esclavos. Sabemos también que muchas mujeres esclavizadas lucharon y apoyaron a los ejércitos nacionales durante las guerras de independencia contra los colonizadores europeos. Previo a la independencia de las colonias, los cimarrones habían creado palenques a lo largo del continente, de norte a sur; algunos de ellos perduraron muchos años antes de ser descubiertos[13], y otros existen hasta el día de hoy[14]. Muchas veces se registraron encuentros entre cimarrones e indígenas quienes también luchaban por su libertad y la recuperación de sus territorios. De estos encuentros se generaron alianzas de paz y defensa entre ambas comunidades donde el intercambio de bienes y mujeres era una forma común de cerrar un trato, siendo este un capítulo de la historia aún poco investigado.

El siglo XXI vuelve a encontrar a las mujeres afro e indígenas en situación de extrema vulnerabilidad y peligro, indefensas ante las autoridades y responsables por su propia seguridad y la de su familia. En mayo del año 2022, los medios de comunicación informan que un grupo de campesinas indígenas y afrodescendientes decidieron unirse y hacerse cargo de la defensa de sus tierras y poblados en Oteapan, estado de Veracruz (México). Veracruz es un estado con una alta presencia indígena y afromexicana; ante la adversidad y la indiferencia e ineficacia de las autoridades gubernamentales, las mujeres mayores de la comunidad se organizaron y tomaron acción directa en la defensa de sus poblados. Son campesinas acostumbradas a utilizar el machete como herramienta de trabajo, el cual por la noche se convierte en arma de defensa de su poblado; así surgen las "macheteras de Oteapan". El periódico *Cambio Digital*, en su publicación del 18 de mayo, informa que con "machetes y palos en mano, docenas de mujeres de todas las edades, recorren cada noche las calles de sus barrios y colonias en Oteapan. Sus ojos escudriñan cada rincón, especialmente donde el alumbrado público está ausente, tan ausente como los encargados de la seguridad del pueblo". Transformadas en guardias vecinales o grupos de autodefensa, mujeres de varias localidades en la zona decidieron protegerse de los robos de motos, vehículos, casas, asaltos y el cobro de sobornos a los negocios locales. Estas mujeres, con machete y una linterna en mano, son pioneras en hacer una intervención directa sobre el problema de violencia e inestabilidad presente en Oteapan y el resto de México. Luego, se les sumaron algunos hombres de la comunidad vigilando las calles en motocicletas y manteniéndose en contacto con las macheteras a través de WhatsApp. La vigilancia nocturna del barrio no se propone matar a los delincuentes, pero en caso de ser necesario, serían capaces de cortar una mano o un pie, anuncia una machetera quien prefiere permanecer anónima. Casos similares de mujeres organizadas como autodefensa de sus comunidades han surgido en otras zonas de México, así como, en varios países de notoria presencia indígena y africana en América Central y del Sur.

Finalmente, nos referimos en este informe a Brasil, país que posee el número más alto de población afrodescendiente en el mundo después de Nigeria. A pesar de, o tal vez, debido a esta particularidad numérica, la situación general de las comunidades afrobrasileñas ha sido históricamente de pobreza, discriminación y marginalidad. Brasil y los Estados Unidos comparten ciertas similitudes, en cuanto a los aspectos históricos, sociales y políticos referidos a las comunidades afro. Ambos países se desarrollaron a partir de una economía agraria de plantaciones y latifundios, sustentada por abundante mano de obra africana esclavizada. Ambos países mantuvieron relaciones diplomáticas con Sudáfrica durante el *Apartheid*, ignorando el boicot impuesto por la Organización de las Naciones Unidas y el resto del mundo. Tras obtener la independencia de sus conquistadores a ninguno de los nuevos gobiernos, brasileño y estadounidense, les interesó integrar en forma equitativa la población afro al resto de la sociedad; por el contrario, ambos estados a través de leyes y narrativas discursivas aseguraron el mantenimiento de una clara separación entre los grupos étnicos legitimando la practica social y política de otorgar privilegios a unos y castigos a otros. En la actualidad, la población afrobrasileña y afroamericana enfrentan obstáculos similares en sus sociedades, tales como, el acoso y persecución por parte de grupos neonazis, la existencia de un sistema judicial y carcelario discriminatorios y la brutalidad policial, entre otros.

Desde los años 1990 las luchas y protestas de las organizaciones afrobrasileñas cuestionan la veracidad de su "Democracia Racial" denunciando el racismo sistémico presente en el país y el abuso policial sobre sus comunidades ignorado por las autoridades. El movimiento Black Lives Matter en Brasil es el más grande en Latinoamérica y se centra en la denuncia de los llamados "homicidios por racismo". Existe un número elevado de organizaciones e instituciones afro en Brasil con distintas características políticas, religiosas, y socioculturales. Una institución pionera en la lucha por los derechos humanos de las mujeres afrobrasileñas es Geledes[15], creada en 1988 por la activista Dra. Sueli Carneiro. Geledes es una institución política no gubernamental de mujeres que tiene la misión de luchar contra el racismo y el sexismo, la validación y el empoderamiento de la mujer afro en particular y su comunidad en general. Esta institución ha participado en intervenciones políticas, a nivel nacional e internacional, denunciando el racismo existente en la sociedad brasileña y contribuyendo en el diseño de políticas públicas para que el lema de "oportunidades para todos" se realice. Geledes ha sido un referente para muchas organizaciones de mujeres afro en todo el continente que centran su activismo en la esfera política manteniendo una agenda feminista. La junta directiva de la institución está compuesta exclusivamente por mujeres afro, mientras que los equipos de trabajo están integrados por hombres y mujeres de diversas etnias. Su trabajo se centra en el área de los derechos humanos, educación, comunicación, salud y entrenamiento vocacional de la mujer afrobrasileña.

Conclusiones

Las circunstancias que rodearon el asesinato de Breonna Taylor motiva la reflexión crítica sobre el estado de vulnerabilidad en que se encuentra la mujer afrodescendiente en los Estados Unidos. Hechos y circunstancias similares continúan siendo parte de la experiencia cotidiana en la vida de mujeres afro en todo el continente americano. La tesis sostenida en este capítulo es que el caso de Taylor debe ser considerado como otro ejemplo en el vasto espectro de abusos y arbitrariedades históricamente enfrentados por la mujer afro en el mundo. Frente a la adversidad, el estudio destaca algunas de las formas de organización creadas por la mujer afrolatinoamericana con la intención de enfrentar y resolver en forma colectiva los desafíos inmediatos presentes en sus comunidades. Fueron mencionados como objetivos logrados la resignificación, reafirmación y reapropiación de la cultura afro a través del arte junto a la construcción de viviendas para madres solteras; la ayuda profesional para recuperar la autoestima de la mujer; la creación artesanal de tapices que cuentan la historia del "lugar" arrebatado como forma de sanación espiritual y de obtener cierto beneficio económico; el entrenamiento político de futuras lideresas en las zonas de conflicto y la vigilancia armada de las comunidades en riesgo. Todas estas alternativas tienen como base común la urgencia por controlar y eliminar la violencia cometida contra las comunidades afro en general y sobre la mujer afro e indígena en particular; urgencia en el empoderamiento de la mujer afrodescendiente y protección contra el abuso doméstico, laboral y policial en los distintos países.

En el año 2004, George Reid Andrews en su libro de historia afrolatinoamericana advertía sobre los nuevos desafíos que las comunidades afro iban a enfrentar en el siglo XXI como consecuencia de las políticas capitalistas neoliberales adoptadas durante el periodo de 1980 y 1990 en la gran mayoría de los países. La importancia del impacto dependería del segmento de población afro considerado. Por ejemplo, los campesinos y pequeños comerciantes llevarían la peor parte al enfrentarse a la pérdida de sus tierras y productos frente a la competencia impuesta por grandes compañías y corporaciones. Esto los dejaría con la única alternativa de convertirse en trabajadores no calificados con bajos salarios en dichas compañías. Andrews recuerda que esta situación sucedió en las plantaciones de azúcar en el Nordeste de Brasil y en el valle del Cauca en Colombia. En estos casos, los campesinos quedaron sin tierras, y fueron desplazados a zonas marginales donde el hambre, la malnutrición y el alcoholismo alcanzan dimensiones epidémicas. Al mismo tiempo, en la costa del Pacífico colombiano y en la provincia de Esmeraldas en Ecuador, el auge de la minería intensiva y la industria forestal se expandieron hacia las tierras que habían sido el sustento de familias afro durante generaciones. Hombres blancos de negocios con acceso a capital y crédito construyeron tiendas y centros comerciales en la zona que pronto desplazaron a sus competidores locales afro.[16] La situación descripta por Andrews continúa sucediendo intensamente en todo el continente americano; en los Estados Unidos, por ejemplo, varias zonas en las ciudades han sido gentrificadas, o sea, la población local de mayoría afro y pobre es desplazada hacia la periferia y reemplazada por otra población de alto poder adquisitivo que en su mayoría es caucásica. Los estudios sobre la pospandemia revelan que los actuales desafíos económicos y sanitarios globales afectan con mayor incidencia negativa a los sujetos más vulnerables, que son las mujeres afro/indígenas y su descendencia. El siglo XXI nos enfrenta a nuevos desafíos a nivel mundial, entre otros mencionamos: el aumento de enfermedades mentales entre los jóvenes, aumento en la tenencia de armas automáticas en manos de civiles, incidencia del cambio climático que genera nuevas emigraciones internas y hacia otros países, aumento en las crisis económica y política, desaparición de empleos considerados obsoletos ante el desarrollo tecnológico. Por lo cual, se prevé en todos los países el surgimiento de más organizaciones políticas e independientes con nuevas ideas y formas de organizarse en orden de asegurar la supervivencia del grupo y del planeta. A nivel social y político es necesaria la denuncia de los abusos contra los derechos humanos. A nivel académico, es urgente la expansión del canon en los estudios latinoamericanos que combatan la invisibilización sobre la presencia y contribución de las "minorías" en la construcción y desarrollo de las naciones americanas. La sabiduría y experiencia de las mujeres afro e indígenas acumuladas y transmitidas durante generaciones es fundamental para el logro del bienestar común. Por lo tanto, la eliminación del racismo y todo tipo de discriminaciones que garantice el acceso de todxs a los puestos de liderazgo es la única oportunidad de sobrevivencia para la humanidad tal cual la concebimos en el imaginario actual.

Notes

1 Black Lives Matter es un movimiento pro-justicia social creado en el año 2013 por tres mujeres afro: Alicia Garza, Patrisse Cullors y Opal Tometi. El movimiento surge como protesta ante la no condena de George Zimmerman acusado del asesinato del joven afroamericano Trayvon Martin en el 2012.
2 Los desplazamientos forzados en Colombia, considerados delitos de lesa humanidad, se han realizado mayormente en las comunidades campesinas, indígenas y afrodescendientes a causa del conflicto armado interno, la violencia de bandas criminales y el narcotráfico. Existen intereses económicos y políticos que presionan el desalojo de la población civil de sus tierras y territorios (Wikipedia "Desplazamiento forzado en Colombia").
3 Los datos de feminicidios en el 2020 en Brasil y Colombia, los países con mayor población afrodescendiente fueron de 1738 y 182 casos. En México fueron 948 casos. Publicado por *Statista Research Department* (2022).
4 La OEA fue creada en 1948 y actualmente reúne a 35 estados independientes de las Américas. Constituye el principal foro gubernamental político, jurídico y social del hemisferio. Sus pilares principales son la defensa de la democracia, los derechos humanos, la seguridad y el desarrollo.
5 Población y Política Públicas. Población Afro en Uruguay: ahora visibles, pero aún sin políticas. Fondo de Población de las Naciones Unidas, 2011.
6 Marvin A. Lewis, *Afro-Uruguayan Literature: Post-Colonial Perspectives,* Bucknell University Press, 2003.
7 Logros recientes incluyen la inauguración de la Red Afrodescendencia Resiliente para elaborar la estrategia de territorialización de la dimensión étnico-racial afro para el periodo 2020-2025.
8 Bill Ashcroft, Gareth Griffiths & Helen Tiffin, *The Post-Colonial Studies Reader* (New York: Routledge, 1995), 391.

9 La Fundacion ASVIDAS es una comunidad de mujeres afrodescendientes víctimas del conflicto armado en Mampuján (Colombia), creada con el fin de buscar la manera de expresar, relatar y documentar los hechos ocurridos a través de la realización de telares, de aquellas experiencias dolorosas producto del desplazamiento, para recordar sin deseos de venganza, realizar procesos de sanidad interior y elaboración de duelo que las conduzca al perdón, reconciliación, restauración del tejido social y construcción de paz.

10 Según un informe de la Organización de las Naciones Unidas, Colombia es el país más mortal del mundo para quienes defienden los derechos humanos. En el 2018, hubo 7,8 millones de personas internamente desplazadas en Colombia, más que en cualquier otro país. Muchas de las víctimas son líderes de comunidades indígenas y campesinas, pero las mujeres negras cada vez corren más peligro en las provincias occidentales donde se concentra la población afrodescendiente de Colombia.

11 Comisión de debate sobre "Alternativas de participación y coordinación de los pueblos negros, afrocolombianos, raizales y palenqueros en tiempos de aislamiento social: una construcción colectiva".

12 Penaranda, B. y D. J. Sulewski., 2018. "Las Mariposas de Buenaventura, Colombia: Sostienen la vida, construyen la paz". *Middle Atlantic Review of Latin American Studies*, 1(2), pp. 36–42.

13 Quilombo Dos Palmares fue un palenque creado en Brasil que duró casi noventa años resistiendo el ataque de los colonizadores portugueses.

14 San Basilio de Palenque, en Colombia.

15 Originariamente, Gelede, es un tipo de sociedad secreta femenina de naturaleza religiosa fundada en las antiguas sociedades "yorubas". Expresa el poder de la feminidad sobre la fertilidad de la tierra, la procreación y el bien de la comunidad (Portal Geledes, The Geledes Black Woman Institute).

16 El proyecto del gobierno colombiano de construir una vía de acceso entre el océano Pacífico y el mar del Caribe resultará en la creación de infraestructura que facilite la instalación de nuevas empresas en la región del Choco, dando como resultado la destrucción del comercio local y la agricultura de autosuficiencia desarrollada por familias afro.

14 Breonna Taylor: Reclaiming Hope, Joy, and Community in the Midst of Tragedy

Sabrina T. Cherry

The spring and summer of 2020 will remain one of my life's most unforgettable seasons. What many thought would be a short interruption of usual activities spiraled into a pandemic further exaggerated by racially charged murders, international protests, and a reckoning unlike any other I have witnessed. In this chapter, I describe my experiences of living and working as a Black woman in the Southeast during the height of the COVID-19 pandemic and after the killing of Breonna Taylor. More specially, I describe what it was like to reclaim hope, joy, and community in the midst of such a dire tragedy.

Autoethnography

Autoethnography invites authors and readers into an alternative way of defining and understanding lived experiences. Instead of the researcher remaining positioned as a removed or distant observer of circumstances, they become an acknowledged part of the situation or circumstance (Ellis et al. 273). Autoethnography enables the author to engage in equally personal and profound research, a process that requires that we dissolve the silos of statistics and engage in the inner work of seeing ourselves, processing our responses to life events, and telling our stories. Parallel to the experiences of the researcher or author, readers are invited to engage more deeply with the co-creator of the content in ways that may foster more intentional learning and action.

For many social scientists, autoethnography and many other categories of qualitative research are foreign and sometimes ostracized (Khankeh 635; Isaacs 4). Social scientists are often taught to be objective, distant, and observant rather than subjective, intimate, and engaged (Ngunjiri et al. E1). Therefore, the work of autoethnography requires a level of vulnerability. This vulnerability encompasses what is felt when working within a discipline, such as Public Health, where funders and researchers are only sometimes welcoming of nonconventional research methods while sharing one's intimate life details. Furthermore, it is this vulnerability I embrace in the writing and publication of this chapter.

Who Am I?

Autoethnography privileges the writer's voice, which does not exist without clarity of the writer's positioning. I am a first-generation college student from a small, rural town in South Carolina. I learned about higher education from my cousins, one, in particular, who often invited me to her college campus and allowed me to visit her during major celebrations. My high school choir director took me and a few of my classmates on a trip to Atlanta, where we toured the Atlanta University Center. A few years later, my cheerleading coach invited me to go back to Atlanta with her, and I visited the campus that became my undergraduate academic home: Morris Brown College.

While at Morris Brown, during my four years of undergraduate study, I learned about Black liberation, Pan-Africanism, the Society of Maat, and the Black Hebrew Israelites. Atlanta taught me about Black pride, excellence, and the importance of a quality education rooted in well-rounded, Black history – a history encompassing Black folks throughout the diaspora and not just within the United States.

Living in Atlanta and attending Morris Brown taught me things my tight-knit community in South Carolina knew but never directly articulated. I was reminded of the value of family, faith, connectivity, and achievement for the greater good of others. I took those lessons with me. I took those lesson gems to The Gambia, West Africa, where I served as a United States Peace Corps Volunteer. I took them to Las Vegas, Nevada, when I was hired as the University of Nevada Las Vegas's first Wellness Coordinator. As a young adult, I brought them back to the east coast as I resettled in Atlanta. More than a decade later, I brought those same lessons to North Carolina when I accepted my first full-time faculty position and a year later when I spent a semester in the United Kingdom as the Faculty Resident Director at Swansea University.

My experiences at home and abroad grounded me in community, including family, connection, and a strong sense of belonging. They also helped shape my perceptions of being Black while abroad and in America. They grounded my commitment to engage in meaningful work that benefits communities I most closely align with. These communities include – but are not limited to – communities with other Black folks, communities of women of color, communities of historically marginalized groups, and communities of intentional, engaged, and thoughtful allies. This commitment is the foundation for what and how I approach my career in Public Health.

Stories: More Than Statistics

At the time of this writing, I celebrate 22 years of working and volunteering in the field of Public Health. Although I now work in academia, it is a place I never thought I would be. My time as a graduate student watching research in action was some of my most formative professional experiences. Based on what I saw, all researchers were focused more on grant dollars than community citizens. It baffled me that someone could write so deeply about a community without spending significant time among its members. Often, the focus of this work involved people who looked like me.

Million-dollar grants and disengaged Principal Investigators (PIs) led me to shrug off academia until I met other researchers forming another way. I can count the number of scholars I have been mentored by who fall into the latter category on both hands. They are those who invested in the communities with whom they hoped to work. Those who considered hiring a program coordinator as equally essential as ensuring they traveled to the communities where the coordinator would work. Those who sought research projects for more than the trending topic were the scholars and mentors who led me back to academia. They showed me there were and remain other possibilities, particularly within the social sciences. Some of them empowered me to embrace that I could and wanted to tell stories. Consequently, one of my greatest joys is facilitating research that involves reading about, engaging with, and retelling the stories of others (Cherry 12; Cherry et al.).

Six years ago, I relocated. My current hometown is different. It reminds me of a healthy and needed balance between growing up in rural South Carolina and the fast-paced and thriving scene of Atlanta. We have beautiful beaches and a gorgeous waterfront. There are more restaurants than one can name, many parks, and walking trails. People are friendly and welcoming. Our university sits as one of the many pillars of the community. My new home lacks the diversity to which I have grown accustomed. The African American population is around 18% (U.S. Census 2020). When it comes to communities of other races and ethnicities, the population includes 7% Hispanic and close to 2% Asian, American Indian or Alaska Native, and Native Hawaiian or other Pacific Islander. Unlike where I grew up and unlike the place where I spent nearly a decade and a half of my life, my present community is where I resided during the COVID-19 pandemic and when the killing of Breonna Taylor took place (Grassroots Project 2022). It is here where I have wrestled with notions of home, connection, and belonging. Within this place and over two years, I became more intentional about reclaiming hope, fostering joy, and becoming rooted in the community.

COVID-19

I identify as a public health practitioner first and an academic second. With this professional identity in mind, the onset of COVID-19 caused great concern. When I heard the news, I was co-leading an alternative spring break trip to Atlanta for a few undergraduate students. My number one priority became making sure we remained safe and made it back to our campus. After we resettled, I began to follow the trends: what did we know, and what was yet to be determined?

As panic grew, I watched the number of cases across the globe swiftly rise. In the spring of 2020, the World Health Organization's (WHO 2020) dashboard indicated 91,700 COVID-19 cases in China, 873,800 in the United Kingdom, and 525,780 in Italy. Other countries took aggressive measures from the onset, including closing borders and limiting non-essential travel (Chen et al. 2020; Haug et al. 2020). And what of the United States? We dragged, delayed, ignored the trends, and blasphemed our public health experts (Vestal and Ollove 2020). I continued to monitor the statistics, particularly in cities with significant Black populations. As of October 2020, the number of people diagnosed had quickly grown, including in Fulton County, Georgia, which includes the metro city of Atlanta, with 31,000 cases; Harris County, Texas, which includes Houston: 159,000 cases; New York City: 500,000 cases; and New Orleans: 13,500 cases (CDC, 2020). From coast to coast, we witnessed the pandemic and its rapid spread among some of the most vulnerable populations.

Persistent Problem of Health Disparities within the United States

When People of Color (POC) die, others justify it (Dionne and Turkmen 2020; Logie 2020)! Early during the pandemic, public official commentators began to surface explaining why there were a disproportionate number of Covid-19-related deaths in Black and other POC communities. Reporters asserted that unhealthy diets, obesity, substandard living conditions, and crime-ridden neighborhoods were partly to blame. These rationalizations pointed to the same narrative: "It is your fault that you're dying!" Some courageous, honest, and informed experts who clarified these misconceptions spoke above the clamor despite the finger-pointing (Poteat et al. 2020; van Dorn 2020; Wright II and Merritt 2020; Yancy 2020). As much as one could cite obesity or diet, what of the unsafe working conditions, systemic predatory lending practices perpetuating poverty, inequitable job opportunities, and unequal pay (Singu et al. 2020)? What of the unseen, non-essential, yet essential workers not permitted to work from home? What of discrimination in health care and the number of uninsured and underinsured patients who were denied access to care? What of failing policies that continue to limit and restrict access to affordable care (Fortuna et al. 2020)? These questions seemed to be hanging in the ether, remaining unanswered as some attempted to understand the inequitable spread of the virus.

As the blaming continued, so did the dying. So did the crippling of communities and the sinkhole of poverty (Pereira and Oliveira 2020). So did the widening educational gap as we pivoted to remote learning (Hoofman and Secord 2021; Lancker and Parolin 2020), and so did the pressing need for expanded mental health care as parents tried to navigate coordinating childcare and school-related alternatives for children, ensuring that some semblance of learning was taking place while working outside the home and trying to remain safe (Rashid and Yadav 2020). As alarming infection rates within communities of color were broadcasted across multiple media outlets, very few addressed the underlying causes of these spikes, and even fewer seemed to be willing to do something to address them.

Social Injustice

Many of us were over the pandemic after just a few weeks. We were tired, we were concerned, we were weary, and we were grieving. At the onset of COVID-19, two deaths in my immediate family and several friends and family members were diagnosed with the disease within a short span of time. To further complicate the pandemic's reality, Breonna Taylor's killing (Grassroots Project 2022) became trending global news.

I recall following the headlines and my hesitation to read more while being unable to turn away from the horrific details. As more details were revealed, I felt my heart uttering, "Here we go, once again." Pictures of Breonna Taylor began to surface, as did information about her work and commitment to helping others. The more I learned, the more I thought, "This could have been me." In my home, on any given day, this could be me.

As has been the case on other occasions where suspected routine engagements with police officers turn fatal, protests erupted. While I processed the chain of events surrounding Breonna Taylor's murder and contemplated my placement within my relatively new community, I also struggled to resolve what it meant to be physically distant from loved ones during such dire civil unrest (Anderson 2021). Civically, I was challenged to engage while remaining cognizant of my health and vulnerability. It became a daily battle and weighed heavily on my heart and mind. In those moments, I reflected on the impact of stress and trauma on the body (Chinn et al. 2021). It became glaringly apparent that these exact exasperated conditions serve as the prelude to poor health outcomes for people who look like me (Felix et al. 2019).

I was reminded once again that living in my new city was different. If I were in a more familiar community, I could process my grief in a flurry of spaces with easily accessible like-minded people I knew and trusted. I would know where to go, what agencies to seek out, and how to engage. In my new city, I needed to figure out where to turn. I battled with being crippled with fear by staying in my home. I feared for my life when I did something as routine as going for a bike ride.

As I watched the United States and other parts of the world respond (Cheng et al. 2020; Haug et al. 2020), I still had to work. I was expected to be present for virtual meetings with my camera enabled. Instead of acknowledging the growing civil unrest within our country (Anderson 2021), many conversations centered on small talk about the weather and lighthearted discussion about visiting the beach for daily sand and sunshine. My heart ached as I slowly dismantled any expectations that those I worked with knew, cared for, or desired to engage in what was happening in my heart and head. Close relationships grew distant, and distant relationships became mere acquaintances at best and strangers in other instances. As I longed to heal my heart, respond to injustice, and be present with the organizations where I held membership, it became apparent that I needed to reevaluate the work and personal circles where I communed.

During the summer of 2020, I realized more than ever how much I value and hold close to the communities I am connected to – communities where I live, work, serve, and learn. It was painful to experience such crumbling pain while watching others appear grossly unbothered. Although I knew many of my colleagues and neighbors were dealing with their unique challenges, I found myself wondering repeatedly – do you see me? And what do you see when you see me? I grieved the phone call that never came and the email or text message asking about my well-being. Many whom I loved grew enormously silent, further confusing my mind while crushing my heart.

The Reclamation

By the end of June, I desperately needed some time away. As much as I knew I wanted to be careful and follow Public Health recommended guidelines related to physical distancing, I needed to see my family. I needed to be with those I love and care for and who loved me. I needed to be reminded of the joy, laughter, and celebration. As I drove to South Carolina at the end of June, I thought about how often I see and experience the anger we carry as Black folks, Black women, and historically marginalized groups and the collective grief we pick up along the way (Felix et al. 2019). I contemplated how our passions seek to kill us if not couched in care, family, and rest. I knew I had to come out of where I had begun to dwell. I had to remember to laugh. I traveled back to my hometown, found peace in that small community, and allowed it to feed my soul. It was everything I needed and more than I wanted. My family and I laughed, talked, reconnected, and grieved.

After returning to North Carolina, some friends and I started regular Zoom catchups, which I found refreshing. While work-related, virtual meetings quickly became a burden – especially those lasting three to four hours – time with girlfriends was renewing. I also began participating in monthly chats with my sorority sisters, which fueled my joy.

Slowly and intentionally, the community was redefined (Anderson 2021; Chinn et al. 2021). Virtual spaces took on new meaning as I indulged in Instagram and Facebook live gatherings, an online four-week class hosted by the National Association for the Advancement of Colored People (NAACP, 2020) titled Black Civics Summer, and reengaged with my sorority's alumnae chapter. Some ongoing activities never stopped, such as a virtual women's group I co-led, but I knew that while the latter activities were necessary, they were insufficient.

A few other national efforts helped my heart during the summer and fall of 2020, including GirlTrek's Black History Bootcamp (GirlTrek 2022). Over 21 days, participants received mini-Black History lessons on Black women from the United States and abroad whose work is considered groundbreaking. The daily email included a playlist – music (literally) for my soul – links to related YouTube videos, other lectures and interviews, and an action item for the day. I ended those 21 days feeling more informed, stronger, and better equipped for the journey ahead.

Soul Care

While I engulfed myself in an intentional community, there were other inward facing rituals I needed, within my control, and necessary aspects of my soul care. The first was reading, which I began doing with abandon. I had books for nearly every part of the day: morning, afternoon, and two bedtime books. I read deeply and widely on a range of topics, from religion and spirituality to politics and women in leadership. I read about financial planning, publishing, writing, and public speaking. I read about justice, hope, and Jesus. Reading helped to guide me in processing my emotions and redirecting my attention. These readings included Michael Bernard Beckwith (2007; 2009; 2012), Austin Channing Brown (2018), Dharius Daniels (2020), Lewis, Williams, and Baker (2020), and Howard Thurman (1976; 1977, 1981).

As I was reading more, I was inspired to write more. I developed a regular schedule for my blog (Cherry 2020b). I journaled nearly every day. I sought freelance opportunities for writing and ramped up my scholarly writing. Writing helped heal my heart.

Finally, I began pushing myself beyond my limits. This meant getting up earlier to have morning devotion time, exercise, write, and have breakfast. It meant going to bed at a reasonable time each night so I could get seven to eight hours of sleep. It meant turning my phone on "do not disturb" for set periods throughout my day to have quiet and exclusive focus time.

Prolonged Justice Work and Community

Time and time again, I was tempted by the knee-jerk reaction to do "all the things" everywhere with every group, but I reminded myself that justice work is for the long haul (Cherry 2020a). This work neither happens overnight nor do we stop after one singular victory – no matter how monumental it is. We keep fighting. We keep pushing. We keep working to move the pendulum for Black folks in the United States and abroad, our LGBTQIA+ communities, and Latinx and Asian Americans. We leave no stone unturned when it comes to dismantling racism, sexism, classism, homophobia, ageism, xenophobia, Islamophobia, and other forms of discrimination. We keep fighting in every area of our lives with every resource we can.

Three years later, I remain committed to showing up. I will keep doing my part. I will keep teaching and writing, and engaging in my new community. I will keep voting and protesting with my dollars, as well as supporting small businesses, minority-owned businesses, and women-led businesses. I will make missteps, and I know there will always be someone, somewhere, who claims I am not doing enough. I am committed to doing what I can, with what I have, in ways I feel led.

However, I also acknowledge that prolonged justice work cannot be done in silos. I need and value community; this community is not limited to equity-seekers and barrier-breakers. I need a loving, deep, and supportive community (Anderson 2021; Chinn et al. 2021). I need and deserve joy (Pham 2020). I need to and will intentionally create moments of pleasure. I seek reasons to hold fast to hope despite shifting external circumstances.

Perhaps, above all else, I choose love. I will continue to love despite the hate that has become palpable. I will continue to love you despite the name-calling and blatant racism. I will continue to love because hate truly is too much to bear. I choose consistently to love holding as truth Rev. Dr. Martin Luther King, Jr.'s quote, "Darkness cannot drive out darkness. Only light can do that," and Audre Lorde, who stated, "Your silence will not protect you."

Conclusion

According to James Baldwin, "We can disagree and still love each other unless your disagreement is rooted in my oppression and denial of my humanity and right to exist" (NewsOne Staff 2020). I have learned a lot throughout the prolonged pandemic and following the killings of Breonna Taylor and Ahmaud Arbery, and George Floyd (Brown 2020; Gipson et al. 2020). I have learned about reimagined communities. I have learned about engaging in civil conversations with those who want to foster meaningful dialogue. I have learned how to care for my heart in prolonged seasons of sadness, anger, disappointment, and hurt. I have learned to love people from afar and make no qualms about distancing myself from spaces where I am unable to show up as myself fully. I am learning to allow room for my continued personal growth.

In the fall of 2020, I moderated a panel on gender leadership. During our discussion, I was reminded how many populations and subpopulations operate in the margins. I was challenged to continue pushing my conversations and efforts toward initiatives that leave no one behind. I saw an opportunity to do what I wished so many had done for and with me: to not pit one effort against another but truly embrace that we are better together.

I am committed to continue talking, shifting, and shaping until we have a new normal – to be revisited as cultures are reimagined, and perspectives change. I move forward and close this chapter with a commitment to compassionate care in healing and reconciliation. I remain grounded in my intentions – now more than ever – to reclaim hope, joy, and community in the midst of tragedy.

Bibliography

Anderson, Ronald E. "Community during the Pandemic and Civil Unrest." *International Journal of Community Well-Being* 4.3 (2021): 293–298.

Beckwith, Michael Bernard. "Day Mind Fast Soul Feast." *A Guide To Soul*. Agape Publishing, 2007.

Beckwith, Michael Bernard. *Life Visioning: A Transformative Process for Activating Your Unique Gifts and Highest Potential*. Sounds True, 2012.

Beckwith, Michael Bernard. *Spiritual Liberation: Fulfilling Your Soul's Potential*. Simon and Schuster, 2009.

Brown, Austin Channing. *I'm Still Here: Black Dignity in a World Made for Whiteness*. Convergent Books, 2018.

Brown, Deneen L. " 'It Was a Modern-Day Lynching': Violent Deaths Reflect a Brutal American Legacy." Vol. 5. *National Geographic* (2020).

"CDC COVID Data Tracker," *Centers for Disease Control and Prevention*, 2020. covid.cdc.gov/covid-data-tracker/.

Cheng, Cindy, et al. "COVID-19 Government Response Event Dataset (CoronaNet v. 1.0)." *Nature Human Behaviour* 4.7 (2020): 756–768.

Cherry, Sabrina T., Kathleen deMarrais, and Cheryl Keita. "Medication Adherence among African American Women Who Have Been HIV Positive for 10 or More Years." *Journal of Black Studies* (2020): 0021934720921518.

Cherry, Sabrina. "Small doses." *Small* 10 (2015): 12–2015.

Cherry, Sabrina T. "Persist and Persevere: Being Jesus-Centred on the Long Road of Justice-Focused Work." Christian Courier. 12 October 2020a. http://www.christiancourier.ca/news/entry/persist-and-persevere.

Cherry, Sabrina T. "Carter's Blog Corner." 2020b https://sabrinatcherry.com/blog/.

Chinn, Juanita J., Iman K. Martin, and Nicole Redmond. "Health Equity among Black Women in the United States." *Journal of Women's Health* 30.2 (2021): 212–219.

"COVID-19 Map." *Johns Hopkins Coronavirus Resource Center*, coronavirus.jhu.edu/map.html.

Daniels, Dharius. *Relational Intelligence: The People Skills You Need for the Life of Purpose You Want*. Zondervan, 2020.

Dionne, Kim Yi, and Fulya Felicity Turkmen. "The Politics of Pandemic Othering: Putting COVID-19 in Global and Historical Context." *International Organization* 74.S1 (2020): E213–E230.

Ellis, Carolyn, Tony E. Adams, and Arthur P. Bochner. "Autoethnography: An Overview." *Historical Social Research/Historische Sozialforschung* 36.4 (2011): 273–290.

Fortuna, Lisa R., et al. "Inequity and the disproportionate impact of COVID-19 on communities of color in the United States: The need for a trauma-informed social justice response." *Psychological Trauma: Theory, Research, Practice, and Policy* 12.5 (2020): 443.

Felix, Ashley S., et al. "Stress, Resilience, and Cardiovascular Disease Risk among Black Women: Results from the women's health initiative." *Circulation: Cardiovascular Quality and Outcomes* 12.4 (2019): e005284.

GirlTrek. "Black History Bootcamp." 2022. https://blackhistorybootcamp.com/.

Grassroots Project. "This is Breonna Taylor." 2020. https://www.standwithbre.com/.

Haug, Nils, et al. "Ranking the Effectiveness of Worldwide COVID-19 Government Interventions." *Nature Human Behaviour* 4.12 (2020): 1303–1312.

Hoofman, Jacob, and Elizabeth Secord. "The Effect of COVID-19 on Education." *Pediatric Clinics* 68.5 (2021): 1071–1079.

Isaacs, Anton N. "An Overview of Qualitative Research Methodology for Public Health Researchers." *International Journal of Medicine and Public Health* 4.4 (2014).

Khankeh, Hamidreza et al. "Challenges in Conducting Qualitative Research in Health: A Conceptual Paper." *Iranian Journal of Nursing and Midwifery Research* 20.6 (2015): 635–41. doi:10.4103/1735-9066.170010

Lewis, Stephen, Matthew Wesley Williams, and Dori Grinenko Baker. *Another Way: Living and Leading Change on Purpose.* Chalice Press, 2020.

Logie, Carmen H. "Lessons Learned from HIV Can Inform Our Approach to COVID-19 Stigma." *Journal of the International AIDS Society* 23.5 (2020).

NAACP. "Black Civics Summer 2020." 30 August 2020. https://www.youtube.com/playlist?list=PL_f_FMiWxsGdXLY33kFYnHyLoLkSHlgrZ.

NewsOne Staff. "10 Quotes from James Baldwin That Will Change Your Life." NewsOne, 2 August 2021. https://newsone.com/playlist/ten-quotes-james-baldwin-happy-birthday/

Ngunjiri, Faith Wambura, Kathy-Ann C. Hernandez, and Heewon Chang. "Living Autoethnography: Connecting Life and Research." *Journal of Research Practice* 6, no. 1 (2010): E1–E1.

Pereira, Marcos, and Ana Marlucia Oliveira. "Poverty and Food Insecurity May Increase as the Threat of COVID-19 Spreads." *Public Health Nutrition* 23.17 (2020): 3236–240.

Pham, Kim. "Celebrating Black Joy as an Alternative Form of Resistance and Reclaiming of Humanity." 1 February 2021. https://voiceofoc.org/2021/02/celebrating-black-joy-as-an-alternative-form-of-resistance-and-reclaiming-of-humanity/

Poteat, Tonia, Greg Millett, LaRon E. Nelson, and Chris Beyrer. "Understanding COVID-19 Risks and Vulnerabilities among Black Communities in America: The Lethal Force of Syndemics." *Annals of Epidemiology* (2020).

"Quick Facts: Wilmington, N.C." *U.S. Census Bureau*, https://www.census.gov/quickfacts/wilmingtoncitynorthcarolina

Rashid, Shazia, and Sunishtha Singh Yadav. "Impact of Covid-19 Pandemic on Higher Education and Research." *Indian Journal of Human Development* 14.2 (2020): 340–343.

Singu, Sravani, et al. "Impact of Social Determinants of Health on the Emerging COVID-19 Pandemic in the United States." *Frontiers in Public Health* (2020): 406.

Thurman, Howard *Jesus and the Disinherited*. Abingdon Press, 1976.

Thurman, Howard. *Disciplines of the Spirit*. Friends United Press, 1977.

Thurman, Howard *With Head and Heart: The Autobiography of Howard Thurman*. Houghton Mifflin Harcourt, 1981.

U.S. Census. Quick Facts. Wilmington N.C. Retrieved from https://www.census.gov/quickfacts/fact/table/wilmingtoncitynorthcarolina/PST045223.

Van Dorn, Aaron, Rebecca E. Cooney, and Miriam L. Sabin. "COVID-19 Exacerbating Inequalities in the US." *Lancet (London, England)* 395, no. 10232 (2020): 1243.

Van Lancker, Wim, and Zachary Parolin. "COVID-19, school closures, and child poverty: a social crisis in the making." The Lancet Public Health 5.5 (2020): e243–e244.

Vestal, Christine & Ollove, Michael. "Politicians Shunt Aside Public Health Officials." 18 June 2020. https://www.pewtrusts.org/en/research-and-analysis/blogs/stateline/2020/06/18/politicians-shunt-aside-public-health-officials

"WHO Coronavirus Disease (COVID-19) Dashboard." *World Health Organization*, https://covid19.who.int/.

Wright, James E., and Cullen C. Merritt. "Social Equity and COVID-19: The Case of African Americans." *Public Administration Review* (2020). doi: 10.1111/puar.13251.

Yancy, Clyde W. "COVID-19 and African Americans." *Jama* (2020). 323(19):1891–1892. doi:10.1001/jama.2020.6548.

Notes on Contributors

Cristina R. Cabral, Ph.D., is a poet, professor, activist, and literary critic born in Uruguay. She received her doctorate in Romance Languages from the University of Missouri, becoming the first Afro-Uruguayan ever to receive such a Ph.D. in the United States. She has published numerous articles and essays about Latin American literature and the *Candombe* from an Afrocentric cultural and sociological perspective. Her articles have been included in various collections, among others, Ramsay & Tillis *The Afro Hispanic Reader and Anthology* (2018), and Harris & Tillis *The Trayvon Martin in US: An American Tragedy* (2015). Cabral's poetry has formed part of Latin American literary collections such as Mercedes Jaramillo & Lucia Ortiz *Hijas del Muntu* (2011), Myriam DeCosta-Willis *Daughters of the Diaspora* (2003), and Alberto Britos *Anthology of Black Uruguayan Poets* (1990). Winner of the Casa de las Americas prose prize in 1986, her literary books include *Conversación entre pájaros* (2023), *Telaraña* (2018), *Memoria y Resistencia* (2004), and *Desde mi Trinchera* (1993). Currently she is a professor of Spanish language, literature, and Afro-Hispanic culture at the University of North Carolina Central.

Sabrina T. Cherry, Ph.D., is Associate Professor of Public Health at UNC Wilmington. She has worked for over 20 years within the field of public health. Dr. Cherry's professional experience started as a Peace Corps Volunteer in The Gambia, West Africa. One of her major projects included partnering with leaders across the continent to focus on Gender and Development (GAD) initiatives aimed at helping young women and girls create sustainable income resources. As a public health practitioner, Dr. Cherry collaborated on Community Health Needs Assessments (CHNA) for the Greater Atlanta

Affiliate of Susan G. Komen for the Cure and two rural Georgia hospitals; provided co-leadership on the expansion of the Community Outreach Program at Northside Hospital; provided technical assistance to faith based, mini-grant recipients in Southwest Georgia; and worked on a food insecurity and medication-adherence pilot study for Persons Living with HIV/AIDS (PLWHA). Her primary research interests are religion and health, global health, and community-based equity initiatives. She earned a Master of Science Public Health (MSPH) degree from the University of South Carolina, a Master of Theological Studies (MTS) from Emory University, and a Doctorate of Public Health (DrPH), as a well as a Certificate in Interdisciplinary Qualitative Research, from the University of Georgia.

Angela Y. Douglas is a scholar-activist, and a seasoned political scientist, strategist, and entrepreneur. She completed doctoral coursework from the University of South Carolina prior to accepting a position in the Political Science Department at the University of North Carolina Wilmington. From campaign politics to community development, Douglas has been actively involved in leadership positions, recently serving as a City Councilmember and Mayor Pro Tempore for the City Council in Chester, SC. Accordingly, during the 2020 election cycle, nearly all major national presidential candidates reached out to her personally to garner her support and endorsement in efforts to win northcentral South Carolina. Currently, she is the CEO and Principal Strategist for Douglas Strategy Group, where she assists governmental agencies, small businesses, and nonprofit organizations with strategic planning, public engagement, policy development, and sustainability. Her business has generated nearly $5 million dollars of grants and funding for clients, and she has published book chapters associated with her scholarship. Douglas continues to conduct research and speak on rural politicking in the south, social capital, US public governance, and policy making in the United States.

Emmanuel D. Harris II, Ph.D., is originally from Indianapolis, Indiana, and he received his master's and Ph.D. from Washington University in St. Louis, where he was a Chancellor's Fellow. A Professor of Spanish at the University of North Carolina Wilmington, he teaches all levels of Spanish language as well as Hispanic culture and literature. In addition, he instructs various classes in Africana Studies where he formerly served as Director of the program. In 1996 he was awarded Teacher of the Year at Washington University and has been honored to have a service award established in his name in 2000 at Baker University where he formerly instructed. Harris has published various books, and his numerous articles can be found both nationally and internationally in academic journals and edited volumes. He is the award-winning English translator of the Afro-Peruvian novel *Malambo* by Lucía Charún-Illescas and also the translator of the collection of short stories *Over the Waves and Other Stories / Sobre las olas y otros cuentos* by the Afro-Cuban writer Inés María Martiatu, which was a featured selection of the Cervantes Institute in Chicago. Harris co-edited the volume *The Trayvon Martin in US: An American Tragedy* and is currently writing *Black Soil: The Allen Family Farm Story*. He has been recognized by UNCW for Outstanding Dedication to Mentoring and Supporting Latino Graduates and is the two-time recipient of the Discere Aude Award for excellence in mentoring.

Sheka Houston, D.Ed., is a passionate educator that has the desire to inspire all she encounters to become the very best versions of themselves. As a teacher, Houston was awarded teacher of the year by her peers. She has spent the last 18 years in public education, 13 of which has been in administration while also serving as AVID District Director. She has also served as the district facilitator for Title IX and the teacher evaluation protocol. Houston is a certified grant writer through Research Associates and has received multiple grants to include EIA ($6000.00) PPG ($1500.00) and NetLead Mini-Grant ($1000.00). Houston has been trained in many programs: A Framework for Understanding Poverty, The Ron Clark Educator Training, Single Gender Training, NWEA Training, and Culturally Relevancy Training. She is a contributing author in the *Women Who Lead Anthology* which features outstanding women with extraordinary achievements from all industries and careers. Houston also serves on the Board of Girls on the Run, Tri-County, and South Carolina; serves as a Girl Scout Troop Leader; serves on the Juneteenth Celebration-Chester Committee; and is a proud member of Delta Sigma Theta Sorority, Inc. Entering the field of education through the alternative certification program, Houston transitioned into education from the real estate industry where she was a million dollar producer after hosting a workshop on self-esteem for a group of young ladies in a local community pageant. She is also the co-founder of The Knowledge Academy for Girls, where she is able to live out her original passion that drew her to education in the first place and this is cultivating young girls. Houston and her husband of 23 years, Jerry, have two beautiful daughters, Elizabeth and Isabella who are truly her inspiration, as she leads and inspires through the lens of a mom.

Athena M. King, PhD/MPA, is Assistant Professor in the Department of Political Science, Geography, and International Studies at Old Dominion University (ODU). Prior to this, she was an Assistant Professor of Political

Science at Jackson State University (JSU). Dr. King received her PhD in Political Science (American Politics) and a master's degree in public administration from the University of South Carolina-Columbia. Her major field is American Politics, with research emphasis in U.S. racial and ethnic politics, African American politics, environmental justice, urban policy, electoral behavior and American Political Development. Dr. King's current research includes projects on implicit bias against women faculty in the Academy, Black electoral complexity, environmental justice in the legislative context, and a book proposal on policy entrepreneurs that foster new or entrench existing racial/ethnic policies in the US. She has published in PS: Political Science and Politics, the National Political Science Review, The Journal of Race and Policy, and 21st Century Urban Race Politics: Representing Minorities as Universal Interests (the latter for which she and her co-authors were awarded the Outstanding Author Contribution Award, Research in Race and Ethnic Relations by Emerald Group Publishing Limited in 2014). In addition, she has co-authored book chapters in *Minority Voting in the United States and Whose Black Politics? Cases in Post-Racial Black Leadership*. Dr. King has taught also at the University of South Carolina-Columbia, University of Massachusetts-Amherst, Framingham State University, and Eastern Michigan University.

Tiffany Lane, Ph.D., is Associate Professor and Coordinator of the Bachelor of Social Work (BSW) program at the University of North Carolina Wilmington (UNCW). Lane held a two-year appointment at Norfolk State University in the Ethelyn R. Strong School of Social Work as Director of the BSW program. Prior to that, she was a tenured Associate Professor and Program Chair in the Social Work Department at West Chester University, PA. Lane has published scholarly articles in various academic journals, and book chapters have been presented at numerous national conferences centered on social equity. She has been awarded grants focused on community development and academic success. Her interests include child welfare services, issues impacting youth who age out of foster care, and African American youth's academic and social success in low-resourced communities. She is a race worker who seeks to disrupt systems and institutions of oppression through scholarship, presentation, and hosting events that seek to center marginalized groups, particularly African American women. She holds a Bachelor of Social Work from West Chester University, PA, a Master of Social Work from Howard University and a Ph.D. from Morgan State University. Lane is the founder of Almatine's Goodies, an initiative to support older foster care youth enrolled in post-secondary institutions. She serves on West Chester University's Academic Success Program Board in West Chester, Pa, and the Youth Scientist Academy Board, Wilmington, NC.

Julia A. Lynch, Ed.D., is a Visiting Assitant Professor at the University of North Carolina Wilmington in Educational Leadership and the Co-Coordinator of the Curriculum & Instruction Master's Program. Generally speaking, her scholarship explores teacher identity and arts-based inquiry practices within rural education contexts. She operates primarily from a BlackMothering epistemology with a critical sociocultural framework to engage in education that promotes equity and social justice in rural education teaching and learning. A Black poet scholar, she engages in critical qualitative research that attempts to center the lives and experiences of other Black scholars while also disrupting normative research that fails to honor the authenticity of the researcher or culturally sustain the community of participants.

Kimberly Eison Simmons, Ph.D., is Associate Professor of Anthropology and African American Studies at the University of South Carolina where she has served in different administrative positions. She received her B.A. in Spanish from Grinnell College and her Ph.D. in Anthropology from Michigan State University where she was also a Researcher-in-Residence with the African Diaspora Research Program. Much of her research focuses on the cultural construction of identity, race and gender, color/colorism, women's organizations, and Black ethnic groups in the African diaspora (focusing on Afro-Dominicans and African Americans). She is the author of *Reconstructing Racial Identity and the African Past in the Dominican Republic* (University Press of Florida, 2009) and coeditor of *Afrodescendants, Identity, and the Struggle for Development in the Americas* (Michigan State University Press, 2012). She is currently working on a book project on global Blackness and the natural hair movement. She is the former president of the Association of Black Anthropologists.

Tammy Taylor, Ph.D., is a dedicated educator who has committed her life and career to the service of others. She has spent 24 years as a public educator, serving in a plethora of roles including teaching fourth and first grades, respectively, as Instructional Coach, Instructional Coordinator, Curriculum Facilitator, Director of Early Childhood and Elementary Education, Director of Title I and Testing, and Director of Accountability and Special Projects. Her most recent role has been her service as an elementary principal. Taylor has served on a variety of committees and boards over her career as an advocate for students and public education. These include First Steps, Chamber of Commerce, and the South Carolina Association of School and Title I Administrators. She has a strong background in Early Childhood Education, curriculum development, and literacy and foundational reading skills. Taylor has been trained in the tenets of the national movement to increase reading skills – Reading First. She served as a partner teacher and Reading First Initiative team member. Taylor is passionate about teaching and learning and keeps her skills honed through her affiliations with a number of professional organizations. She is a member of the Association for School Curriculum and Development, The National Education Association, The South Carolina Education Association, Kappa Delta Pi, the National Association for Professional Women, and the International Reading Association. She received her PhD from the University of South Carolina. Her passion for validating the experience of the principalship and the impact on students' achievement drives her research focus. This research focuses on the leadership experiences of four African American, female principals and their experiences: challenges and successes. Taylor is married to Keith Taylor and the co-founder of The Knowledge Academy for Girls. She's passionate about working with youth and has worked with young ladies to create a sense of value and self-worth by teaching them to understand, accept, and fulfill their purposes in life.

Aaron Treadwell, Ph.D., is Assistant Professor of History at Middle Tennessee State University (MTSU). His areas of expertise are Black spirituality with an emphasis on the African Methodist Episcopal (AME) Church; U.S. history with an emphasis on sociopolitical activism; African American history; and public history with an emphasis of data archiving. Before coming to MTSU, Treadwell taught History and Religion at Florida Agricultural and Mechanical University (FAMU) from 2015 to 2018. He also taught at Howard University, Howard Divinity School, and Edward Waters College (EWC). Currently, he is the founder and archival engineer of the A.M.E. Digital Archives project, which houses information on every church in the denomination (7,000+). Treadwell is also an Ordained Itinerant Elder in the African Methodist Episcopal (AME) Church, where he presently serves in the South Nashville Conference, in the 13th Episcopal District. He is a graduate of Howard University, with a Ph.D. in History (2017) and has degrees from Florida State (B.S. 2008), Emory University (M.Div. 2011), and Florida Agricultural and Mechanical University (MASS 2013). Aaron Treadwell is married to Jade Treadwell, and they have two children, Carter and Miles Treadwell.

Keryn G. Vickers, Ed.D., is a native New Yorker who resides in North Carolina with his family. He is the inaugural Director of the Watson College of Education, Student Success Center at the University of North Carolina Wilmington. His dissertation research, "Lift as We Climb: Investigating

Nontraditional Pathways and Strategies to Executive Leadership for Black in Predominantly White Institutions and Historically White Universities" stems from his unique life journey. More recently, Vickers began applying the Groundwater Approach to better analyze a broad range of industries and systems in private and public sectors. Throughout his career, Vickers held several roles as a higher education administrator, adjunct professor, reverend, entrepreneur, civic engager, coach, mentor, motivational speaker, and humble servant leader. He often focuses on leading and mentoring the underserved, underrepresented, underprivileged, and disenfranchised populations. However, Dr. Vickers recognizes that servant leadership first starts at home with his children! To know Dr. Vickers means you know he loves his children, family, extended family, and friends.

Bisola Wald is a Ph.D. student in Curriculum and Instruction, minoring in African American and African Studies. She serves as a graduate instructor, researcher, and program assistant within the teacher education and licensure program and Teacher Scholars of Color program at the University of Minnesota. She started her career in education in the spring of 2005 as an English professor at Venusa College in Merida, Venezuela. She has served as a professional educator, treasurer and charter school board member, teacher coach, diversity and education facilitator, webinar host, podcast guest and co-host, and professional development trainer. As an Intercultural Development Inventory (IDI) Qualified Administrator, she partners with educators and school leadership to develop and expand their capacity to effectively engage diversity, equity, inclusion, and retention. She is passionate and strategic about birthing equity through antiracist pedagogy and decolonizing education. As a first-generation Nigerian immigrant raised by a Black feminist mother, she teaches, leads, and writes out of the intersectionality of her own faith, ethnicity, and gender along with the social constructs of race and class.

Louis Lee Woods, Ph.D., is a Professor of African American History at Middle Tennessee State University (MTSU). Graduating Phi Beta Kappa, Dr. Woods received his B.A. degree in Africana Studies from SUNY Stony Brook. He obtained his M.A. and Ph.D. in African American History from Howard University. Dr. Woods' research has appeared in several peer-reviewed academic journals including the *Journal of Urban History and the Journal of African American History*. During his time at MTSU, Dr. Woods has served as the Presidential Fellow for Social Justice and Equality, Africana Studies Program Director and President of the Black Faculty and Staff Association.

OMPLICATED

A BOOK SERIES OF CURRICULUM STUDIES

Reframing the curricular challenge educators face after a decade of school deform, the books published in Peter Lang's Complicated Conversation Series testify to the ethical demands of our time, our place, our profession. What does it mean for us to teach now, in an era structured by political polarization, economic destabilization, and the prospect of climate catastrophe? Each of the books in the Complicated Conversation Series provides provocative paths, theoretical and practical, to a very different future. In this resounding series of scholarly and pedagogical interventions into the nightmare that is the present, we hear once again the sound of silence breaking, supporting us to rearticulate our pedagogical convictions in this time of terrorism, reframing curriculum as committed to the complicated conversation that is intercultural communication, self-understanding, and global justice.

The series editor is

Dr. William F. Pinar
Department of Curriculum Studies
2125 Main Mall
Faculty of Education
University of British Columbia
Vancouver, British Columbia V6T 1Z4
CANADA

To order other books in this series, please contact our Customer Service Department:

peterlang@presswarehouse.com (within the U.S.)
orders@peterlang.com (outside the U.S.)

Or browse online by series:

www.peterlang.com

9 781636 679211